Praise for WHAT REMAINS

"One of the best memoirs . . . a small masterpiece . . . devastating and beautifully written."

—New York Post

"Bittersweet and tender."

—The New York Times Book Review

"Remarkably tender and moving."

—People

"Elegant . . . moving."

—New York Daily News

"[Radziwill] tells her story with graceful discretion and quiet power."

—The Plain Dealer

"A moving testimony to the tenuous nature of love and life."

—USA Today

"It's impossible not to admire the author's courage and devotion and skill."

—New York Newsday

"A stunning memoir of love and loss . . . Carole Radziwill is a natural storyteller."

—O, The Oprah Magazine

"Powerfully affecting . . . a highly compelling read."

—Vogue

"Carole Radziwill has written an unsparing, unsentimental, and inspiring memoir. A spirited journalist with a novelist's eye for detail, she delivers a stunningly honest story about life's great joys and deepest pain."

—Christiane Amanpour, CNN, Chief International Correspondent

"Love and loss, family and friends, fate and fortune: these themes pervade this beautifully written . . . courageous, and compelling memoir."

—*Library Journal* (starred review)

"*What Remains* is a testimony to the human spirit. It is beautifully and honestly written. The reader feels he or she has peeked into the author's soul and glimpsed courage, wisdom, and love."

—*Bookreporter.com*

"A fascinating tale."

—*The Daily Telegraph* (London)

"A beautifully written and deeply moving memoir."

—*The Irish Times*

"*What Remains* explores the complexities of marriage and the importance of friendship with unflinching honesty. . . . This vivid and honest memoir is a tribute to the author and a testimony to the resilience of the human spirit."

—*Birmingham Post* (UK)

WHAT
REMAINS

a memoir of
fate, friendship, and love

Carole Radziwill

Scribner
NEW YORK LONDON TORONTO SYDNEY

SCRIBNER

1230 Avenue of the Americas
New York, NY 10020

First Scribner trade paperback edition 2007
SCRIBNER and design are trademarks of
Macmillan Library Reference USA, Inc., used under license
by Simon & Schuster, the publisher of this work.

For information about special discounts for bulk purchases,
please contact Simon & Schuster Special Sales:
1-800-456-6798 or business@simonandschuster.com

DESIGNED BY KYOKO WATANABE
Text set in Granjon

Manufactured in the United States of America

17   19   20   18

Library of Congress Control Number: 2005296802

ISBN-13: 978-0-7432-7694-8
ISBN-10: 0-7432-7694-9
ISBN-13: 978-0-7432-7718-1 (Pbk)
ISBN-10: 0-7432-7718-X (Pbk)

For Anthony

[The wise] will start each day with the thought . . .
Fortune gives us nothing which we can really own.

—Seneca

Prologue

Show me a hero and I will write you a tragedy.

—F. Scott Fitzgerald

Friday, July 16, 1999

Three weeks before my husband died a young couple smashed their plane into the Atlantic Ocean, off the Massachusetts shoreline, well after the mid-July sun had set. It was reported in the news as 9:41, but I knew the general time, because I had spoken to the woman less than an hour before. The pilot was my husband's cousin, John Kennedy. His wife, Carolyn Bessette, was my closest friend. She was sitting behind him next to the only other passenger, her sister, Lauren. A still, hot summer day had melted into a warm and sticky night. A quiet night, unremarkable except for the fog, which rolls in and out of New England like a deep sigh.

While we were still making plans, before they took off from Caldwell, New Jersey, she called me from the plane.

"We'll fly to the Vineyard tomorrow, after the wedding. We can be there before dinner."

It was a short conversation, because I was going to see her the next day. I was staying in her house, their house, on Martha's Vineyard, with my husband, and they were taking a simple trip. One they'd made many other weekends, from a small airport in New Jersey to the islands off Massachusetts—a well-worn ninety-minute path up the coastline.

I hung up the phone and opened the book I was reading and an hour later she was dead. Afterward I tried to find something to explain what had happened—was it cloudy, were the stars out? But the night was ordinary. It usually is, I think, when your life changes. Most people aren't doing anything special when the carefully placed pieces of their life break apart.

They flew a lot that summer, from the city to the Vineyard, and we called each other every day if we weren't together.

3

"We're getting a late start. I'll call you in the morning."

It takes seconds to plunge into an irrevocable spin in a small plane—into what the Federal Aviation Administration calls a *graveyard spiral*. According to the accident report, the plane broke the surface of the ocean three minutes after the pilot sensed a problem. At 9:38, he made a curious turn. One hundred and eighty seconds later, the last thirty of them aimed directly at the water, their stories ended abruptly.

I wonder if he felt the awkward motions of the plane in those minutes, the changes in speed or direction. It's likely he did not. If you close your eyes in an airplane, you don't feel up or down. You don't feel yourself tilting right or left. You don't feel anything, really, and your senses tell you it doesn't matter. Clouds were hiding the familiar strings of lights that paint the coastline. He might as well have been flying with his eyes closed.

"I need to talk to you," I said.

My husband, Anthony, was dying and we were all trying to pretend that he wasn't, that everything was fine.

"I can't hear you, Lamb. I'll see you tomorrow, okay?"

The accident report shows the pilot made a turn after passing Point Judith, Rhode Island—he turned east, away from the coast, away from where he was going. And then another turn, and then another. It was puzzling to everyone, including the investigators, and after months of plotting radar signals, studying twisted pieces of wreckage, constructing maps and charts, and speculating about state of mind, they confirmed what they had suspected—the pilot was disoriented. He may have turned, some suggested, hoping to spot something familiar. A landmark like the lighthouse at the tip of Gay Head, blinking a steady twenty-mile stream of light, muffled that night by thick, black air. He might have scanned the dark sky for Noman's Land—the empty island you can see clearly in daylight from the beachfront of their Martha's Vineyard home.

Perhaps he felt a slight tilt of the plane, but it was more likely that the instrument panel caught his attention, his compass shifting slowly.

He may have tried to correct it, turning the rudder slightly—or adding pressure to the controls. But when it doesn't *feel* like you're turning, it feels wrong to correct it. He wouldn't have corrected it enough. He wouldn't have corrected it at all. He would have followed what his senses were telling him to do—an overwhelming feeling of what he should do—and it would be exactly the wrong thing.

It's possible that nothing felt unusual in the plane as his altimeter began to unwind, marking a perplexing descent. Slowly at first, then at a sickening rate. It is likely he was watching this helplessly. His senses, of no use to him, telling him to ignore, even then, irrefutable evidence. The handful of controls all showing deadly readings. She may not have noticed any of this. She wouldn't have seen the airspeed on the control panel, pegged in the red, reflecting the quickening pace of the ocean rushing up to them.

We were staying in their house because Anthony wanted to be on the Vineyard that summer, and I went along with it. In June when we arrived I gave the ambulance drivers a paper with directions to the house, and they taped it to the dashboard. "It's the chance of a lifetime," Anthony had said to me in a restaurant in New York before we left. "I don't know why you can't see that. We have the summer off, we can spend the days on the beach, have margaritas at sunset."

There were sunsets that summer, and when I noticed them I was grateful. But he was dying. It was likely, but unmentionable, that he wouldn't be going back to the city, and for everyone but Anthony it was hard to think of margaritas. It irritated him when I didn't play along.

One hundred and eighty seconds. John might have felt annoyance, perhaps, before panic. Frustration, and then fear. His pulse accelerating as one replaced the other. The water would be as black as the sky—like concrete, at their rate of descent. It is possible that he thought for the entire three minutes that they were going to crash, probable that he thought it for thirty seconds.

It was a new plane and I wasn't familiar with it. It bothered me that I didn't know where she was sitting. The accident report recorded passengers in the *aft-facing seats,* but I couldn't picture her there. When I rode along, we settled down on the back seat and read magazines under the small light. If there were other passengers she sat up in the front. One weekend a year before, there were five of us going to the Vineyard. Carolyn was sitting next to John and her door popped open over the ocean. She stretched her arm into the clouds to grab the handle and clicked it shut. It was quick and smooth and insignificant to her.

But in the dark, on this night, did she sense his frustration and impatience? Did she dismiss it? We were all frustrated and impatient that summer. She was sitting directly behind her husband, the backs of their seats touching. He could have, if he had wanted, reached a hand around his seat to her. Her sister was beside her.

I sometimes mark time now in three-minute intervals. When I am talking on the phone, or walking around the city, or sitting on a plane, I glance at my watch and reflexively mark the time. There is so much that can happen in three minutes. It's enough time to think you can fix things.

I'm sure she was reading magazines. She always took a pile of them because she scanned them quickly and she didn't like to run out. She sounded tired when I spoke to her. Her voice was soft. She was trying to distract herself. We were all trying to distract ourselves. It was a bad day, if you had to choose one, to die. There had not been enough time.

"I love you," she said before she hung up. And then again, "I love you." We always said this to each other, but I didn't want to love anyone that night. I was tired, and I didn't say it back. "I know," I said instead.

You never know when something is going to happen to change your life. You expect it to arrive with fanfare, like a wedding or a birth, but instead it comes in the most ordinary of circumstances. The Roman goddess Fortuna snaps her fingers and changes the channel— click. I was sitting in a chair, reading, preparing for one death, and then *click.* It was silent. Was there a noise? I always thought tragedy had a sound. I always thought there was something you would *hear*. We were holding our breath until Anthony died. Believing that everything else would wait.

Carolyn had a theory about relationships.

"You're much happier when you wait," she used to tell me. "The ones that come to you are the only ones worth anything, Lamb. It's like standing on the shore and spotting something in the water. You can splash around to try to get it, or you can wait and see if the tide brings it in."

I was thinking this while I stood on the shore one day, dreading what the tide would bring. Her makeup bag, a luggage tag.

The weekend before, we were all at the house. She came early in the afternoon, and John flew in later. Effie made a big dinner of grilled fish and roasted potatoes, pie for dessert. John had arranged for him to be there that summer. He cooked for us and maintained our routine—dialysis in the morning, the beach during the day. A table set for dinner at a planned time each night. We welcomed diversions. We'd have dinner, linger at the table, play Bartlett's if we were up for a game.

We had friends staying for the weekend and we were all sitting in the backyard, waiting for John, and suddenly a plane was right above us. He flew low, buzzing over the house before he landed, a fun thing. He broke up tension. He always knew to. A sort of childish but innocent thing to do, flying over us, dipping the left wing. *Just like him.* We all looked toward the sky.

"Hey!" We waved. Except Anthony, who just shook his head, a reflex after so many years. Anthony's eye roll and John's sideways smile. *I got you, Principe.*

"He's here!"

Carolyn looked up, smiling, squinting, her arm in front of her to block the sun.

"He's crazy," someone said, laughing. He brought people to life. He could relax a room, and we counted on him for it. He flew over the house and dropped a dash of exhilaration on the weekend.

I would come to think of it as my summer of tragedy. I was reading love stories, the classics, one after another. You could lose yourself
in someone else's heartbreak while you held your breath for your
own. I brought a stack of books and piled them in the bedroom next
to *Lady Chatterley's Lover,* which John picked up one day. "Do you see
what your wife is reading?" he said to Anthony, shaking his head.
"It's worse than I thought." Carolyn was reading *Light in August.* We
had no time for a badly told story.

I wonder if in those last three minutes he called out to her. I have
learned that engines sound different at that rate of descent—a whin-
ing noise and much louder as the plane starts into a corkscrew. There
was a hard shift to their flight in the last thirty seconds. Did he call out
to her, panicked, his voice strained?

Three minutes, one hundred and eighty seconds, is enough time
to think through whether he should tell her, and then to struggle with
his decision. It is plenty of time to consider who would be waiting for
a phone call on the shore. It is the length of an average story on the
evening news.

It was a fairly ordinary accident, all in all. The plane dropped
neatly into the water after its pilot lost his course. For all the experts,
the theories, the newspaper ink, it was a simple crash. A small plane
dropping out of an unlit sky.

I was reading *Anna Karenina* by a light in the living room. The
window near me looked out onto a pond, and then farther, to the
water where they lay for four days. Their crash didn't disturb a soul,
until later. I was sitting comfortably in a room where I had seen them
days earlier. In the house where we'd agreed to meet the next evening,
before she hung up the phone.

Thirty seconds is what it would have taken me to read a few para-
graphs in my book. Thirty seconds and I am completely absorbed in
a scene in someone else's story. Thirty seconds, after Anna Karenina's
final and fatal decision leaves her kneeling awkwardly on the railroad
tracks—the train a split second away from her inelegant end. It is
enough time to become anxious, then calm and then anxious again—

as you might do reading an account of the end of a life. I may have paused once, put a marker in the book, and taken a sip from a glass on the table. This is very likely what I am doing as my best friend rushes to the end of her life, in water visible from the window of the room where I am sitting. Enjoying an unusual moment of quiet calm in an otherwise restless summer.

We dressed for dinner that summer. We'd come in from the beach, take long, cool showers, and slip into floor-length skirts. Long gowns and bare feet. We dressed for dinner every night, and our husbands liked it—it lifted us up for a moment. We could pretend it was all the way we had once imagined a summer like this—suntanned shoulders and salty kisses.

Anthony looked thin and small in his bathing suit, his legs knobby like a boy's. His face was strong and handsome.

I was surprised when Carolyn called from the airport. I didn't think she'd be coming. She had mentioned that she might not come. There was a wedding, and we were all doing our best. We were holding our breath, trying to pass time while we waited for Anthony to die. When you're waiting for someone to die, passing time is the cruelest thing to have to do.

She had started a tradition the Christmas before. Christmas dinner, just the four of us. "Every year we'll do it. Don't you think we need a tradition?" she had asked. "Marta will come and cook a big Christmas dinner."

"It sounds great," I replied, caught up in her enthusiasm.

I don't have many things left. What I kept is mostly in boxes now, stored away. You go through what remains and there isn't a lot that is meaningful, except your memories.

There is another scene months before this night. I am with John on this same route. I am his only passenger, and we are flying in the old plane, the one with his father's initials and birthdate on the tail wing—529JK. The trip takes one hour and forty-three minutes from the time we park his white convertible in the corner of the lot in Caldwell to the time we touch down on the runway of Martha's Vineyard.

"You slept the whole way!" he says, laughing, when we land.

"Oh, I know," I say. "I'm sorry."

He climbs out and reaches for my hand.

"Don't be," he says. "It's a compliment."

But I am reading a book by the window on a different night, and as his cousins fly up the foggy coastline, my husband sits next to me watching a movie he doesn't care about, then goes to bed. When he wakes up they will be missing.

Once it was the four of us, with all of our dreams and plans, and then suddenly there was nothing.

Beginnings

Where to start is the problem, because nothing begins when it begins and nothing's over when it's over, and everything needs a preface: a preface, a postscript, a chart of simultaneous events.

—Margaret Atwood, *The Robber Bride*

1

Saturday, August 27, 1994

I'll start with the fairy tale.

Orson Welles said to Gore Vidal once, in an interview about a movie he was writing, *If you want a happy ending, it depends on where you stop your story.* My wedding, then, might have been a good place to stop. I never dreamt of myself in a wedding dress, but here I am. White, naturally, and silk gazar, because I'm told this is what they are making them from this year. "Keep it simple," I say to the designer, a family friend of my fiancé's who called in June to say she would design the dress. We trade sketches back and forth—mine a woman with a Scarlett O'Hara waist and saucy, flirty mouth. A woman, I imagine, who knows a proper card stock, knows to register at Bergdorf Goodman, to get listed in *Town & Country*.

It is simple, elegant: long chiffon sleeves in August because I am conscious of my freckles, but otherwise perfect. I am standing in this dress at the edge of the floor where parquet meets the green lawn like Jay Gatsby on the terrace gazing out. For a brief moment I go unnoticed beneath the edges of the tent, under the billowing soft silk, at the fringe of light fingering through the baby's breath candle chandelier. Famed party designer Christian Tortu was flown in from Paris to create it.

The sky, if I were to step from under the tent and look up, is full of stars. The dark ocean, even, is lit up tonight, because my mother-in-law has thought of everything—has tucked lights into the foliage along the dunes. The night is all twinkles and light and sparkle. The tinkling of crystal, trickles of laughter, silver clinking on porcelain.

Seashells carefully picked, artfully scattered on the tables. Off-duty policemen stand in the shadows along the path to the beach. Music floats out and drops on the waves like bubbles. The ocean slaps onto the sand, like faint applause, behind me.

The Polish prince and the small-town, working-class girl. This is the moment when my worlds collide—Kingston, Suffern, American royalty, my ABC News career. This is the crossroads. Everyone raises a glass to futures, beginnings.

My uncle Benny has one arm around the senator, the other stretched out in front of them holding a camera. My mother is talking to the news anchor, my father having a cigarette behind the bar. John poses patiently with two of my cousins. Uncle Jimmy is laughing with the movie director at something one of them has said.

Anthony's stepfather, Herbert, is elegant in his classic navy suit, sipping champagne from fluted crystal. His gaze is fixed on my mother-in-law, in pale green Armani and white gloves, her light-brown hair brushed back to frame an extraordinary, elegant face.

My uncle Freddy and aunt Marsha are seated next to the Rutherfords of Newport. Marsha is animated, her laugh carries over the music, the Rutherfords quiet. Buddy is here, too—Governor Roemer when I met him in Baton Rouge on a story. "So happy for you," he whispered to me earlier in the night. He is here with someone, a friend, and I know it's likely we won't see each other again. There's no reason for our paths to cross. I have his letters piled neatly, tied together with string.

Tony, my cousin's boyfriend, watches everything closely, drinking a beer. He'll call a popular radio station tomorrow to report the celebrity sightings here in his rough Yonkers accent. They won't believe he was a guest until he gives them enough detail, describes what Melanie Griffith was wearing. The DJ will make crude jokes about the bride; he'll call me a *gold digger.*

I have the vantage point of Fortune. Standing in the middle of this, I now know how it all turns out. There will be love and loss and luck and fate—the tent is lousy with it.

Bobby Muller in his wheelchair is getting a drink from the bar. Six months earlier we crossed the Mekong River on a rickety wooden ferry, heading to the medical clinic he built in Cambodia to make prosthetic limbs for land mine victims. I'll win an Emmy next year for the story and call him from the lobby of the Roosevelt Hotel with the news.

Our friend Judd holds a crowd rapt in the corner with his repertoire of stories from the road. He pulls them out like aces from a deck of cards. He'll die of a brain tumor soon after his twins are born. Two of the couples dancing will divorce before the year is out. A heart attack will kill my uncle Sal a few weeks shy of his son's wedding, but tonight he is hearty, slapping someone's back, telling a joke. The celebrated artist talking to the young girl in the hat will die in three years from a sudden bout of pneumonia.

Fortune. Fate. But there are people here, too, who will fall in love. Our friend Kissy will get assigned to the Balkan war and meet her husband Jamie in a bar in Croatia. I sit Anthony's friend Beth next to Tony, and they fall in love. My sister marries the boy she came with.

I am watching Anthony now. He is handsome and strong, dashing, like the pictures I've seen of his late father, Stas, the gallant prince. His hair is grown out, wavy and brushed back the way I like it. He'll look up for me, spot me here in a moment, and smile. I will not see the bump tonight. I won't see it until the end of our honeymoon on a beach in Hawaii.

Women in red lipstick and men in cream-colored pants with dark sport coats are sipping cocktails against the ocean breeze. It is a perfect wedding—the bride and groom in love, a Louis Armstrong song, the air tingling with *future*. People fall in love with one another all over, and with life and colors and music. They form instant relationships with people they will never see again.

Linda, my oldest friend, is having a baby any day, so her mother, Vivian, has driven out here alone. I spot her chain-smoking Winston menthols, sweet and anxious. A familiar sight, and I am happy she is here. She hugs me tight and quick in the long receiving line, but I lose her in this crowd and don't speak to her again. She'll find out she has lung cancer next week while I'm on my honeymoon. Linda will tell me at her funeral that she spoke of tonight often. "You were like another daughter to her," she will say.

My four-year-old niece Theresa is singing onstage with the band. My brothers are laughing, heads thrown back. Teasing Mike, I suspect, about driving his rusted Duster to the house in the procession of black sedans. Explaining to the valet about the rope around the steering column holding the passenger door shut.

My mother-in-law is dancing with Hamilton, smiling at something he has said. Anthony whispers to Holly, and she gives him a playful punch. They call me over. The handsome groom, the lovely bride. *They'll have beautiful children,* someone is surely saying. You do this at weddings, imagine the future.

This is my ball. The carriage arrives in the morning to whisk us away for three weeks. We fly to Australia and dive off the Great Barrier Reef. Anthony teases me about the huge potato codfish. "They're swarming you, Nut." Then he says to the dive master, loud enough for me to hear, "Aren't there sharks in these waters?" I'm new to diving and half-scared, treading water as he takes pictures of me from the boat. "Stop it, Anthony!" I yell at him, and then laugh, trying to be mad. I fix the video camera on him in the car while he's driving. It's late, and we are heading down winding country roads to the Mount Cook Lodge. "Tell them," I say, referring to our imagined audience—all of the people we think are as thrilled as we are about this marriage. "Tell them about the poor little bunnies that got in your way." He winks at me, at the camera.

How sweet, you would think if you watched it. *Look at how sweet they are together.* Young and in love, we return to New York and to messages on the answering machine from people who missed us. I write thank-you notes and put the pictures in a scrapbook. We go back to work, flushed from adventure.

I am fortunate, you might say, and that could mean anything. I will tell you what happened and let you judge for yourself.

2

Most people think Fortune is something good—to have a *fortune,* to be *fortunate*—a word that implies advantage, like "luck." We use prefixes for bad fortune: misfortune, ill-fortune, unfortunate, but Fortune goes both ways. The Romans personified it in the form of a clever but dispassionate woman who coolly disperses both the good and bad with a flick of her wrist. The goddess Fortuna. Good fortune from her left hand out of a cornucopia filled with gifts—things like straight teeth, a good job, a two-car garage in the suburbs. Bad fortune from her right hand holding a ship's rudder that changes direction, triggering car crashes and untimely deaths. A gesture from her, and the place you thought you were going is no longer in front of you. We call it fate when there is no logical path from then to now. When the man misses a train, then shares a taxi with his future wife or when the cautious woman daydreams through a stop sign at a busy intersection and is hit by a speeding truck. When the man who loves to fly dies in a plane crash. We shake our heads. It's fate, we say.

Every Tuesday afternoon in Suffern I took a bus from Airmont School to Sacred Heart for religion class, where Sister Teresa taught us not to sin. There was an implicit promise of reward for that, but I didn't think it was so simple or personal. My life at the whim of a fickle, apathetic woman made much more sense to me. As a young girl I thought misfortune would befall my father. I thought he would drive his car off the bridge in an ice storm on his way home from the restaurant he owned in Yonkers. The Tappan Zee Bridge with its thin strip of guardrail and the Hudson below, a blanket of black ice on the asphalt. I stayed up alone on these nights, watching for his headlights in the driveway. Standing on the edge of my bed to see out the window, careful not to wake my sister. When the lights appeared I crawled quietly under the covers and tried to sleep in the restless night. It was never peaceful, and I still dread nights, the quiet. When the unforgiving ring of a telephone is impossible to ignore.

The phone didn't ring in the house on Madison Hill Road in the middle of the night. My father's blue Mustang never skidded off the bridge, but twenty-six years later the phone rang late at night in the house on Martha's Vineyard, and I knew.

In seventh grade I had Mr. Durrwachter for biology, and Caroline Garritano was in my class. It was 1976 and *Jaws* was the scariest thing most of Suffern Junior High had ever seen. *Welcome Back, Kotter* was launching John Travolta. My parents were watching *Roots* and following the Patty Hearst trial. Jimmy Carter was elected president and the Yankees were losing, but I was concerned with other things.

I was a quiet twelve-year-old fascinated with the junior high cool kids. The girls, really. The ones who walked down the halls in twos and threes, glossy-lipped with strawberry flavored Kissing Potion, unaffected by pimples and lunch tables and bus lines after school. The girls with feathered hair who hung out at Sport-a-Rama ice rink on Friday nights watching the older boys play hockey, wearing Puca beads and mood rings. They sat in levels in the bleachers, sideways so they could talk to one another, and flirted with the boys between periods, arranging and rearranging themselves like patterns in a kaleidoscope. They wore Frye boots and chinos and kept Salon Styles in their back pockets. I was still wearing hand-me-downs from my older sister—stiff Wranglers and pilly sweaters—and when I saved up enough to buy carpenter pants, they weren't the right ones. They were missing the telltale hammer loop on the left side.

My hair was long and straight, and I wasted hours with the curling iron trying to create what they seemed to be born with. They carried cassette recorders and played Peter Frampton on the hill at lunch. They left a trail of Love's Baby Soft in the halls. And then there were the Garritano twins, Caroline and Suzanne. They wore Charlie.

The twins created energy around them, a palpable squirm of adolescent girls hoping to tag along with them to the mall. Caroline and Suzanne moved through seventh grade as if they had been handed an envelope with directions on the first day. They were not frantically trying to create themselves, like the rest of us. You can see it in Suzanne's yearbook photo—the one on its own separate page above lines of junior high yearbook prose about life and fate.

Everyone I knew wanted to be where the Garritano girls were—the cafeteria, the movies, or Nicky's Pizza. They hung around at the school some days after the last bell, and rumors of what went on rippled through lunch tables and slumber parties. They reigned over the playground, sitting on swings. Unhurried, letting their feet brush the ground and watching the boys hop around them like popcorn.

One rainy day after school let out, after I was already on the bus and the school was deserted, Suzanne and Caroline snuck into the old janitor's quarters at the far end of the hall. It was strictly off-limits, which made them predictably intriguing. There was a dumbwaiter here that dropped from the main floor into the basement—the kind with doors that opened from the top and bottom like a sideways elevator.

They had a boy with them that day—Eddie Meyer from the hockey team. Suzanne's boyfriend, though the twins weren't possessive. But he was Suzanne's boyfriend this day, so he let her in first, watched her squeeze through the horizontal doors, and then followed after her with Caroline. The three of them were cramped, sitting hunched in the tight space, and when the elevator dropped to the basement, Eddie and Caroline got off. Suzanne tried to follow them, sticking her head out awkwardly through the doors, and the top door of the dumbwaiter dropped down on her shiny long hair, crushing her neck. It happened too quickly for her to call out or make a noise. But the dumbwaiter doors, solid metal, were loud when they closed,

and Eddie and Caroline turned around. Of course she was dead
already.

There was an eruption of grief the next day. Principal Parparella
broadcast the news over the crackly public-address system, and clus-
ters of teenage girls formed—sobbing their stories to school coun-
selors and to boys they had crushes on, carefully wiping mascara
streaks from their faces. There were legends forming already—
romantic stories of Suzanne's last words. *Tell Eddie I love him,* echoed
through homerooms. Weepy girls who barely knew her pooled in the
cafeteria and crowded into big hugs in the halls. And they all got out
of class. The school cut a lot of slack in absences for the next few days.
It was easier to excuse an absence than to talk about what had happened. It was easier to excuse an absence than to tell a twelve-year-old
about Fortune. That it was not personal, really.

I gave a name to these sobbing girls later, when we were grown
women. I spotted them again in the wake that shook the world one
July when I was too close to Fortune's rudder. I called them *tragedy
whores.* Even as adults, they cluster in groups, feeding on these occasions, where they reap the reassuring comfort of connected souls.
That is the small reward and point of the wake. They are eager par-
ticipants, playing with Fortune from a safe distance, then going home
to husbands and children, unmarked.

Tragedy whores don't feel the foundation break apart beneath
their feet—the reeling blast of emptiness, though to watch them you
might think so. They're voyeurs. They feed like coffin flies on drama,
embroiled in virtual grief and the illusion of heartbreak. They all have
stories they want to tell, *insist* on telling, proclaiming their link to
tragedy. Emotional rubberneckers.

I didn't like them at twelve, and I hated them at thirty-five.

Suzanne's funeral was the Super Bowl of tragedies for Suffern
Junior High. The church was standing room only; the young parents
sat bravely in the front row beside the spitting image of their dead
daughter. Everyone wanted a view. When the young and pretty ones
die, the tragedy whores get seats up front. They love the melodra-

matic story. That the deceased had an identical twin sister still walking around was a windfall.

The climactic moment, however, was not witnessed by the hundreds in the church, but by an unprepared twenty-five seventh-
graders in Mr. Durrwachter's first-period science class. Eighteen
hours after the dumbwaiter crushed Suzanne Garritano's neck, Caroline walked into class with her jacket on, sipping Coke through a
straw. The rest of us were frozen, knowing we should turn away,
but not quite able to. Caroline was uninterested. She walked to the
front of the room, without a glance to the rows of desks, and said
in a flat voice, her arm stretched out, holding a piece of paper, "I
can't come for class, Mr. Durrwachter. My mom wrote a note." Mr.
Durrwachter looked at her and nodded. He took the note and stared
unblinking as she turned and walked out, unconcerned with his
reply.

Caroline Garritano saw her sister dead in the dumbwaiter and
then excused herself from class sipping Coke through a straw. She
knew about Fortune.

3

There are three places that define my early life, and you can drive to
all of them in half a day. The city, where I live now; the Rockland
County suburb where I grew up; and another small town about an
hour's drive upstate.

The city, New York, is the place I longed for since the nights in the
back bedroom at Tante's wedged into her trundle bed with four fid-
gety brothers and sisters, listening to the buses go up First Avenue.

Watching the lights in other buildings. Her five-story building was on the corner, with a thick black double door. The corner where my father, on leave in full army uniform, waved down a cab to take my mother, pregnant with me, to the hospital and a man saluted him from the back of a limousine. The corner where Grandma Binder raised my mother, in the building across the street.

Suffern, New York, is the suburb, where I went to school and played the flute and hung a David Cassidy poster on my wall. It was where I lived with my brothers and sisters, my mother and father, and Grandma Binder for most of my young life. It's a sleepy town forty minutes north of Manhattan, over the George Washington Bridge, up the Palisades Parkway. A shapeless bundle of families too far from the city to borrow its identity, too close to find its own. Sacred Heart Catholic Church marks the entrance to downtown. The old Lafayette playhouse, the post office, and twelve beauty salons line Main Street. The Avon plant sits just up the road on Route 59.

The small town upstate is Kingston, my moveable feast.

Kingston is anchored by *time*. Kingston is an *era*. At the end of the day, no matter where we have been in our lives, the DiFalcos are firmly tethered by the ghosts of Kingston.

Kingston memories flash through my head like old home movies—Grandma Millie mugging for the camera with hands on her hips and her eyes shut in a smile. Her friend Norma, up from Queens for the summer, standing on the back porch in her housedress. People moving in jerks and fast-motion like 8-millimeter frames. Mouths moving, always smiling, happy like they didn't know better, didn't know you could be somewhere else. Uncle Joey picking out the chords of "Stairway to Heaven" on his guitar. Grandpa DiFalco at the stove stirring his red sauce, orange fly strips hanging over his head. My father holding a fishing rod off the dock. Aunt Maryann at the oak table in the Knotty Pine room, her cards laid out for solitaire, a wineglass beside her, filled to the rim. It is upstate New York in the seventies. Anything can happen or nothing can happen, and either way is fine.

The city of Kingston was a town with schools and historical sites, restaurants and churches. It had an order—businesses where people wore suits and white shirts to work. There were neighborhoods of houses with paved driveways and aluminum siding, but this was not *our* Kingston. The closest we came to that Kingston was in August, when my sister and I had our birthdays in the same week, and Grandma Millie took us to Luigi's for pizza and cannolis.

Our Kingston was in a small alcove called Mount Marion on the banks of Esopus Creek. There might have been another world beyond there, but we didn't need it. Once you turned off Old King's Highway onto Clint Finger Road, you drove through a patch of woods and the road closed up behind you. Mount Marion was where we went to be outside of order.

Grandma Millie's father, Pellegrino, bought the property in Mount Marion for four thousand dollars in 1954, and after Millie retired from the phone company in New York, she and Grandpa moved in, leaving their apartment on Fifty-Eighth Street in New York City, where they raised my father and his three brothers and sister. It was a lot and a one-story house, but Grandpa added a second floor—a clumsy jumble of rooms he put together from a kit that made it look like two different houses stuck together. There were never fewer than half a dozen cars and motorcycles in the driveway, parked at odd angles and in various states of disrepair—one or two on cinder blocks, waiting to be hauled off to the junkyard. A large square gravel patch in the front yard stood in for a driveway, and the grass was knee-high right up to the door. There was a big weeping willow tree in the side yard that shaded Grandma Millie's vegetable garden.

There were two large rooms downstairs—the living room with a TV and couch that doubled as extra bedding, and the Knotty Pine room. Grandma and Grandpa's room was off the living room next to the room where Norma stayed.

The Knotty Pine room was part of the original house and was named after the pine-paneled walls Grandpa bought with a rare windfall from the track. It creeps, somehow, into every story that is repeated about those summers. It had French doors on the side, which I thought made the house sophisticated, and a long oak table right down the middle.

On the side wall, beside the French doors, was a scuffed wooden dresser and a mirror wedged with old photos. The drawers of the dresser were stuffed carelessly with Grandpa's betting sheets, shotgun shells, and unpaid bills. It was the only neat room in the house, because Grandma gave us a dollar or two every week to clean it up.

A makeshift wooden ladder led up to a loft, where my older sister and I usually slept. It had two twin-sized mattresses on the floor, and boxes of letters, papers, and discarded knickknacks stacked in the corners. There was a fluorescent mural on one wall that had been sprayed by one of Grandma Millie's adopted strays on an acid trip. At the back of the Knotty Pine room a door led out to a screened-in porch. From the porch you could see all the way down to Esopus Creek, which divided the short strip of houses where we were and the rental cabins across from us. The creek was muddy green, with tree branches hanging low on both banks. We often bathed in it because the plumbing in the house was unreliable. We kept a bottle of Flex Balsam shampoo out on the dock and when the mood struck, we jumped into the creek in our shorts, soaped up, and then swam underwater to rinse, leaving a trail of soap scum. Then we dried off in the sun on the dock. The water in the house was no good for drinking, even by the flexible standards of my grandparents. Grandpa had jury-rigged a hose with a pump to bring in the water directly from the creek. We could wash the dishes with it, but it had to be boiled first for drinking. On Saturday mornings Grandpa filled the back of his brown station wagon with empty milk jugs and drove over to Maryann's friend Jeannie's house in Lake Katrine, a town over, and filled them up from her tap.

Mount Marion as we knew it orbited around Grandma Millie. The house was like a termite mound of wriggling, rotating DiFalcos, each one cheerfully bringing new members to the colony. Grandma Millie was their queen, heaped right in the middle. She was three hundred pounds, with a raspy voice and a mischievous wink. She had a jowly face marked with bright-red rouge and creamy green eye shadow caked in the creases. She wore cheap rubber flip-flops and big, bright muumuus that she bought on sale at Montgomery Ward—whether it was eighty degrees out or ten. She was always smiling, a fleshy mass of love; everyone competed for her attention, from the box boys at the Pink Store to the old ladies who ran bingo. There was a place here for everyone.

Aunt Maryann was her daughter, my father's younger sister. She was large like her mother, with the same grin and the same wayward wink. She also inherited from Millie a chameleonlike ability to be any age at any moment. She had a head of thick black hair that she made bigger with an even thicker black hairpiece when she went out. She lived in Mount Marion year-round and ran the house like an Egyptian princess with shimmery blue eyelids and clingy outfits. She was perfectly certain of where she should be at any given moment; most often it was at the head of the long oak table in the Knotty Pine room with a glass full of Riunite.

In the summer the air in Kingston was thick with mosquitoes and the Mount Marion house was a centrifugal fusion of love, cigarettes, and sticky wine. It was a hot spot for a revolving "rat pack" of twenty-somethings that included my uncle Joey, aunt Maryann, my other "uncles"—Freddy, Johnny, PJ from Fifty-Eighth Street, Jimmy from the cabins across the creek—and whoever else might be passing through. Millie collected people like green stamps, cashing them in when she needed a favor. She found them, and Maryann carefully worked them into the routine. Millie stumbled upon Tammy in the butcher department at Waldbaum's and befriended her for the discounts and good cuts. She brought Tammy home and Maryann matched her up with Johnny.

Tammy and Johnny were doomed from the start. Tragic lovers. After years of dating and infidelity and boozy shouting matches on the dock, there was nothing left for them to do but get married. Johnny had a deep, hoarse laugh and spent one summer in a full body cast after he broke his neck in a car accident. I remember him sipping beer through a straw in The Kingston Hospital. His brother PJ died young from too much whiskey but Johnny lived, ten years longer than he was supposed to. "His liver," the doctors gravely told Tammy one hospital stay. "You should make arrangements." She went to Seamon-Wilsey for an urn. Jimmy and Freddy went to visit him during this fluorescent-lit vigil and brought him a meatball parmigiana hero from Angelo's. He walked out of the hospital proclaiming the healing powers of a good meatball parm and drank his way through ten more years. Tammy moved out after that, but according to family legend, she routinely drove by Johnny's trailer for the rest of his life, affectionately waving the urn and yelling out her window, "Die already, you son of a bitch."

They were in and out of jobs, all of them—construction and odd labor. A few of them made a decent living bringing pot from the city and selling it in the Kingston bars on weekends. When Grandma Millie got wind of this, she wanted a piece of the action and started growing her own pot in the vegetable garden under the weeping willow. During card games in the Knotty Pine room, Larry sat at the table with a big mound of it and a pack of EZ Widers and rolled perfectly shaped joints that he stuffed into cigarette packs.

Maryann brought Larry home from People's Choice, a popular bar where she worked, and he hung around for three years. He was famous for his skill at rolling joints and for teaching us all to drive a stick shift. Learning to drive a stick shift with Larry was a rite of passage in Kingston. You didn't really *arrive* until Larry put you behind the wheel of his green two-door Subaru and ran alongside the car, yelling through the driver's window, "The clutch is on the left, no, the left!" One summer, my younger brother found the brake just inches before lurching the Subaru into the creek. After that we practiced in the field across the road. Larry was fifteen years old when Maryann discovered him in the bar, and he was devoted to her. I was twelve that summer, but in my eyes he was big, sitting around the table in the Knotty Pine room, drinking beer and playing cards with the grown-ups.

Our family spent almost every summer weekend in Kingston. My parents packed us into our white wood-paneled station wagon—four of us squished in the backseat, my older sister up front, in the middle. We drove up Route 17 making up songs, picking fights, and yelling out landmarks: Motel on the Mountain, Angel Bridge and Devil Bridge, Red Apple Rest.

"We're almost to Red Apple Rest," my mother would say. "And we're not stopping unless it's quiet!" And then we watched out the windows, hushed, for the big, red wooden apple that meant hot dogs and cotton candy. It loomed large and as animated in our unshaped stories as the optometrist's sign in *The Great Gatsby,* marking our entrance to Kingston and the summer the way the big, round spectacled eyes marked East Egg.

The bridges were just past Sloatsburg, and the Tuxedo Motel. They were a pair of cast-iron structures built high over the water, higher, it seems, than they needed to be, and we personified them. The black one was Devil Bridge, because it was dark and rusty and looked sinister. When we approached it we all yelled out, "Devil Bridge!" and my sisters and I crossed our fingers and raised our feet. Angel Bridge came up next and was shiny and unspoiled, with glinting silver beams. "Angel Bridge!" we all yelled, and then my brothers crossed their fingers and raised their feet. We were quiet and serious as we approached the bridges, ready to act. I don't remember what the consequences were if we didn't raise our feet, but I never considered testing fate.

Two or three times a summer Grandpa loaded the grandkids into his rusted brown Cadillac, and we took the Thruway north to exit 24, then I-87 to Saratoga—the upstate town where the Rockefellers, Whitneys, and Vanderbilts summered—to the racetrack, where I caught a glimpse of another life. A life of wide-brimmed hats and white gloves, of pressed slacks and pastels. Of people getting out of fancy cars. I saw boys like the one I would later marry, with neat khaki shorts and blue blazers. Clean, short hair. They sat in a separate part of the track, in boxes, eating sandwiches, while we ate in the greasy restaurant, thrilled with our big plates of the breakfast special.

Grandpa taught us about the horses, boxing trifectas, and long shots. Grandma Millie taught us to steal. She called it night-raiding. She dressed us up in black clothes, a big festive event—like Halloween—and equipped us with pillowcases and flashlights. We were instructed to fill the pillowcases with crops: corn from the Boises' farm, tomatoes and zucchini from the garden next door. Apples from the orchard at the end of the dirt road. She had us pumped up like Little League champs. There were anywhere from five to fifteen cousins here during any given summer, and everyone wanted to go night-raiding, even more so after the neighbor fired his shotgun at my brother and me, as we ran dropping the pears we had taken from his tree.

During the day Millie carried on a more sophisticated subterfuge at Waldbaum's, slipping choice cuts of meat into the great folds of her housedress. She had an ideal shape for camouflage and could tuck a small bag of groceries beneath her enormous breasts. I went with her on one of these shopping trips. She wheeled her shopping cart through the store, filling the large area with lower-priced items and setting more expensive things, like meat, in the front—where you might put a purse or a baby. Then she draped her breasts over the cart and leaned forward, pushing it along with her body. I watched her make a five-pound roast disappear this way. Her arms stretched out along the sides; she looked simply relaxed on a slow, heavy stroll through the store. She hummed to herself, glanced casually, like the other shoppers, up and down the aisles. She pushed her way to the checkout line, where, still leaning over, she set the items from her cart out on the belt. When the cashier had rung her up, chatting with her the whole time—they all knew Millie—she wheeled the cart out of the store and emptied her housedress onto the front seat of the car. A box of Devil Dogs had found its way in there, too. She didn't think of it as stealing so much as *pocketing* stuff.

Millie possessed a number of traits that I have since learned are peculiar, but when I was ten, nothing she did seemed unusual. She seemed like anyone's grandmother, a huge, huggable mass of unconditional love who slipped us cigarettes and pocketed things from Waldbaum's.

The police were called to the house once, to fish a dead deer out of the creek, and there was a brief panic about the pot. Millie saw the black-and-white car with roof lights snaking down the road, and she called for backup.

"Maryann, get out there quick. The cops are coming! Get Freddy!"

Johnny and Freddy ran out and propped an old pickup canopy against the side of the house to cover the crop, and when the officers pulled up, Millie sauntered out the front door in her muumuu with a fly swatter, swatting the air at imaginary flies. Painting a picture, in her mind, of a woman with nothing to hide.

She led the officers around to the creek, where they found the deer, chatting them up like a southern belle. After that, she replanted the marijuana on a remote patch of the Boises' cornfield directly across from our driveway. It wasn't on her property, and she had room for a bigger crop. My aunts and uncles were making a nice side income by this point, selling pot to the Mount Marion summer population.

Kingston was a town where the same dramas repeated every payday somewhere along Route 9W—at People's Choice or Partners or the Dew Drop Inn. Women left their boyfriends, then went back, and then clung to another man in the bar. There were fistfights, tears, and whiskey with beer chasers. Led Zeppelin played on the jukebox, and my aunts and uncles were in the middle of all of it. My grandparents' house was at the dead end of a winding dirt road, and all the walls between adulthood and adolescence dissolved behind their door— especially the year I turned ten, when I was allowed to stay for the whole summer with my older sister, away from the watchful eyes of our parents.

The loft was the best place to be. I liked to sleep there, because I could lie down on the floor, lean over the edge, and have a front-row seat to the theater going on below. Wide-eyed and fascinated, I watched the Knotty Pine group passing out six-packs of Schlitz and smoking up cartons of Marlboro reds or Larry's cigarettes. Maryann kept everything in check; she oversaw nighttime operations, which was when everything important happened. She set their schedule, loose as it was. She decided where, when, or even if they'd go out. There were nights that the group of them sat so long at the oak table—getting up only to pee in the bathroom by Grandma's room, if it was working, or off the back porch—that the bars would close, and they'd stay up all night in the house, getting drunk and playing cards. Those were the best nights. If they remembered anyone was in the loft, they would shout up, "You better be asleep. Don't make us come up there!" Then back to their roundtable. On the nights Maryann bartended they all followed her to People's Choice, where the drinks were strong and often free. We'd hear them stumble in as the sun was rising and watch them wake up in the afternoon—bloodshot and bleary-eyed, and ready to start all over again.

Sometimes they'd let us tag along, and then Jeannie would drive us to the bar and we'd dance by the jukebox while Maryann finished cleaning up. She'd turn the music up loud and teach us to two-step to Donna Summer and Sister Sledge.

Our days were spent in or on the creek, in cutoff jeans and T-shirts— swimming, jumping off the rope swing, and fishing for dinner. We didn't care when the board of health condemned the creek one summer. My uncles just took down the sign. Each of the houses along the creek had a dock, and sometimes I spent entire afternoons sitting on ours with a fishing pole. There wasn't much to catch—mostly catfish and eels—but I loved the simple ritual: picking earthworms out of a can, stringing them on a hook, and waiting for a tug on the line. The dock was also where the rowboat was tied up, and the rowboat led to the cabins.

A boy drowned in the creek one year, just off the falls on a sunny day—the only kind of day I remember. He was older than I was, in his twenties probably, and not a local. The sun was straight over us like a spotlight, and he and his friends were swimming around the deep spot that the rest of us knew to avoid. I saw him go under. I saw my brother Anthony and Matt Nucci running from the cabins. I saw Uncle Freddy diving in.

They said the boy screamed, but I don't remember that, just my brother running so fast and then diving into the deep, muddy spot with Freddy. Their heads crashing the surface to gulp air, and diving down again. The ambulance came, and my brother climbed up on the bank. Silent minutes crept by while the rescue crew put their diving gear on, the rest of us staring at the water, frozen, picturing the body on the bottom of the creek.

We watched from the bank, my brother and Matt still dripping, while the rescue workers combed the bottom for his body. When they pulled him up, twenty minutes had gone by, and he was splotched purple and blue, and bloated—his stomach stretched out like he was pregnant. They pumped his chest and then took him to The Kingston Hospital.

"Twenty-two feet," one of the men told my brother. "You never would have gotten down there, and if you had it wouldn't've helped. He filled up like a Coke bottle and sank. Wasn't a thing you kids could've done."

"They kept him hooked up to life support, but they never got him back," I heard Aunt Marsha tell Maryann the next day. "They said it was his sneakers. Those big leather high-tops. They pulled his feet down just like weights were tied to his legs."

Uncle Freddy had almost drowned once, too, in the creek. It was one of the stories about him that ended with, "That was before Marsha." There was a group on the dock one night dropping acid, and

Freddy jumped into the creek. He started thrashing and screaming, and a nameless man—one of the strays who was staying at the house—jumped into the water and pulled him out.

Neither of these events changed the routine of the Kingston summers.

I learned everything I needed to know about growing up in that cluster of farms and houses and summer cabins. It had the way that some small towns do of harboring eccentrics, like us. We were an unusual assortment of adults and kids, lined up like tipsy ants, weaving in and out of my grandparents' house. We lived exactly on the fray. It was the kind of place where everyone knew what you bought at the Pink Store, the brand of cigarette you smoked, whose car was parked at your house.

Millie's was a house of firsts: first cigarettes, first drinks and petty crimes, first crushes—mine was Frankie McGarrigal.

The McGarrigals rented a cabin across the creek where the other summer kids all stayed. The cabins were one- and two-bedroom shacks painted army green. There were a dozen of them on the opposite side of the creek. They had plumbing and screened-in porches and a big room for playing cards and drinking beer. A flurry of kids ran in and out of the cabins—Kevin Anderson, Matt and Chris Nucci, Judy Pilger—and we followed them, crossing back and forth in a rowboat. But it was Frankie and Chris Nucci my sisters and I had crushes on, and mostly Frankie. Frankie had a speedboat and took his friends waterskiing up and down the creek. He sat on the top of the seat back to drive, one leg propped on the dash, coolly checking the skier behind him. He had silky hair and brown eyes and trickled a sultry cool through our world.

The boys were more interested in my older sister than in me. She knew how to smoke and inhale. But I tagged along anyway wherever they went. We hiked down the falls to Tarzan's Pit and spent the afternoon jumping off the cliff into the water. Then we'd climb up to the rickety wooden trestle that hung over the tiny waterfall to drink beer and wait for the trains to come. We'd show off for one another and stand up as the trains came roaring by with their whistles screaming in our ears. We hung on tight, absorbed in our own danger, the wooden beams vibrating so hard I was sure they would collapse under the weight of the train.

Maryann was my role model, since she seemed to know something about boys. I remember watching her from the loft, getting ready to go out at night. She had a General Electric plug-in vanity mirror and all her makeup arranged on the table in front of her. The mirror had three light settings: daytime, nighttime, and office, and she always had it set to nighttime. The sun had barely set, and she was already drunk but painstakingly precise. She painted herself like a portrait— not a streak, smudge, or uneven spot. She had beautiful skin, a perfect complexion the way heavy women sometimes do—dewy-looking and smooth.

She started at the corner of her eye near her nose and wiped a bold blue shade across her lids with the foam-padded wand that came with the eye shadow. Then she spread it in a slow, even sweep to a point toward her ear, beyond her eyebrow—a solid band of vivid color. And then she repeated it for the other eye. She penciled her eyebrows into a perfect arch that framed her eye shadow. Then she brushed on a straighter line of thick black along the tops and bottoms of her lids and pasted on long black lashes. Her hand was always steady, even when she was holding a whiskey and soda in the other.

She unrolled the pink foam curlers from her hair and combed it into waves and then attached her thick, black hairpiece, teasing it up so that her hair was as big and exaggerated as the rest of her. She wore tight, stretchy pants, tapered at the ankles, and a clingy, low-cut knit top that outlined huge breasts floating like pontoons across her chest. Smooth orbs of flesh pressed against each other, a sharp line plunging down the middle.

It was mesmerizing to watch her routine, ending in time to get to the bar before midnight, pausing at stages to refill her drink and check in on the other rooms in the house. She was the most beautiful woman I had ever seen. I was too young to be aware of sex, but I knew there was some secret Maryann knew that I guessed I'd learn later.

I snuck into her room once and tried to mimic the long, even streaks of color on my eyelids. I thought I would learn something if I could get it just right. I'd find out what it was, this secret. I wiped the blue eye shadow onto my narrow lids, around the small hazel eyes, and in the filtered light of her mirror, I thought I'd done a pretty good job.

I followed my sister to the trestle that night to meet the boys and drink beer. She didn't say anything while we were walking up to meet them, but when we got there, Frankie pointed a flashlight in my face.

"What's on your eyes? They're all blue!"

"What do you know?" I said, trying to sound cool.

I don't know what I had expected; I just thought that grown-up girls wore makeup, and I wanted to be grown-up for Frankie. I tried to shrug it off, act tough, drink a sip of beer, but I knew the moment he pointed the flashlight that I had made a huge mistake. I knew this couldn't be what Maryann spent hours at that table for. I scrubbed it all off with cold water in the bathroom as soon as I could sneak back to the house, leaving them to drink Budweiser and sing along to Zeppelin on the cassette player.

Our lives then were free of horizons; aunts and uncles represented everything I thought life would be. It caught up with them later, of course. Some of the guests of the Kingston house divorced, or died, or were defeated by alcohol and stifled dreams. Our summer days, for many years, were deceptively simple, but everything is different played back on the sober screen of adulthood.

You can drive up to Kingston now in a summer month, follow the winding exit road to Mount Marion, and it's a sure thing you'll catch Ruth Nucci in cabin 5 sitting in a nylon lawn chair drinking a Dr Pepper on her screened-in porch. My grandparents are buried in

Mount Marion cemetery off Old King's Highway. After they died, my father and my uncles sold the house to pay off tax bills, and the new owners tore it down to build a quaint Cape Cod. There is a paved driveway with two cars, and a flower garden where the Knotty Pine room was. The willow tree is gnarled but still standing by the side of the house where Grandma Millie's marijuana plants grew.

I took from Kingston an attitude I am still able to summon, though I do so less frequently: The heady, youthful buzz of beginnings and possibilities. Like Hemingway's Paris. The times we came to life.

4

Life begins with one random and fleeting moment, my first memory. I build the whole story from here. It starts with a road trip, Labor Day 1967. I was riding in the cab of a moving truck on the Palisades Parkway, wedged between my father and my uncle Freddy. I had just turned four. My mother followed behind us in a black Olds 88 with my two sisters, my brother, and our dog, Gigi. My mother was twenty-three and pregnant with her fifth child. Behind the Olds was Grandpa's station wagon, with a mattress tied to the roof and the back packed with boxes.

We were colluders in the cab, the three of us—me, Dad, and Freddy. Trucks weren't allowed on the Palisades, and here we were in the late afternoon sun, zipping along without fear. My father occasionally checked the rearview mirror, grinning. Beating the system, never mind the insignificance.

Behind us was a cramped, thin-walled apartment in Queens next door to the Silvercup Bread Factory and its sour smell of yeast. Ahead of us—the suburbs.

Just two weeks earlier my mother and father were driving to the suburbs in the same black Oldsmobile, looking at model homes in the new neighborhoods. It was what everyone did on the weekends. There was a "For Sale" sign at 15 Madison Hill Road. My dad knocked on the door and handed the woman who answered a hundred dollars to hold the house, or so it's told, and two weeks later we rented a moving truck.

Rockland County was changing dramatically in the late sixties. City families were chasing the American Dream through towns named Nyack, Spring Valley, Tuxedo. They were looking for houses separated by neatly combed lawns on streets with pretty names—an oasis of driveways, garages, swing sets, and picket fences. Suburbia was not yet a caricature of life, but a status. It was for my parents a bold leap into adulthood, a $22,000 mortgage from Dime Savings Bank and $10,000 lent from Grandma Binder.

It was dark when we arrived, and the electricity hadn't been turned on. Grandpa was a handyman by trade, the super of an apartment building on Fifty-Eighth Street—but he had a sort of slapstick way of fixing things. He was like a cartoon character who pulls the plug stopping one leak, uses it to stop another, then steps back and dusts his hands off, oblivious of the water swallowing his feet. He took the meter apart, and when he put it back together, the lights came on. But the meter was broken, and for three years the O&R bill was exactly the same each month, $3.04.

We were unpacked into bedrooms: my two sisters, Elaine and Terri, and me at the end of the hall; my mother and father in the room to one side of us; my younger brother, Anthony, in a crib on the other side. When Richard was born six months later, he moved in with Anthony.

Suffern was an ordinary suburb, filled with ordinary mothers who served pot roasts in Corning Ware. Their husbands carried briefcases on the bus from their jobs in the city. Their children set their places at the table. They all bowed their heads for grace.

By this measure, we weren't ordinary. My father worked as a cook. It was my mother who dressed up to go to work in the city, my mother who got a college degree. Her mother, Grandma Binder, came to live with us when I was six, after she retired from the cafeteria at New York Telephone & Co., and was put in charge of a loose arrangement. My parents popped in at odd hours, around various jobs and my mother's school. Grandma tried to impose a sort of structure, but she was no match for five slippery grandkids, and we ran as unchecked as the dandelions and black-eyed Susans that grew wild in our backyard.

In a sense it was a life every kid dreams about—unruly, wild, unhampered. We had a baseball diamond worn into the side yard, where you could always find a game. We ran through the woods that edged our backyard at all hours of the day and into the night. We were dressed and fed and pointed toward school and the rest was more or less up to us. There was no quiet stretch of time when we were called in for dinner or told to wash up. No hours set aside to do chores or homework. No one checked our report cards, watched the clock when we were out, made sure we brushed our teeth at night. There were no bedtimes or story times except for the few weeks one winter my mother read us the first half of *Treasure Island*.

There was an infrequent and arbitrary use of discipline and attempts at order. One year family meetings were introduced, a sort of family court run by my mother, during which our shortcomings were pointed out and we were allowed, in turn, to point at one another. There was a chore chart and a meal schedule laid out. There were a handful of these meetings at best, so they were quickly forgotten, and disorder resumed.

I developed two traits as a result of my childhood: an obsession with order and a devotion to detail. I line up details and study and rearrange them until they please me. The simplest task is thought out, well-ordered, planned. I am unable to leave a thing to chance.

We turned our basement into Grandma Binder's apartment—a cramped bedroom with a living area and kitchenette. Her Singer

sewing machine, the kind with a floor pedal, was wedged in by the
TV, next to a clear plastic sewing box with fabric scraps and hundreds
of spools of colored thread that she used to make aprons, splurging
only on the s-shaped rickrack she sewed around the hems. She hung
picture puzzles of Austria on the wall and grew pots of African vio-
lets on the windowsills; they thrived somehow in that basement. She
was known in the neighborhood for her green thumb. Mrs. Merrick
showed up at our door one day with a pot of dirt and a limp stalk and
Grandma Binder had it back to life in a week.

There was no furniture in the house to speak of, outside of
Grandma's apartment. There were beds to sleep on and a couple of
mismatched chairs and a bookshelf, but the rooms gave an overall
impression of emptiness. The previous owners left gold satin floor-
length drapes in the living room, and they looked extravagant in the
empty space. For years we posed for pictures in front of them closed
so that the bare wood floors, the empty room, made it look like a small
theater. As though we had just ended the school play and were
crowded around my mother taking a curtain call.

We ate downstairs at Grandma's, arranged around her table. She
cooked Austrian foods that our friends had never heard of—boiled
pig knuckles and kraut nödel. She had a thick, clotted accent and
struggled with English. She watched *Guiding Light* while we were in
school, hoping to improve it.

Grandma lived in New York City for thirty years on Seventy-
First Street, the Upper East Side. When she arrived, Seventy-First
Street was not an address people dropped at dinner parties. It was
called Yorkville then, a name that went the way of the rotary phones
and rabbit ears in their apartments. She raised my mother alone in a
small ground-floor apartment. Her older sister Johanna lived across
the street. We called her *Tante,* the Austrian word for *aunt.* They
were linked by blood, by relatives in Austria, and Tante was loyal
but not warm. She was not a woman who forgot mistakes. She
thought it a duty to preserve them. She was small and firm like my
grandmother, and she came to America first and respectably, with a

husband. Grandma Binder left behind a son in Austria and a cloud of secrecy surrounding my mother's father. His identity was never discussed. For this, Tante kept my grandmother in a perpetual prison of atonement that she neither resented nor shunned. There was a distinct pecking order: Tante, then Grandma Binder, then my mother. This was simply how it was. Grandma Binder and Tante were quiet and serious—staid women from a generation that expected difficulties and hard work. There was pride about owning things, admonitions to be careful. They parceled out information in tiny bites on a need-to-know basis, and there was little, in their view, that anyone needed to know.

The DiFalcos were cheap wine, cigarettes, loud laughter. Their faces were colorful, their movements exaggerated. They told big stories and filled up space. They were unable to leave a room without marking it somehow. My mother's family, on the other hand, was quiet and resolute. They drank coffee in cups with saucers; they sat up straight in their chairs. They were in constant struggle, these temperaments, from where we kids stood: the DiFalcos' clamorous simplicity, the Binders' stern wall, and my mother parked uneasily between them.

My father grew up on Fifty-Eighth and Second Avenue with his brothers—Sal, Benny, and Joey—and Maryann. It was the kind of city block that was typical then: self-contained like a small town. A tight neighborhood at a time when you counted on the kindness of strangers—on other adults, the neighborhood policeman—to watch out for the kids. He was handsome—muscular and square-jawed, always with a cigarette dangling from his lips. He was one of the gang on Fifty-Eighth Street and had a quiet, James Dean kind of cool.

He was twenty-two when he spotted my mother on Sixty-Ninth and First Avenue, sitting on the corner next to Julia Richman High, from which she had just graduated with honors that spring. She was brainy and pretty, drawn to the guy in the leather jacket. I like his stories because he doesn't tell them much, and when he does they're casual but vivid. Nothing is left out. We know about the years busing tables at the Copa, with Dean Martin and Frank Sinatra hanging out in the kitchen. We know about motorcycles and street fights and hotwiring cars from Potemkin Cadillac on Sixty-Ninth Street with his buddy Vezzie. We know about Eddie Nine-fingers and the fight with Duke for my mother. We know he and Sal and Benny enlisted in the army in 1962 and that he was promoted from private to sergeant, which made him practically a war hero in my family.

My father was a high school dropout with a motorcycle and a leather jacket, a pack of Marlboros rolled up in the sleeve of his T-shirt. And he was the first person to give my mother information she could do something with. "You're smart, Helen," he told her. "You should go to college." Then they walked hand in hand through Central Park singing, "two lost souls on the highway of life . . . " and she married him.

I think my mother had a different sort of life in mind, a more complicated one that she had expected but thought had missed her. Girls on Seventy-First Street were to get married and have children and it was assumed that was enough, a vague sense of respectability that always involved a man, and children, and very little of the woman herself. My mother made her choices early, before she was ready to, perhaps. At a time when there was a slight shift in what was expected of women. The idea of a career, a college education, was possible yet seemed just beyond her reach. She had a baby when she was eighteen, an age for trying things on, and four more before she started supposing a life for herself. She was caught between the pretty picture and this other thing that was yet to be defined.

I think there was a point in the beginning when she was thrilled with this family she had made. When she loved the madcap drama of five babies, a handsome husband, a pretty new house in the suburbs. The paint peeled faster than she expected, of course.

She was good with occasions. Our birthdays were filled with neighborhood kids and balloons and a Betty Crocker marble cake.

We carved pumpkins every Halloween and picked from a chest full of costumes. On Easter we dressed up and drove into the city to Tante's.

At Christmas she put together an extravaganza of food and toys. There was an improbable number of presents under the tree, and there was food in the house for weeks. Neither of which we could afford, but reality was put on hold. The empty house filled up magically, with furniture in the living room and a life-size poster of Santa Claus tacked to the wall. There was a big fir tree, borrowed chairs, stackable plastic tables draped with red-and-green tablecloths. Boxwood garland hung from the ceiling and wrapped around the banister; a wreath went up in the hallway. Cars crowded our driveway by noon on Christmas. My father started cooking on Christmas Eve and finished Christmas night. There were giant aluminum trays of baked ziti, calamari, and eggplant parmigiana. Food appeared like the miracle of the loaves. The sensation lasted through New Year's, until all the food was eaten and all the needles were off the tree. We were characteristically late in taking everything down.

Then, however, there was the rest of the year to get through.

I was seven when my dad bought a restaurant in Yonkers and called it DiFalcos. It was on Kimball Avenue, three blocks up from Yonkers Raceway. It was a family restaurant, where you could get a chicken parm with a side of spaghetti for $2.50, cheese lasagna for $2.25, and free refills on soda. My mother waitressed here at night and on weekends. Sometimes on Sundays I would go with her to help. She would let me carry the baskets of bread to the tables, clear the dishes, fill up sodas. They struggled to keep the restaurant open and never seemed to save a dime, no matter how hard they worked. There was a flush of optimism one year when they bought a brown-velvet love seat, fancy teak bookshelves, and a brass tea cart with wheels. But DiFalcos didn't survive, and then there were years of unpaid bills, foreclosure notices, and food stamps. My father took a job at Stella's Deli. He moved easily within his space, wherever his space happened to be, like a man who had planned it all.

My mother was different. She wasn't like the other mothers on the block, exchanging casserole recipes and sewing patterns. Like all little girls, I watched my mother carefully. If she had been the sort to bake cookies or play bridge, I am certain that I would have played bridge, too. But she wasn't.

My mother wore short skirts with go-go boots, which were the style then. She was a *pretty* mother. She had Boswell's *Life of Johnson* and *The Complete Works of William Shakespeare,* and they were both marked up in the margins. She was a *smart* mother. She was inconsolable when my father took the car to work one Saturday and she missed the Sears white sale. She was a *sad* mother. She screamed, furious, if towels were not washed, when the toilet paper ran out. She was a *mad* mother. I can't find an adjective to hang onto.

My mother had no language yet to describe what she was feeling in 1973. For a year she drove white-knuckled over the Tappan Zee Bridge to the restaurant, willing herself not to drive off. Then at twenty-seven, with five children, she started her retreat. She put a lock on her bedroom door and enrolled in Rockland Community College.

There was a family vacation when I was eight, the only one I remember. We drove through Pennsylvania to Hershey and toured the chocolate factory, and I remember the smell of the chocolate and the great conch machines that stirred and smoothed it out. I remember the Hershey Motor Lodge with the five of us squirming in a bed. We rode horse-drawn buggies in the Amish country in Lancaster. We drove through Civil War battlefields—Gettysburg and Lexington— stopping at the chambers of commerce to pick up self-guide cassette tapes of reenacted battles. I have a vivid memory from that trip of my mother listening to the battle of Gettysburg with headphones in the front seat of the car. She gave me headphones, too, and I listened to the sounds of cannons and guns, the screams of dying young boys, and watched the tears run down my mother's face. You remember when your mother cries. Tears came at odd times. As though she saved them until she couldn't hold them anymore.

5

As families go, I held up Linda's as the standard. Linda Rosenfeld appeared in my driveway two weeks after we moved to Madison Hill Road. My sister and I were jumping rope. She was with her mother, Vivian, across the street at the Merricks', and Vivian sent her over. "Go and say hi," she said, nudging Linda and her little sister, Nancy. "I'll be right there."

They had ponytails and were dressed in matching short sets, with bathing suit straps sticking out from under their shirts. Nancy was two years younger but taller, Linda chubby with crooked bangs. Vivian joined us from across the street, and we played hopscotch while our mothers talked on the front lawn.

Linda lived three houses up the street, number twenty-four. She had the same bedroom as I did, upstairs at the end of the hall, and our birthdays were three days apart. We made a well-worn path across my front lawn to hers, and after a while the grass stopped growing there.

It was nothing for me to be out of sight for hours at a time. No one worried about me. If I wasn't home, I was at Linda's house or somewhere with Linda. We spent afternoons in her basement holding talent shows and beauty pageants, writing plays and hosting game shows. We had skateboarding contests with Joey Tiso and the Spiegals. We explored fossil land in the woods at the dead end of Madison Hill—a burned-out, flat patch of land with buried metal, plastic junk, and rocks with animal skeletons hardened in them.

When our dog, Gigi, had puppies I gave one to Linda, and we named him Cocoa. Gigi was a pedigreed poodle, dropped off late one night under mysterious circumstances by my uncle Joey. It's the sort of story that was a cliché in our house. Like in the movies if a man meets a woman on the train, they'll become lovers by the second act. If there's a pedigreed poodle at the DiFalcos', it was delivered suspiciously and late at night. Then Gigi muddied the bloodline during an illicit romp with a German shepherd, and Cocoa was born. The DiFalcos could never quite summon a proper appreciation for lineage.

Linda's father was an accountant; he wore a suit and tie and carried a large briefcase. And except for his toupee, he was like all the other fathers who drove to work each morning and returned in time for dinner. Then he and Vivian divorced. They were the first ones on the block. It separated them from the string of nuclear families that lined Madison Hill the way our weedy lawn separated us.

After her divorce, Vivian reinvented herself. Like a lot of mothers in our neighborhood, she'd had no reason to think she would ever take a job outside her home. But now she had to go to work in an office. From our view, little changed, though. She was still home by 5 p.m. and making chicken cacciatore. She drove us to Girl Scouts and band practice. She consoled us when Cocoa died of a heart attack after getting knotted up in his chain one hot July day trying to mount Sparky, Linda's cat. Then Vivian explained the birds and the bees.

My admiration for Vivian was inexhaustible. She seemed everything my own mother was not. She sat down with us at dinner and asked about school. She signed permission slips and made grilled-cheese sandwiches. She kept potato chips and Ring Dings in the cabinet. She read trashy romance novels and had copies of *The National Enquirer* in her bathroom. She was available always, it seemed, at any time of the day, to drive us somewhere. She was my idea of the proper American mother.

Vivian married young, had children, and didn't pursue anything else. But she encouraged Linda to study and go to college. My mother was less specific; she told me to be independent. It was the only advice she gave me. Everything I did was tied to the quest for independence. I washed my own clothes, found my own way home from school, paid "rent" when I started making my own money. "You have to be independent," she said. So at fourteen I rode my bike to the Wendy's just over the Jersey border in Ramsey. I filled out an application and lied about my age, and they hired me. I possessed a certain proficiency at work. I paid attention and I followed direction, and I sensed that these skills, somehow, would be my ticket out of Suffern. I applied at Caldor Department Store shortly after this, and they hired me in customer service. The pay was better, and I had more responsibility. At Caldor I had some authority. I handled returns and customer complaints. I resolved things. I made decisions. If your blender was defective or you bought sheets the wrong size, I took care of it. If someone needed to be paged over the speaker system, I was the one who paged them, and at a quarter of nine I announced, "Attention Caldor shoppers, we will be closing in fifteen minutes. Please bring your items up to the register."

6

Grandma Binder died my junior year in high school. My father came home and found her collapsed on the floor of her bathroom. She'd been lying there for hours, too weak to move. He carried her to the car and drove her to Good Samaritan Hospital.

Grandma Binder was never sick—it was an indulgence she didn't permit herself. Even in her seventies she walked the mile to Grand Union for groceries a few times a week. Then she went to the hospital with my father and didn't come back. Now is when I developed an uncertainty about hospitals, a nagging distrust that I filed away after her funeral and pulled up again at thirty, when hospitals were part of my routine.

My mother was waiting for me when I got home from school, and I knew why she was there. The phone rang this morning, too early, and when I picked up the extension, a man's voice said, "She took a turn for the worse. You should come as soon as you can."

"Grandma died." She didn't wait for me to shut the door. "During the night. Your dad and I went this morning, but she was already gone."

"Gone where?"

"She was in her hospital bed, very peaceful. She just looked like she was sleeping."

Where was the doctor? I wondered. I had an image of doctors whispering around her, this woman not dead yet but dying, and not wanting to disturb her so she'd look peaceful in the morning. So my mother could tell us she looked like she was sleeping.

"They did what they could, Carole. It was too late."

Even at sixteen I was skeptical. I imagined interns shuffling in groups through sterile hospital wards—straight-A'd from medical school, fresh from their Hippocratic oaths. During the doctor's morning rounds, leading a pack of them, he pulled the curtain around her bed. *This one took a turn for the worse,* and then he instructed his interns on the fine points of informing next of kin.

"Pneumonia," her own doctor had said two weeks earlier, and then he sent her back home. "She's fine, she just needs rest," he told my mother. So Grandma rested and then got worse and my mother called the doctor and he told her again, "She needs rest."

After she died I remembered a conversation I wasn't supposed to hear, seeing Grandma at the door of my mother's bedroom, standing in the hallway. "I'm scared, Helen," she said. Her voice was ragged. She was standing in her nightgown, and I was not supposed to see that.

When she got to the hospital, they started running tests. My mother was relieved. Now they will figure out what's wrong, she thought, and took the next train home. Grandma didn't have pneumonia. Her kidneys had failed, and Sister Joseph Rita greeted my mother with this blunt news as she entered the emergency room.

"We gave her last rites."

They didn't have dialysis equipment then, so they moved her to New York Hospital that night. My mother took us to see her. The next day she died of heart failure.

My mother was serious, but there was nothing otherwise unusual in her manner or her voice to mark the occasion for me. Nothing in her expression that I could file under "death." She might have known it would be easy with me. It wasn't that I didn't care or that I didn't love my grandmother; I was just not surprised by this. I knew misfortune was simply a stumble from a curb, a distracted turn on a highway, one careless doctor away. After she told me, I walked to the back bedroom to watch out the window where a bus would pull up and my younger sister would step off. She was my grandmother's favorite and the kind of little girl who thought Fortune was personal. She thought misfortune happened to bad people, that if she smiled and made her bed she'd be spared. My little sister thought Fortune picked favorites.

I watched from the window. The last moments of one life she knew and the first moments of another. It was a peculiar fascination, I suppose, but I was trying to understand the things no one explains. I was curious about death—about the power it has to change life so completely. The dead slip out quietly and leave furious holes in their wake. It's Fortune's strong suit. She keeps catching us unprepared, again and again. *Life,* we say at dinner parties or while we're tsk-tsk-ing the evening news, *is so short,* and then she proves it.

I wanted to see what would happen to my sister in the hall, on the other side of the door—what it would look like, her life changing. I wanted to see her physical response, how her body reacted, so I watched at the window, waited for her to run across the lawn to my mother in the hall. The bus pulled up and she got out, waving to her friends, to the driver. She was grinning the way kids do, excited to go to the next thing. She ran across the grass, jumping onto the steps. I watched the last few seconds of a life she had grown used to. *Don't open that door—run away before they say it.* She could just as easily have turned down the street and gone to play at the Ochs'. She could have had her life for another few hours.

Tante came from the city for the wake at Wanamaker & Carlyle, the funeral at St. Anthony's in Nanuet. They had Grandma's hair done for the viewing, and her forehead was blue where the makeup had rubbed away from kisses.

After Grandma died, I found her passport in one of the boxes my mother had packed. The girl in the picture was unsmiling but pretty, and I wondered about the plans she had made for herself before taking that picture and getting on the boat to America. It was a life she might have been angry about missing but she wouldn't have permitted herself to dwell on her loss. On the dresser in her bedroom was a mirrored vanity tray with a matching comb and hairbrush arranged carefully next to a tarnished gold compact and several crystal perfume bottles. Reminders of the life she might have imagined for herself at one time. Before ill-timed pregnancies, before circumstances recast her in a new country as a single mother when there was shame in that.

My grandmother had secrets, and my mother inherited them. It seemed everything was a secret. It was a secret that businesses had failed, that the house was perched on foreclosure, that we were on welfare for a time. The mundane, even, was a secret. I did not know, for instance, where my mother worked. Where she was going, what time she'd be home. When she was not home, I would sneak into her room and look through her pictures. She kept them loose in her desk drawer, in no order, hundreds of photos stuffed in bags and envelopes, and I took them out one by one, careless with fingerprints. She would have been angry if she'd caught me. I knew this, but I was too young to understand privacy. I thought it was harmless, sneaking in there. I just wanted to look. I thought they would tell me something, reveal something, although I couldn't imagine what.

I held them up close and studied the backgrounds for clues. I lingered on the photos of my mother as a child. Black-and-white photos, the edges yellowed and slightly warped. Here she is at eight, holding her dog Brownie; at sixteen in a frilly white dress on a chair in Tante's apartment, her hair around her face in tight blonde curls, her legs crossed at the ankles, long white gloves on her hands. There were no pictures of a father. Her father wasn't discussed in our house. There was a sound bite: *He died in the war before I was born,* and that was all.

There was a picture of Tante and my grandmother in a cemetery in Austria, *September 1963* stamped on the back. They were each on one side of a tombstone, their brother Frank's. *Franz Binder.* My grandmother's name. She had two children, yet she never changed it.

It took me fifteen years after Grandma Binder died to ask Tante. She was ninety-six and in a nursing home in Tinton Falls, New Jersey. I went to visit her several times before I got the nerve.

"Who was my mother's father?"

She was propped up in a twin bed with the radio on and looking straight ahead as she always did. Her eyesight was failing, but her stare was still hard and unyielding.

"I knew you'd be the one to ask," she said without surprise. "You always asked too many questions. It's too long ago now to talk about it."

But I knew she wanted to tell me. It had been too long to keep a secret, even for her. I looked back at her with the same hard stare.

"His name was Nick. He was nobody. He was married. Your grandmother worked for the family."

I was silent.

"Your grandmother was wrong to see him. She shouldn't have and that's that."

"Did you know him?" I asked.

"I met him once or twice. He was tall. Italian. It doesn't matter. He had a wife and children."

I was stunned. *Tante knew him? She met him? Were they in love? Did he love her? She got pregnant and never saw him again?* Tante turned away from me.

I had waited a long time to ask. Three months later she died in her sleep.

7

There were three men in my house when I was growing up, besides my father. And I was in love at various times with all of them—Bucky Dent, Hawkeye Pierce, and Robert Redford. My mother hung a poster of Redford in our stairwell, his sultry gaze held fast with thumbtacks, and for years he watched us come and go.

So it seemed perfectly natural that one day I would follow him out of his office and chase him down Forty-Sixth Street into a cab.

It was Linda's idea. We were sixteen and bored on a Thanksgiving holiday. Linda and our friend Maria and I took a train into the city. I was wearing Maria's rabbit fur, glamorous, pretending I was famous while Linda and Maria followed me into buildings and took pictures. "Oh my God, is it her?" they gasped, laughing.

My mother said Redford had an office in the Warner Brothers building at Rockefeller Center. We went into the city without much more of a plan than running into him at work. We made it as far as his lobby before backing out under the stares from security.

"Let's go in the bank," I said. We were loitering, looking for something to mark our adventure. "Maybe he's in there, making a deposit." We giggled at the thought of Robert Redford just hanging around, doing the ordinary things other people in New York do.

"What are we *doing*?" Maria was laughing. I peered into the front window of the bank, trying to see past the tinted glass, and then I saw his reflection as he walked by right behind us.

"Oh. My God." Linda's body froze and her eyes popped open, wide with a giddy mix of fear and joy. Fortune dropped Redford in our laps. He was bigger than the president. *The Electric Horseman* had just come out, which would have been a forgettable movie if we hadn't been so love-drunk for The Sundance Kid, Hubbell Gardner, and Jay Gatsby. There was nothing he couldn't be forgiven for.

"Oh, my God," Maria screamed, unembarrassed.

"Oh, my God," the three of us shrieked in unison. And before we could think, we were following him. He was walking east on Fifty-First Street toward Fifth Avenue, and people butterflied to the sides, fanning out and double-glancing. The sidewalk parted for him like a holy sea, and the three of us chased him right up the middle.

"Hurry, he's hailing a cab!" Linda yelled. We got to the cab as he was getting in and shutting the door. He was looking straight ahead, saying something to the driver, and Maria opened the front door and threw in a ten-dollar bill. "Here. Don't charge him. Take this for his ride."

The cab screeched away, and we walked back to the train station. We sang "The Way We Were" off-key and imagined Redford with his blue, sparkly eyes and angled jaw, flashing teeth and dropping anecdotes on the *Tonight* show. *Well, Johnny, there was a funny time with these girls once, in New York.* . . . It didn't occur to us that he had thousands of these stories, that this one would be instantly forgotten.

Years later I tried to remember that moment when a man came to life from a poster in my stairwell and what it aroused in me. I attached to him all the utopian illusions of my sixteen-year-old self about boys, fame, love. I tried to remember what that afternoon was about. The rush of power we felt that day when we willed a thing to happen and it did.

I remembered how once I felt a giddy sense of invincibility that has gone almost unmatched in the years since that afternoon with my two girlfriends, skipping carelessly through the city. I tried to remember Redford and that it wasn't personal. We weren't chasing the man, after all, but the poster, a caricature. A caramelized, glittery concoction of Jeremiah Johnson and Bob Woodward and Gatsby and Sundance. Of horses and beaches and Katharine Ross and white teeth. Of windless days of sun shining on an ageless face. We knew him intimately without ever speaking a word to him.

This was my first glimpse of mania—of crazy, blind desire for a

stranger with a well-known face. A stranger who unwittingly repre-
sents something for the adorer, entirely personal and unpredictable. A
stranger who is so completely formed in the minds of others that one
wrong move, a sentence spoken or not spoken, an expression or gesture, can excite extreme emotion.

It was my first glimpse of losing yourself and hanging every
heightened emotion on another human being's shoulders. A human
being in the sense that he walks standing up. In every other regard not
human, but godlike, able to clear a New York sidewalk simply by
stepping on it.

I'd like to think I had a nagging sense of embarrassment that day,
that somewhere before the train back to Suffern I realized how silly
it was to chase after a stranger like that, a man with his own life, trying to get home after work. I'd like to think I felt bad about it. It
seemed so harmless, three teenagers acting silly. But then years later I
was on the other side, going to the opening of the ballet. I went out
with John sometimes before he and Carolyn were married, so she
wouldn't have to. There were rows of photographers facing us, walking backward and shouting out, "John, this way. John, over here."

Photo assassins, I called them. They tried to be familiar, yelling out
things they thought they knew about him. "Hey, John. Who's the
girl? Hey, Sunshine, over here! Look over here. What's your name?"
All against a loud backdrop of rapid-fire camera clicks.

I suppose it's not acceptable to protest the travails of fame, even
when it's unsought. I witnessed it from the sidelines. You have to
remove yourself to stand in the middle of it, smiling.

When I was dating Anthony but before many people knew, I
had dinner with Linda and Maria. We were catching up—we were
all in different lives, and by then a year or two might go by between
dinners. Linda brought up Redford, and we laughed. "Maria and I
went to Hyannis last summer, to see if we could find John Kennedy,"
Linda said. They giggled a little, exchanged sheepish looks, because
we were older now. They didn't know about Anthony, that I was
dating John's cousin, and I didn't tell them that night. "I thought

maybe we'd get lucky again," Linda said with a laugh. I laughed, too, nervously.

It hadn't occurred to me what it might be like from Redford's view, to be *inside* the cab.

8

After the summer of '99, the summer they all died, I took a Walkman with me everywhere. I read the Philosophers in 90 Minutes series, and I discovered Mary Cantwell. She wrote *Manhattan, When I Was Young,* and I don't think there's a better love story or tragedy about the city anywhere. I found it when I was living in other people's houses when I was afraid to go home to an empty apartment. I marked it up and took it with me, trading Cantwell's thoughts for mine, tracing her journey from Bristol, the small town on the coast of Rhode Island where she grew up, to her magazine career in New York in the fifties.

I took her on my long walks. I went to her places. Her 21 Perry Street, her 232 Hope Street. These are my 969 Park, my Madison Hill Road. Like me, she seems always misplaced, running away, then looking behind her. We'd be a terrible pair, the two of us, both looking for a thread to follow, both grabbing the loose ends. She, too, is escaping.

I walked along Perry Street one morning looking for the *most secret of all the Village's secret gardens,* which Cantwell said was between West Eleventh Street and Perry. When she lived here in 1962, you could get a key to the garden only if you were renting one of the houses from St. John's Church. I was thinking of her apartment, with the concrete urn and Paul McCobb couches, looking for the garden, when I came abruptly upon Sant Ambroeus restaurant on the corner of West Fourth.

I hadn't been to Sant Ambroeus since the night before Anthony died. We ordered takeout, and I left him alone to pick it up, pasta pomodoro and a tricolor salad with parmesan.

It was the same place, but our Sant Ambroeus wasn't here; it was on Madison Avenue, and it was old and well-mannered, with white-satin walls and fake geraniums. *The coffin,* we used to call it, because of the puffy satin walls, the waiters solemn in jackets. It was our place. Now I stumbled across it in its new downtown location, cheery with large windows, the waiters in pink button-down shirts. The geraniums were still here, but not fake. It was a strange feeling, the past reshuffled, memories rearranged.

When I think of Cantwell's Bristol, I think of Suffern. I think of a butterfly flapping its wings in a jungle in Brazil and creating an earthquake on the other side of the world. I think of what might not have happened if I'd stayed there. When I think of Suffern, I think of longing for something else. I think of Chris Nucci sitting on the hurdy-gurdy in Kingston, after I have just started an internship at ABC, asking, "Who do you think you are, Barbara Walters?" The question was rhetorical and wrapped in a sneer that suggested a girl from Suffern had no business being there. I was embarrassed but I thought he was probably right. *Who do you think you are?*

Suffern was a fenced-in, cheerful town, where not much happened, and a lot of people were happy with that. I never was. By the time I was in high school, I felt a sort of low-grade panic about my future and a gnawing embarrassment about my past. I was at an age at which I thought I should have a picture of an adult life in my mind. I longed to see the world on the other side of the fence, my nose pressed up against the town limits sign.

The city held, I thought, every adventure I hadn't imagined. I thought it might be a place to reincarnate, to pull a whole new existence from the chatter of crowded streets. I fell in love with it when I was small and my mother used to take us on weekends to Tante's apartment. It captivated me—the noise, the grit, the busy, crazy flow of it all.

I loved the same things then that I do now about the city—walking along Madison Avenue to Central Park, watching the lights in other buildings, soaking up energy from the people in Union Square. Listening to the buses out the front living room window of Tante's apartment.

She lived in the same fifth-floor railroad flat for fifty years. Her apartment had a smell of old things—piles of yellowed newspapers, pictures and letters wrapped with rubber bands. Layers of paint so thick none of the doors closed shut. The musty odor of a life lived and then boxed up. It was a safe smell, comforting. It said, *I have managed it all this long.*

I could sit sometimes as a little girl on the stoop of her building and watch the people walk by with their stories. In bed at night, I listened to the steady, soothing sounds of the street. Everything was moving; something was going on behind all those doors stacked on top of one another.

I loved the procedure of those weekends—watching the tall brick apartment buildings that lined the drive from the George Washington Bridge to the East Side along the FDR snapping by through the car window, pressing my face up against it, searching for the Seventy-First Street exit. My father let us out in front of the building and disappeared to find parking. The rest of us raced one another up the stairwell to the fifth floor, elbowing for the lead. Tante was always waiting for us in the hallway, peering over the rail as we ran up.

When Anthony and I moved into an apartment on Park after we were married, we got into a fight the first night. A silly fight that was

really about things that were bigger than we wanted to talk about—
marriage, a new mortgage on Park Avenue, cancer. I left angry at
midnight to walk around the city, and I ended up on Seventy-First
Street. I walked out because I wanted to feel the city on my skin. I still
do that, walk around aimlessly at odd times of the night. The feel of
the city comforts me.

You're lucky if you have a place like Tante's apartment, a place
where you can remember the time when you were safe. I found myself
in Tante's foyer—the small room inside the front door before you get
buzzed through the second—because I knew it would look the same
as it did to me when I was five. Like two people watching the moon
from opposite ends of the world. My five-year-old self and my thirty-
one-year-old self staring at the same cracked pink-and-black tile,
smelling the same mildew mixed with smells of old cooking.

There had been times in the city at Tante's, or dancing in Linda's
basement, or fishing off the dock in Kingston, that I was excited with
what life had given me. Times I felt perfectly complete. Then I left all
of that. I went too far to go back, but I didn't know that until I was
grasping for something familiar and safe and there wasn't anything
for me to hold on to.

Discoveries

We used to drink it at the Radziwills' when I stayed with them for the shooting. You should have seen those Polish princes putting it away.... Good blood, of course; aristocrats to the tips of their fingers.... Oh, how it brings back the old days! You people who never stayed with the Radziwills don't know what living is. That was the grand style.

— W. SOMERSET MAUGHAM, *The Razor's Edge*

1

We create narratives for people, because they are simpler than the complexities of real lives. Everyone wants a good story, with a prince and a princess and a villain. When narratives change, it's unsettling, because whether or not they're our own, they help to define us, and we don't want to let go of them. In my own narrative my husband was brave and I was selfless, the two of us dancing a tragic dance of love. Cancer was our villain. It wasn't so simple, of course, but this was our story.

The hardest part of moving on is cleaning up and collecting the scattered bits and pieces, the noise, the buzzing in the head. Making decisions about what to keep, what to give away. I kept a box of odd things. Anthony's belt still bent at the notch where he wore it, his bike shorts and a wrinkled T-shirt, his good-luck cuff links, a gold locket, and our wedding bands. I kept the framed photo of John and Carolyn's dog, Friday, that she hung up at every hospital and a book of poems with John's doodles in the margins. I kept the amethyst ring from Carolyn, a tape recording of her phone greeting, and the gold Cartier toe ring she surprised me with one night in the city our last summer together.

And then I packed them away one by one as they worked free from the memories attached to them.

Ultimately what remains is a story. In the end, it's the only thing any of us really owns. Some people write to explain their lives, others to escape them. I write partly out of a compulsive habit to keep things organized. Partly because our story is all that remains of our lives together, and I was afraid of losing that, too. But this is *a* story of my life, not *the* story. Who could ever begin to tell it all?

I looked for God and meaning in all the usual places: the Bible, a yoga retreat, a mountaintop in Peru. I had my numbers and my cards read and went to see Beatrice the psychic, who said I'd meet my next husband in Europe and I'd be wearing a floral dress. But the closest I came to solace was in philosophy and in fiction: logic and truth. I was a permanent step behind and at constant risk of falling further. It took me a certain time, for instance, to understand what had happened to Anthony—that he was gone and I had lost a husband, that I was a widow—because I kept backing up to the phone call that night in the Vineyard. *They're not here yet and I was just wondering, are they there? With you?*

Among the voices in my head was one that chided me for calling the coast guard, the air force, for saying it out loud. In my fantasies, if I hadn't been so quick to think it, maybe we would have found them—John wandering the property, Carolyn asleep upstairs. She would be sheepish, I imagined, at putting me through all of that, and he would laugh it off. *Oh, Carole, you're so dramatic!*

I kept only one eye on the details when Anthony died three weeks later, making sure I got them right—the music, the guest list, the ashes delivered by sunset. The other eye trailed behind, trying to figure out, still, how this had happened. Playing it over and over to see how it could be fixed.

There are days I feel as though the interesting part of my life has happened to me. The curtain has come down, the guests have gone home, and I am here alone, waiting for a ride. This life, the one I made for myself through varying amounts of design and chance, seems to have started and stopped between twenty-five and thirty-five. I moved to the city. I found a career. I married a handsome man. I met Carolyn.

2

Before I was a wife or a widow, I was a journalist, and that started in Annette Kriener's office at ABC, on Sixty-Seventh and Columbus. Really it started ten months before on an ordinary January morning, watching TV in my parents' kitchen. The space shuttle *Challenger* exploded, and an entire life occurred to me. From a thirteen-inch black-and-white television I saw a completely different world develop, beyond Suffern. I watched the coverage and became absorbed with the network news anchors, and I made up my mind. As far-fetched as it seemed, I wanted somehow to be *there*. I wanted to tell the story, not watch it.

I began going to job fairs for college students interested in media careers. There had been months of these fairs, to no avail, and this one, I'd decided, would be the last. I was tired and on my way out but handed a résumé to an older man from ABC-TV who said he would pass it on to the right person and who also wondered whether I'd like to get a drink sometime. I didn't have the drink, but there was a phone call anyway, and then a moment in which I picked out what I thought a woman in New York would wear to an interview at ABC News. I chose a black-wool skirt and a matching peplum jacket, and I fixed a pearl pin to the collar, because I had seen Holly Hunter wear a pin like it in the movie *Broadcast News*. I pulled my hair back neatly in a ponytail. I took the Red and Tan Lines bus from Suffern to the Port Authority on Eighth Avenue, and then the subway to Sixty-Seventh Street and an elevator to the tenth floor.

The young girl in *Broadcast News* organized her life early in the direction of journalism, writing to pen pals, cultivating an almost disturbing obsession with language and facts. I wish I could say that as a child I sat each evening captivated by Walter Cronkite. That I hoarded newspapers in my room and collected the big stories in scrapbooks. I wish there were a defining moment in my childhood I could pick out—my family huddled around the TV watching the Watergate hearings, maybe. Instead I can instantly summon any given episode of *M.A.S.H.*

I am nervous in the subway in my black suit on my way to Annette Kriener. She is the budget controller for the news show *20/20* with Barbara Walters and Hugh Downs, and she has an enormous amount of power. She is rumored to have started and stopped careers with a phone call, and she is known as the *dragon lady* around the office, though I don't find this out until I am working there. Had I been armed with this information, I might not have taken that subway ride, and this story would have worked out differently. I was quite successful, for some time, getting from point A to point B on what I didn't know.

I have an interview that isn't stunning or awful, but just good enough for her to offer a nonpaying internship. I snatch it up like the Golden Ticket. Forty hours a week filing videotapes, making dubs, and taking phone messages for *20/20*.

"Can you start Monday?" she asks. Though it's more a directive than a question.

Oh, my God, I think, and answer, "Yes."

"You can get an ID across the street at Forty-Seven West." I am dismissed. Then, she adds as I walk out, "Oh, and we don't really dress up that much around here."

I have a moment of panic after I leave her office that repeats itself intermittently for the first two years I am here: the irrational certainty that when I get in the elevator Peter Jennings will be inside, that he'll eye me suspiciously and then ask a question about a congressional race or what I think of the shift in Middle East policy. I will freeze and then blurt out something ridiculous; he'll see I'm overdressed and know instantly I am a fraud. He'll make one quick call from his office and I'll be gone. The questions vary. *Who are the nine Supreme Court justices? What did you think of Gorbachev's speech to the UN? Where did you say you went to college?* But this day the elevator is empty.

A woman in the security office tells me to stand in front of a white screen. She takes my picture, presses it into a plastic badge, and now I am Carole DiFalco, Intern, ABC News.

I'm a third-year English major at Hunter College, living at home with $300 in the bank, student loans about to come due, credit card bills, and a car payment for a brand-new Datsun. I sell the car right away and buy an old Toyota from my new boss, Mike Drucasian, for $150. It is rusted, and the driver's seat doesn't have a back, so he rigs up a wood brace with a seat cushion. I have to open the door with a screwdriver, but the engine runs well enough to get me to and from the city. I have a copy of *How to Talk with Practically Anybody About Practically Anything,* by Barbara Walters. This is what I'm equipped with to make my way through ABC.

I start in November 1986 on the bottom rung and my strategy is simple: now that my foot is in the door, I will not take it out. I interviewed a politician once who defined *relentless* as the ability to come back, time and time again, until your opponent gives up his will to resist. I am relentless. I love everything about news—the journalists in wrinkled clothes, the cigarette smoke, the energy in the newsroom before Peter Jennings goes on the air. I love the way reporters always know the inside story and the shorthand way that they talk. I love the stories they tell about getting the story—the chases, the near misses and dead ends. I love the cold dark of the editing rooms, where producers huddle with editors and create the piece frame by frame. I love the frenzied *crashes,* the last-minute feeds, the terrifying quiet of control rooms when stories air.

I love picking up my coffee at Elite diner two blocks from the office and eating my lunch at my desk because it seems like a New York thing to do.

I observe a few things early on: few people at ABC went to public school or Hunter College or spent summers in Kingston. I notice that the production associates' cubicles are papered with Ivy—three Harvards, a Columbia University, and then me. I learn that *Dunster House* is Harvard and that people never tire of saying it, because while it might be boorish to announce you went to Harvard, you can say *Cambridge* repeatedly or drop the name of the house you pledged to make the same point. I notice that the Ivy Leaguers rarely have to master the videotape library.

I learn that everyone has a footnote. There is the producer related to a von Bülow, the associate producer whose father is a famous reporter at the *Times,* the young production associate at *20/20* of the Welch's grape fortune. Anthony's footnote is, of course, his family. I don't have a footnote, or a tagline, or a phrase between two commas, but I suppose later Anthony's is tacked onto me. *She's married to Anthony Radziwill, Jackie O's nephew.*

As an intern I start and end my days in the basement, behind the Dutch door of postproduction. The *20/20* producers bring me audio-cassettes to be transcribed and Beta tapes to be dubbed, and I fill out the work forms and send them out. I relieve the production secretaries on the phones every day, while they all have their breaks. And once a week, I stay late to clean the supply room. I spend hours sorting the paper clips, Post-it notes, and cartridges of typewriter ribbon. I label the three-ring binders and reporter's notebooks according to size and style. I am obsessive, and it pays off. In what I consider a vote of confidence and a good omen for my career, Annette Kriener lets me order the supplies, and I approach this with a solemn intensity. I make it my business to know which producers like the razor flair markers in black and which prefer navy. I know that they all favor the small reporter's notebooks on the road and the legal pads in the office, and I stock accordingly. I run the supply system like the Pentagon, as though our national security depends on it.

At night I waitress at the Ramapough Inn in Suffern, and on Saturdays I work for Pam Hill. Pam is a senior vice president at ABC and executive producer of the news show *Closeup* and was looking for someone to work for her part-time. Her assistant asked if I would be interested.

Pam and her husband, the *New York Times* reporter Tom Wicker, have a brownstone on Eighty-Fourth Street and two other homes, in Canada and St. Lucia. They hire me to "organize" them. I think it could be a huge break—if I am impressive enough at her house, she might hire me at *Closeup*. If I can keep the houses outfitted, I think, my career in news is made.

She leaves lists of errands—*pick up the dry cleaning, call US Air and cancel reservations, rebook earlier flight back from New Hampshire*—and stacks of catalogs littered with Post-it notes: *send this to St. Lucia!, send this (black m.) to Canada, send two of these to St. Lucia and one to Canada.* Every Saturday I arrive by 10 a.m., go straight to her office on the third floor, and work all day. It is fairly straightforward: order the items marked in the catalogs, charge them to either her credit card or Tom's, ship them to the right home. I have things running smoothly until one Saturday when I order two of everything she has double-underlined in *Williams-Sonoma*—one set for each house, I think. Too late, I realize the mistake.

"Whose card was it on?" she asks when I tell her what I've done. I tell her Tom's card, and she seems relieved, but it is my last assignment for her. It takes weeks to straighten out, and just after the card is finally credited, the fiasco all untangled, I get a paying job as a production secretary with *Closeup*—$225 a week.

As a production secretary, my job is to assist the producers and associate producers. I man the phones, sort the mail, stack the morning newspapers for them to pick up. I book their travel and keep compulsive track of their profiles. One producer goes to Washington often, and I know always to book him a room at the Ritz, never the Mayflower across the street from the bureau. Another prefers American Airlines, so I learn ways around the company policy requiring travel on Continental. I memorize their employee ID numbers, sign their travel vouchers, collect their cash advances from the credit union, and babysit their children when they are out of town. One producer always takes calls from B——, a detail I learn the first time I refuse to connect her when he is in a screening. He calls me into his office later that day to tell me, "You are *always* to put her through. Oh, and if my wife calls, tell her you moved my car for alternate-street parking and dropped your barrette in the backseat." There is nothing I am unwilling to take care of.

But the action is on the phones. I have a chunky, flesh-colored phone on my desk with the extensions of all the producers. The telephone, or, more specifically, the person answering it, is critical. This is a time before cell phones, voice mail, or e-mail. A time, still, of *While You Were Out*, the pink slips on which you check a box to indicate whether the caller was returning a call, expected to be called back, or left a message, in which case you wrote it down on the black lines at the bottom. The phones are a lifeline. *I'll transfer you* is a solemn promise, a contract. There are producers calling from the lobby of the Commodore Hotel in West Beirut, from satellite phones in Moscow, and in my mind, a disconnected call might be the difference between life and death, or worse, might cost us a story. The phone connects me to places I read about in the papers and hear the veteran producers discuss in the halls. On the other end of the phone are the places in my dreams, where I imagine I will go one day to cover a story. I want to stay at the Commodore, with its well-stocked bar and talking parrot in the corner. I want to be asked at the front desk, "Do you want a room on the car-bomb side or the artillery-shell side?" I want to have stringers and drivers and sources and call from the bombed-out Holiday Inn in Sarajevo, where electricity is unpredictable but there is an espresso machine in the lobby. I want to be reached at the American Colony Hotel in East Jerusalem, conducting off-the-record interviews with members of the PLO. This is where I have set my sights.

In the meantime I am happy logging stock footage and running tapes to the editing rooms behind the newsroom. We call it *slant track*—a group of cold, dark, windowless rooms named after the angle that video ran through the old-style tape machines. They have a bank of monitors and two chairs, one for the producer and one for the editor. This is where it happens—the flotsam becomes a three-minute news spot. I sometimes sneak in and stand quietly in the back and watch them. The producer next to the editor, sitting in the dark, pointing, rewinding, forwarding frame by frame, sometimes screaming. *Cut—no, dissolve fifteen frames, play that sound bite.* Weaving together sound bites and b-roll and file footage and rushing to feed the piece to the control room, where it will be dropped into the show.

I am eventually assigned small research projects: collecting articles on the drug war, compiling crime statistics, tracking down archival footage. *Call the Washington desk—find out what gun control legislation is pending on the Hill.* The best way I see to be promoted to PA is to *be* a PA, so I squeeze research in between phones, travel itineraries, and tape searches.

Pam Hill's *Closeup* is canceled in the spring of '88, and the staff is folded into what we call the *long-form programming unit*—that is, anything that isn't the evening news or a weekly magazine show. By now I am doing more research than travel or phones. I make research books for a series of one-hour specials ABC airs called *Burning Questions,* each on a different subject: education, drugs, the environment. I do time-consuming and expensive LexisNexis searches, pull every relevant article on each subject, and then make up binders with ABC News labels and mark them with a thick black Sharpie by producer name and story number.

I am essentially a production associate with a production secretary title, but I don't mind. The production secretaries are paid hourly, so I get overtime, and I am working enough to get my own apartment— a small studio, a fourth-floor walk-up, over the Raccoon Lodge Bar on York Avenue, that I share with a family of insomniac mice.

After work the PAs go to Peter's on Columbus, between Sixty-Eighth and Sixty-Ninth. The beer is cheap, and the hard-boiled eggs they keep lined along the counter are free. When we tire of the bar, we play pinball in the back room. We like Peter's until someone spots a cockroach, and then we start going to Santa Fe around the corner. We are the young crowd. The old guard goes to the Ginger Man, on Sixty-Fourth Street. Like the Pentagon Bar for Edward R. Murrow and his boys swapping stories of McCarthy, the Ginger Man is for the producers who've been shot at and know which side of the American Colony Hotel in Jerusalem has the better rooms. It is for Charlie Glass, the Middle East bureau chief who was kidnapped in Lebanon. It is for David Lewis, Tom Lennon, Steve Singer, Chris Isham, Pat Cook, John Fielding, Richard Gerdau—the inner circle. The crowd who, if I peeked through the window at almost any time of the day, would epitomize what I think journalists should be. Smoking filterless Camels, drinking Scotch and soda, trading stories of evacuations and military checkpoints, comparing restaurants in Managua. I am enchanted with the world of the Ginger Man in the same way I was captivated peering down from the loft in Kingston at the grown-ups around the table in the Knotty Pine room.

One morning my phone rings. Tom Yellin, the executive producer of *PJR*, is on the other end. "We're interested in Cambodia. Can you come to my office?" Peter Jennings has just created his own documentary unit, *Peter Jennings Reporting,* and a small group is assigned to work in it.

This is an opportunity, and I don't grab for it so much as lunge.

I imagine *villages* and *jungles.* I imagine *refugees* and *guerrilla soldiers.* I imagine that someone has just handed me the phone, Cambodia on the line, and given me permission to step through. I have misty visions of bombs and sources and intrigue in my head, of suspicious men in trench coats slipping me microcassettes. I imagine deals brokered, negotiations, shady characters ringing at three in the morning.

"You'll be working with Leslie Cockburn. I'll have her call you, but expect to be there by the beginning of the year." And then as an afterthought, "You're familiar with the situation there, right?"

I say yes, of course I know Cambodia, though I'm not even sure, at this point, that I can place it on a map.

I have three months to become *familiar.* I spend nights after work in the news library reading back issues of the *Far Eastern Economic*

Review. I comb through *Sideshow: Kissinger, Nixon and the Destruction of Cambodia* by William Shawcross, all 544 pages. My twenty-five-year-old eyes grow wider. I make up research books full of every policy article I can find. I buy a safari vest at Banana Republic.

Leslie Cockburn is producing, and I'm assigned as her PA. Leslie is notorious—a one-word name in the news business, like Madonna. The daughter of a tycoon, she is on a first-name basis with Third World leaders, spies, and rock stars. She carries an Hermès address book full of the private numbers of arms merchants and drug cartel bosses. She has the source no one else can get, the impossible interview. She is famous for it.

She gives me a long list of things to do to prepare for the trip. I have to get visas for the crew to Cambodia and Vietnam and set up meetings with officials at the embassy in Thailand. I make an appointment with Dr. Kevin Cahill, the infectious-disease specialist, for my shots: tetanus, yellow fever, gamma globulin. I fill my prescription for malaria medication. "And call Sathern." Leslie gives me his number. "He's our stringer and will take care of everything." Then she sends me ahead to line up interviews and smooth itineraries, with ten thousand dollars cash and a box of ABC News baseball caps.

On New Year's Eve 1989 I take an overnight flight to Thailand. Sathern picks me up at the airport and takes me to the Oriental Hotel in Bangkok. It's not the Commodore. There are plush white robes and warm slippers, and the laundry is returned wrapped in tissue paper—no artillery fire, but still. It's where the journalists stay.

The documentary is to be called *Peter Jennings Reporting: From the Killing Fields* and will focus on American foreign policy. It will have good guys, bad guys, innocent victims, a culpable government. There will be refugees and insurgents, a front line and coalition forces; guns and money and one of the most murderous groups in history, the Khmer Rouge. Cambodia and Thailand and Vietnam, places where it seems there is no end to war.

The United States has a long history in Cambodia, most of it duplicitous. In the early seventies, as part of its Vietnam strategy, the

Nixon administration secretly dropped close to a quarter million tons of bombs in northern Cambodia, along the Mekong River. And by 1974, Cambodia was simply another casualty of the Vietnam War. When the United States pulled out, it was left shattered. The next year Pol Pot and his Khmer Rouge marched to the capital city of Phnom Penh and emptied it. They tortured and killed close to two million people. The worst act of genocide since World War II.

I have a list of things to do, and it starts in the border town of Aranyaprathet, where Sathern and I head first on a dusty road out of town, at night to avoid the Bangkok traffic and heat. Cambodia is just over the mountain, a few hours' hike. Border towns are where everything happens, in the lawless haze between one country and another. They are hideouts for illegal gunrunners, jewel traders, and military intelligence officers. Sathern has a list of names and numbers for everything I'll need. He knows everyone, or if he doesn't, he knows what they cost. As stringers go, he's the best.

He has set up a meeting with the Thai generals so I can get permission to film in the refugee camps. The camps are run by the United Nations, but nothing happens without a nod from the Thai military. The meeting with the generals is a formality. I sit in a tent across a metal folding table from three men. They regard me suspiciously. *Americans,* they must think, *sending a woman to do a man's job.* They examine the business card I hand them and seem reassured by the logo. The cards are not even real. PAs don't get business cards, but someone told me to bring a box of them. So I cut out an ABC logo from letterhead before I left and took it to a print shop by my apartment. I ordered three hundred cards, and except for the cheap paper they look as good as the official ones. I am winging this, all of it.

I ask their permission to film, I ask for access to the people inside the camps. I get our names on the list, and then money trades hands, paperwork is filled out, ABC News caps are passed around.

We stop at Site 8 because it is famous—the refugee camp under control of Khmer Rouge soldiers. This is understood more than stated, and affirmed by their telltale green caps. There are nearly thirty-five thousand refugees in Site 8, many of them used as mules to carry food and ammunition to the secret military camps over the border.

I go back to Aranyaprathet a few weeks later, alone, to get footage of these camps. I have the name of a local cameraman who freelances for WTN, World Television Network, and, according to rumor, runs guns in and out of the camps on the side. I have no trouble finding him. Aranyaprathet is straight out of the Wild West—you walk into the saloon and ask for the WTN guy, and they all point across the street. "He's over there." He speaks just enough English to understand where I want to go, and he has legitimate equipment, a Sony Beta camera. I hire him for two days, and we drive, then hike, to the KR military camps across the Thai border. The soldiers are young boys with smooth cheeks, thin arms, and expressionless faces. We ask them to march through the trees. We film them riding in trucks. We film them in the camps, bored and smoking cigarettes. Such a fierce reputation, and they look so harmless. My requests do not surprise or startle them; they seem accustomed to this.

To get Peter Jennings to Phnom Penh I have to fly to Hanoi, Vietnam, to negotiate a charter with the president of the state-run Vietnamese airline. I am met at the Hanoi airport by Nuygen, a government minder, who has been assigned to translate and keep his eye on me. To take me to the shops where he gets kickbacks on what I spend. He takes my passport and tells me in perfect English, with a French accent, that I can have it back in four days.

I am booked in the VIP hotel, the one for diplomats, though when I arrive it is filled mostly with French and Australian businessmen. I check into my room and make phone calls, report back to the foreign desk, and two hours later Nuygen is still waiting in the lobby. "Would you like to see where your Senator McCain was shot down, Miss Carole?"

I meet with the president of the airline the next day, and through Nuygen we agree on a price for a charter flight and make a plan for me to deliver the cash. We don't discuss currency, we make assumptions, and I make the wrong one. The next morning I have six thousand dollars in my shoulder bag, and I stop at a bank to convert it to Vietnamese dong. The president, when he sees this, is enraged. "No, I understand," I tell Nuygen, who looks worried, trying to keep up with the translation. "Tell him, please, I'll convert it back." There is another fee for the transaction at the bank, but I return within the hour. Everyone is happy.

Carolyn will make me tell these stories again and again.

I'm learning the ropes: how to talk to guerrilla fighters and negotiate with presidents of airlines, and where to find the best exchange rate on the black market. I know now to always carry cigarettes, and lighters with the ABC News logo. Bartering tools are almost as good as cash in third world countries.

I have the coalition military generals standing by to take the camera crew and Leslie to the front lines. It is a dangerous trip through a stretch of guerrilla-controlled territory inside Cambodia touted as the "liberated zone." But Leslie isn't here and the generals are getting anxious. Calls to New York are pointless. "Don't worry," my boss tells me, "it's Leslie."

"It's okay," Sathern says, "we'll stall them."

When she arrives a week later I find her sitting in the hotel café, sipping iced tea in a knee-length skirt and a yellow-silk jacket, and I feel silly, suddenly, in my safari vest. She is cool and composed and offers no explanation. I don't ask.

I hand her a file folder of details: an organizational chart of the Khmer People's National Liberation Front and the Khmer Rouge, schedules and backup schedules, alternate shooting dates with times and attendees. She glances at it and nods indifferently. Leslie knows, and I will find out, that dates and times are meaningless in countries with corrupt military and guerrilla fighters.

When Peter arrives, it goes quickly. We drive directly to Aranya-

wanted to be. All that angst about getting out of Suffern, and it had been as simple as getting on a plane. I was at the beginning of a whole new life. I was seeing where all of this would lead, enjoying the ride, and then a man walked into the room. Or, to be accurate, I walked into the room, and the man stood and reached for my hand.

3

How did a girl from Suffern meet a man with Polish royal lineage going back four centuries? Anthony Stanislas Albert Radziwill, a prince, like his father and grandfather before him. This is where fairy tales come in handy, because the real story is somewhat dull. No glass slipper, white horse, or wicked stepmother. We met at work.

In fact, we met over a murder. In March 1990, Lyle and Erik Menendez were charged with killing their parents with shotguns while they were watching television in their den. And almost everyone in the news business flew to Los Angeles to cover it. "*Primetime* needs to borrow you," my boss had said after *From the Killing Fields* aired. "It's four weeks in Beverly Hills, the Menendez murder." I flew to Los Angeles and went to a suite at the Four Seasons—*Primetime Live*'s makeshift office—and met Anthony.

We had both been at ABC for three years. Anthony was working for *Primetime* with Sam Donaldson and Diane Sawyer, and I had just started with *Peter Jennings Reporting*. He was an associate producer when we met, and I was a production associate, a rung lower.

By this time I had adopted some things—a wry sense of humor and a brown-suede miniskirt, for instance, and the bravado gained by a bit of travel. I was just back from six weeks in Southeast Asia, and no one in the Four Seasons suite knew I'd never been so far from home. *I have seen some things now,* I was hoping to suggest in my manner. *I know some things, too.*

We couldn't have come from two points farther apart, Anthony and I, but I walked into the hotel suite flush with the slippery confidence of youth and an award-winning documentary under my belt. And he took it all in with his own brand of self-possession.

"Hi, Carole, come in," Shelley Ross, the producer, greeted me. She was an attractive brunette with a short, tight skirt and high heels that shot sparks when she moved around the room. "This is Anthony," she said. "You'll be working with him. Are you up to speed on the story?"

I nodded. "I read the research packet on the plane."

"Okay, good. Then let's get started."

Shelley was a barely contained explosion. Anthony was just the opposite, steady and calm, bent over a table with scripts. When she introduced him, he stood and reached for my hand. He wore pressed jeans and a button-down shirt, and he held on for a moment before letting go. "It's nice to meet you."

He was unremarkably handsome. He had a face you might linger on, possibly remember but not place. He was anonymous most of the time. The sort of man strangers wondered about—*What's his story?*—but passed by. He had a straight nose, wavy, thick hair, and a strong jaw. A receding hairline from his father, his mother's defined cheekbones. His shoulders were broad and strong. It was, in fact, impossible not to notice his muscular frame. He had a dark-featured European look—a man you might cast as the playboy count. His eyes were serious if you didn't know him, playful if you did. He turned himself into a British lord, a French diplomat, in an eye wink, to *get* you. He had a subtle, deceptive sense of humor that hummed continuously below his surface. His eyes and his smile betrayed him—if you knew to look.

The story could go anywhere from here. We could lock eyes and ooze passion and show up in the next scene with arms tangled, knees bumping, clothes flung to the floor during a late-night editing session. The ABC "office," after all, was attached to his hotel suite. He could be preoccupied in this introduction and not even notice me. Or we could work closely together, talk too much, develop the sort of friendly relationship that rules out other possibilities.

The smallest detail can change your life. If I had not been called on that project. If I had met him in a large group of people—noisy, in a restaurant—perhaps nothing would have come of it. If he had not said to Shelley loud enough for me to hear, "Things are starting to look up," maybe I would have returned to New York and lived a different life—a more predictable one. I might have moved to the suburbs and had children. Traded work afternoons for soccer games.

I was new to this business and infatuated with it all. I was just beginning to climb the mountain and looking as far as the foothold in front of me. Anthony was ahead of me, and I think of him smiling down at me that afternoon, a bit bemused.

He was born in Lausanne, Switzerland, and was sent to elite boarding schools in London. His family had a country home in Henley on the Thames and a townhouse in London that stood in the shadow of Buckingham Palace. His parents divorced when he was thirteen, and when he was sixteen his father died, and he moved to New York to live with his mother. He finished high school at Choate in Connecticut and went on to Boston University.

He was a prince and the son of a prince, the nephew and godson of a president. He brought centuries of history with him wherever he went. He had a name that was spoken with expectation, a name that made people pause. A name people whispered behind him when he walked into a room. The men around his dinner table, around his Christmas tree, on the yachts of the family vacations, are in history books.

In my childhood pictures, kids played on a rusted swing set or piled on a tattered love seat against a wall in an otherwise empty room. In his, there were wooden toys beneath a Chippendale table, a prince and a president playing backgammon across the room. A glamorous young mother posed with her sister and the vice president. You could see another world in the easy way he walked. The delight he took in movement, his arm stretching out to reach me, legs unconsciously slack and relaxed, an easy smile—I sensed order. He suggested security and straight lines. In my world there were no guidelines, no footsteps ahead of me, no safety net below to catch me.

In the hotel suite the first afternoon he was introduced simply as Anthony. Someone told me later in the secondhand way someone always did: *John Kennedy's cousin. Jackie Onassis's nephew. His mother, Jackie's sister, Lee Radziwill.* Counting backward on the family tree. He carried it effortlessly, the weight of this name, while I was struggling to escape weightlessness.

There was a buzz around him that he seemed unaware of, and later I learned to seem unaware, too. He moved around a room as though in a perfectly timed waltz, delivering the right lines to the right person, turning this way and that. He knew how to work around the heavy name and introduced himself immediately to anyone new, rolling his name off with unassuming ease. He instinctively knew to stand when a woman walked into a room.

He had a steady calm about work: he approached it with an elegant balance of duty and fun. None of it—the hours, the crime, the politics of network news—seemed to affect him. You would never turn a corner to find him in heavy conversation—gesturing and whispering in the hallway. He seemed to transcend it, while still being part of the team.

But he was also a bit reserved, distant. We worked side by side, on many occasions the only two people in the suite. Yet he was the one on the team I felt least connected to. It was my first time in Los Angeles. There was a pack of us in our twenties, with expense accounts, and we took advantage of it, going to different restaurants and bars every night, exploring the city. He kept apart from all of that, and I liked it about him. He was there to work on a project, and he spent his free time at the gym. We were comrades in arms, the whole bunch of us, for those three or four weeks, but he was the one I doubted I'd see again.

One afternoon it was just the two of us in the suite—he reading transcripts, I logging tapes, and the television on low. A news anchor announced a birth in his famous family—his cousin had had a baby girl. I didn't say anything, and he didn't react, but a few moments later he got up quietly and walked to the bedroom. He closed the door, but I could hear him on the phone excited. *Congratulations!*

I remember wishing that we had met covering the Gulf War instead of a murder story. Wished his mock-serious eyes and cocked eyebrow had met mine over the blast of rocket-propelled grenades. A war is sweeping and dramatic, with heroism and bravery. I picture soldiers doubled up in bunkers over Anthony's deadpan impressions of Saddam Hussein. But we exchanged our first glances over two people shot dead eating blueberries in their den. The younger son stopping to reload his shotgun so he could finish off his mother, who was crawling away. It was great television. Beverly Hills, rich private-school kids shooting their parents. We met because this was a story people watched and advertisers flocked to, making it profitable for everyone. We were in the business of telling profitable stories. We would get to do the serious ones, but flashy murder and celebrity profiles would pay our salaries.

4

Our courtship starts and stutters. We meet on the murder story and four weeks later board separate planes to fly back to New York. There is an inauspicious parting—me running up to the suite at the last minute to get something I'd left behind. "Shh." He answers the door, finger to his lips. "My cousin's here for the weekend. He's sleeping." I tiptoe in, keep my head down, and mumble something clumsy about lunch when we get back. But then I'm assigned to a story in Louisiana and become quickly reintoxicated with my job. Everything else, for the moment, is forgotten.

It's a documentary called *Abortion: The New Civil War,* and Buddy
Roemer is the star. He is the governor of Louisiana, and the state leg-
islature has passed a bill criminalizing abortion that he thinks is
unconstitutional. A quietly pro-choice governor in a pro-life state, he
is planning to veto the bill. Peter Jennings sends Ray Farkas and me
to Baton Rouge to cover it.

Ray is an old-school producer. There is nothing that happens to
him that he doesn't line up, clip, and fit into a frame. He is obsessed
with composition and camera angles, the way writers are with words.
He shoots every shot just slightly off center; it's his trademark. He'll
shoot an interview subject from a side angle, instead of straight on,
and get part of the lamp on the table next to him. He is not interested
in the story so much as the camera angles, the composition, the parcel-
ing of the story frame by frame. Life is one long clip reel to Ray, there
for the editing. If Leslie Cockburn is Meriwether Lewis, stamping up
trails and craggy mountains to find the last Shoshone Indian, then
Ray is William Clark, meticulously mapping and recording and
framing it all for an audience.

Governor Roemer's secretary ushers me into his office toward the
end of a staff meeting the first day. He's expecting us. "You must be
Carole, right?" He is just wrapping up his meeting, and he motions
for me to take a seat. He is younger than I imagined, and wears cow-
boy boots with his navy suit, as only southern politicians or rich oil-
men can. I tell him the crew will be arriving later in the day and that
I need to go over his schedule. "I'm not sure I'm crazy about having a
film crew around, Carole." He laughs. Buddy is good-natured, but
Guidry, his chief of staff, is all business. "You can ask us to leave at any
time," I tell him, "and we'll be careful to stay out of your way." I'm
very professional, reciting my lines—convincing, I hope. Guidry, I
can see, will be watching us closely.

In 1988, the U.S. Supreme Court said that states could set limits on
abortion, and by 1990 more than forty states had taken advantage of
the decision. Louisiana passed the most restrictive legislation of all:
doctors who performed abortions could be sentenced to prison for up

to ten years. It wouldn't be criminal to *have* an abortion, but it would be criminal to perform one. Buddy Roemer had promised in his campaign to sign tough antiabortion legislation, and he was now facing a political quagmire. How does he veto an antiabortion bill while still appearing to be pro-life? He will be up for reelection soon.

Ray and I follow Buddy to meetings with lawmakers, to radio talk shows, and to press conferences. We follow him to the Governors' Conference in Mobile, Alabama, where another southern governor, Bill Clinton, is working the room. The conference is a thick haze of backslapping politicians—choreographed movements from group to group of handshakes and practiced anecdotes.

But in the haze Governor Clinton stands out. It is apparent in the way people respond to him that he is the type of man who is used to knowing everyone in a room by first name. Buddy calls, "Clinton, get over here." They are friendly with each other, teammates in southern politics. "Hello," he says to me and introduces himself. There is nothing stiff or rehearsed in his greeting. My ABC News badge is visible around my neck, so I tell him about the piece. Buddy asks him a couple of questions about the issue for our benefit, and he answers them. "This is a good man," he says in a soothing drawl, his hand grabbing Buddy's. "You've got a good story." Then Governor Clinton leans in close to Buddy, who is miked, and says something in his ear that we can't hear, but it's crystal clear when we play the tape back. *Give them fucking hell about that bill, Buddy.* Ray and I get a good laugh out of this when Clinton announces his run for president a year later.

We worked on the story for five months, and Buddy and I became close friends. He introduced me to politics and country music— Machiavelli, Lyle Lovett, and Jesse Winchester. He was divorcing that summer after a long marriage, and was struggling with it. We had long late-night phone calls about wars and men and women and the business of politics. We skipped over small talk completely. And maybe there was a sort of love affair, platonic, but I didn't see it then.

I was too young—or maybe just old enough. Idealistic and caught up in all of this—the intrigue of state politics, a man and a principle, the rise and fall of ideals, a new story.

During the summer I fly back and forth to Washington, D.C., where Ray is doing final editing on the piece. Washington during the week, back to New York on the weekend, and Anthony and I don't meet up again until September, when he calls my office. "Do you want to catch a movie tonight?" He's working late and the theater is across the street from my apartment, so I buy the tickets and meet him there. Afterward we go to dinner at a trendy Mexican restaurant, and the bill comes to $104. I am relieved when he grabs it and then insists, "You paid for the movie."

There are a handful of dinners, and then these dates become regular. It is an odd pattern, arranged without discussion—we don't call from the road but take up again when we get back. Ours isn't a whirlwind romance. It is slow and consistent, and it suits us both for more than a year. There is a unique ebb and flow to the news business, and we are wedded for the moment to our careers. Everything else is second. We both understand: an assignment trumps personal plans, no hard feelings.

We never talk about our families. There is no moment when the relationships are laid out. No moment when he says to me, *The president was my uncle, John is my cousin, Jackie Onassis is my aunt.* He is private, compartmentalized about his famous family and I am relieved. I like the world we are creating, just the two of us. Occasionally he mentions a vacation with his aunt and cousins, a weekend in the Vineyard. There's an odd netherworld, really, where our invisible aunts and uncles and siblings and cousins carry on wordlessly in a back room. In the beginning it is just Anthony, a producer I met at work, and me. Two news junkies who like travel and the chase of a story. By the time we get to our families, almost two years after we met, my anxiety has dissipated. His mother is simply his mother—a woman with a beautiful house, a breathy voice, a cover story in *Life*.

The first winter we're dating we steal out to his mother's house in East Hampton for weekends. It is impossibly clean, with white-cashmere couches in the living room standing on finely made Cogolin straw carpets, handwoven, I imagined, by stooped old women in France. Just off the living room is the small library, which becomes my favorite refuge. The walls and the two sofas and chair are all covered in white and red fabric. The walls, white with thin red strips, are soft and pillowy to touch. The couch in front of the fireplace is white, too, and covered in sketched red Chinese print. The room is cozy and warm and full of family photos: Anthony as a little boy in England in green Wellington rain boots; with his younger sister, Tina; playing on the lawn with his dogs at Henley; the four cousins: John and Caroline and Anthony and Tina, dressed up as angels for a Christmas play.

Our first weekend at the house, Anthony suggests I take his mother's golden retriever, Zack, for a walk while he goes to the gym. I am new here and trying to impress him, so I call Zack from the kitchen and walk toward the beach. Emilia, the housekeeper, watches me quietly. Her English and my Spanish are about the same. I can say "Hola, qué tal?" and she knows how to say "Good morning."

We leave through the side door, and after a few feet Zack just stops and sits. "Come on, Zack," I call to him. He has a blue-leather collar with his name engraved, and I tug on it to get him moving. "Come on, Zack, we're going to the beach." He digs his hind legs into the ground, and it starts to annoy me. *What kind of dog won't go to the beach?* I pull harder on the collar, and he digs in deeper and starts to bark, so I pick him up and carry him halfway down to the beach before I hear Emilia. She's running toward me, yelling in Spanish. "Para! Póngalo hacia abajo!" *Put him down!* There is an electric fence around the property for the dogs that I'm unaware of. Emilia makes motions around her neck and then points to Zack's collar, and I realize I have electrocuted him. I wait for him to go stiff, but after he stops yelping he seems fine, so we keep going and when we get back Anthony is waiting for us, unsuspecting. "Thanks for taking him," he says, smiling.

"Oh, it wasn't a problem at all," I say, giving Zack a big pat.

We're still in the campaign phase of the relationship, all promise and no accountability.

Love's one thing, war's another.

In January, Saddam Hussein fires Scud missiles aimed at Israel, and I go to the war in the Gulf, with Leslie Cockburn again. She wants to do an hour-long news special and sends me ahead to set up the interviews. I pick up my chemical suit and gas mask in London on my way to Tel Aviv.

The Israeli military has its public affairs office set up in the lobby of the InterContinental Hotel. This is where we spend most of our days, in the lobby crowded with bored and restless journalists waiting for the daily briefing and press release. The rest of my time is spent on the phone, confirming interviews, or at our bureau office screening tape with the military censor and then feeding it via satellite to New York. Nights we lie in our rooms on unmade beds, waiting for the alarms to go off. The loud, high-pitched wail blasts like a fire drill, and people stream out with gas masks, no pushing or running, to a makeshift bomb shelter in the basement. Everyone except the news crews. We assemble in the lobby and head out in the direction of the smoke billowing up against a starlit sky.

War, at least this one, from my vantage point in Tel Aviv, is mostly long, uneventful days interrupted by sharp bursts of horror. Two intolerable extremes. Reporters aren't afraid of war zones, or air strikes, the way people should be. They consider it a perk. Some nights I sit out on the hotel balcony watching the CNN reporter file live telecasts across the rooftop. I watch for a few minutes, and then go back inside to watch him on television, and then go back to the terrace again to watch him live. It's odd—the story I see on the television is much more frightening than the one actually happening outside, much more frightening *reported* than witnessed live.

I learn a little about the power of the medium, about moments strung together for television and condensed. Days of war are cut into a two-minute report and then shrunk to fit the average TV screen. To do this to the experience is to distort it. It's inevitable.

When I get back in February, Buddy calls and asks me if I want to go to the White House with him. "The Governors' Ball," he says. "How 'bout it?"

I wear what I think a young woman should, a Nicole Miller cocktail dress, black. It's the only short dress in the room, but I'm winging it again. There is someone to prepare you for such things only if you are the kind of girl *expected* to attend dinners at the White House. If I were the sort of girl people *expected* to grace the halls of ABC, to marry European royalty, I'm sure there would be someone here steering me along. But all of this is so unpredictable, nothing my father or Millie or Grandma Binder could have prepared me for. If my mother has this sort of advice, she has withheld it.

We drive right up to the front door. A guard holds a list, asks our names, then whisks us through to the main lobby. There is a flock of photographers behind a rope, snapping away while someone announces our names for the AP wire and the White House photographers. There is a reception in the East Room, then a receiving line to meet President Bush. A sharp-creased marine stands directly behind him, whispering the names of people as they come through the line. I don't remember what I say as I shake his hand, or if I say anything, but I have a photograph of the moment, and in the photo I'm standing between Buddy and the president, my back to the camera, and they are laughing together about something.

This is actually my second time at the White House, but the circumstances are very different. A few months earlier, when war was just a gleam, I went with my boss to pitch an idea to John Sununu, White House chief of staff. We wanted cameras to follow President Bush as he prepared for war. Reality war. The White House wasn't ready for it. We suggest to John Sununu the relevance of television as an instrument for "recording history," and he looks back at us, unblinking. Unsmiling. Unmoved. "What does television have to do with history?" he asks. Then politely dismisses us.

When I go with Buddy, it's all pomp and glitz.

We eat dinner in the Blue Room, and I sit between the country singer Gary Morris and Marilyn Quayle. Buddy is at another table.

After dinner we file into another room before the entertainment starts, and I see Bill Clinton through the crowd. "Hello, nice to see you again," he says, gripping my hand. "How'd your story turn out?" He is warm, and I am flattered that he remembers me.

The next day Buddy faxes the front page of the *Times-Picayune*. There is a photo of the two of us at the dinner, and the caption reads, "Governor Roemer and his date, Carole DiFalco."

Buddy and I stop off at flirting and Anthony and I inch right along. We are perfect for each other, even if it's not immediately obvious why. More Newman and Woodward than Taylor and Burton. In love we are both the turtle, slow and deliberate.

I like our relationship. We are both on the road a lot, so there are many hellos and many good-byes, and when we come back so many stories to tell. It all works smoothly until a weekend in September, a year and a half after we met. "I don't care. Go," I say to him. He is going to Captiva, Florida, for the weekend with his friend Holly and another coworker. They're going away, and he's assumed there's no need to involve me. I'm in Boston working on a story about the Mob. There is a phone call and a casual mention, *I won't be around this weekend.*

I am suddenly tired of the unspoken rules—of the coming and going as we please. I am angry about this lapse of judgment—wanting to spend a holiday weekend with friends instead of thinking to spend it with me. I am sure he is surprised at my reaction. I am.

"What do you want me to do, Carole?"

"I'm not going to tell you what to do. Figure it out." I know this is a loaded message. It's a test, really, and I'm waiting to see how he scores. But he doesn't know that. We hang up, and I go to dinner, and when I get back there is a message I don't return. And then the phone rings in my hotel room, late.

"I called you. Didn't you get my message?"

"Yes," I answer. And this is all we say.

This is how we fight—silently, stubbornly, neither of us yielding. No passionate explosion, but a slow, quiet burn. We are both determined to finish our own way. I go back to New York the next day, and he goes to Florida. I distract myself with the hearings on Clarence Thomas's nomination to the Supreme Court.

Two months later, he calls late from his office. "Hi, it's me, wasn't sure if you'd be there. Do you want to grab dinner?" And we start back up again in the same easy way. We finish the Captiva business quickly and neatly.

"Did you end up going?"

"Yeah, I did." And I respect him for being outright. He did what he wanted to do, no apology. I like this about him. He tells me about the place they found, the 'Tween Waters Inn—a great cheap motel right on the beach. "I'm going back for Thanksgiving," he says. "Do you want to go?"

I don't say yes or no, but he calls later with dates and flight numbers just the same. "I can't come for the whole weekend," I hear myself saying. "I'll meet you there."

Whether he believes I will actually show up or not, I don't know, but he is sitting out on the second-floor terrace when I pull into the parking lot. "Welcome to paradise," he shouts down, as if he's been sitting there in that spot for two days, watching for me.

This is when the tides change. It's hard through the prism of a hospital bed to remember these delicate little heart trembles, the butterfly wings. It's hard to remember his body muscular and free of lines, running shirtless on the beach and breathless back into our room. But this is how he is the first evening, barreling through the door with big, puffy breaths. "They just launched a shuttle. God, I wish you had seen it!" His eyes are wide. He couldn't wait to run back here, couldn't wait to run back to tell his girl, me.

Just like this, we go from being one thing to another.

We leave Florida in a different gear and cruise into the rhythm of a couple—weekends are assumed, holidays are assumed. *Let's see where this goes.*

5

We rented a house in Sagaponack, Long Island, for the summer—the name, *Sea Song,* painted onto a piece of driftwood at the end of the long pebble driveway. A great field stretched out behind the back deck, and beyond it you could hear the ocean. For a few summers it was our *idyll.*

Sea Song is modest by Hamptons standards—three small bedrooms separated by an open kitchen and living area, furnished with Pottery Barn tables and white slipcovered couches. Sliding glass doors open onto the back porch, where the shrubs are overgrown, and off the side deck is an outdoor shower, the hidden jewel. There are no walls around it, just some well-placed trees offering privacy without blocking the view. It faces east, and in the mornings I turn toward the sun with my eyes closed, letting the water stream down. I paint the landscape in my head—the large field of wildflowers, the ocean beyond. Then I snap my eyes open quickly to catch it.

The Hamptons is a collective name for a string of small beach towns along the east end of Long Island. In some minds, I suppose, it's less a place than an endless round of social climbing and money. And maybe there's that. But for Anthony and me it's simply Long Island, a place of barbecues, bike rides, and long walks on the beach, a place to meet up with our friends in the summer. Holly, Anthony's close friend from *Primetime,* has a house nearby. If it's a slow weekend, and it usually is, she hires a deejay and we clear the furniture from her living room, drink margaritas, and dance all night. Her dad, Pete, and stepmom, Joan, have a home in Bridgehampton on Rose Hill Road. On some weekends we invite Marc and Lori out. Marc works with Anthony and Holly, and his wife, Lori, works at NBC. Anthony's family is here, too. His mother's home is one town over, in East Hampton, a bike ride for Anthony, a ten-minute drive for me. And his cousin Caroline lives down the road from us with her husband, Ed, and their children.

We leave the city on Friday afternoons to beat the traffic and stop at The Palm in East Hampton for steaks and creamed spinach. We get there before the dinner crowd to enjoy the cool air and the peaceful atmosphere of the dark wood and white-aproned waiters.

Anthony wakes up at ungodly hours, always. Weekends, vacations, and summers. "Boarding school, Peanut. They drilled it into us. Up, out, get on with it." He pops with energy, throwing drapes open, switching the news on, soaking the world in. He likes to watch the morning shows at 6 a.m. when the anchors have barely swallowed their coffee.

I like to enter the day in gradually developed stages, but we manage a middle ground. He turns the volume down on the television, keeps the drapes drawn, and leaves me in bed while he goes for his morning bike ride to Radu's Gym in East Hampton. And I pull myself upright before he returns for the next thing—tennis, kayaks, a swim.

"Carole gets up at the crack of noon," he jokes to our friends. It isn't noon, but most mornings it is true, he has run on the beach, gone for a swim, or biked eight miles each way to the gym, before I am up. I still can't manage this sort of enthusiasm for the morning.

On Saturdays we pick up meat loaf sandwiches in the afternoon

from the General Store on Sagaponack Road—warmed on white
bread with ketchup—and go to Gibson Beach at the end of Daniels
Lane. We meet up with Holly, who usually comes with the latest gossip. Our friend Richard is always there with the Sunday *Times* and his
latest girlfriend. Steve, another friend from *Primetime,* brings his
Kadima paddles and hits the small rubber ball back and forth with
Anthony for hours.

We split the rental fee, my first summer here, with John, who
rarely shows up. But Anthony insists he pay his portion anyway. I
meet John the second weekend out. He'd come in late the night
before, after we'd already gone to bed. He walks into the kitchen the
next morning, in his underwear, grinning and stretching a long arm
out to greet me. "Hi, I'm John Kennedy. Anthony's better half."

"Has the old boy left you here alone?" he asks.

He is recruiting me, I can see. Comrades in goading Anthony.
Don't worry, I know. He hasn't got me fooled, he seems to imply with his
loaded smile, the eye roll, the "principe" and "old boy."

I tell him that Anthony is at Radu's and I'm just back from Joe's
body shop in Southampton.

"What?" He perks up. "What were you doing there?"

I tell him I got scratches on Anthony's Jeep pulling out of the
driveway and had to get them buffed out.

"He made you spend the whole morning at the garage with his old
Jeep?"

"It wasn't so bad. I brought a book," I say. I am earnest, not yet ini-
tiated in their game of *got you.* "The scratches were superficial. It
didn't take that long, really. I was only there a couple of hours. It
would have been quicker, but the guy had to finish an oil change." I
chatter on, oblivious, and John's smile stretches out, his head moves
slowly back and forth. I am implicating Anthony with each word.

"I can't believe he made his girlfriend sit alone at the garage on a
beautiful summer weekend while he worked out at the gym. What a
prince!" He laughs.

He repeats this disbelief to Anthony when he gets back, and to his sister and to everyone who comes around over the weekend. *What a prince!*

My first impression of John is *entirety*. He is complete in a way I've never seen. My second impression is that he is aware of the effect he has and does his best to dispense with it immediately. He makes everyone in a room feel at ease. He says his name without the *F.* and without the *Jr.,* "John Kennedy," his hand reaching out. No matter who, no matter where, no matter that everyone in the world knows who he is.

Anthony and John have been sharing a summerhouse for several years, though they are unlikely roommates. John is Oscar to Anthony's Felix, banging through the house, marking his territory like a teenager, leaving trails of movement behind him: a dirty dish, an empty bottle, books and newspapers wrinkled from spilt drinks. If he has been in the kitchen, every cabinet is opened. In the bathroom there are towels on the floor and a toothpaste cap in the sink.

If Anthony is the angel, the English schoolboy, well-mannered, polite, John is the scamp. Every family has one—the one you feel obliged to frown at occasionally, to disapprove of halfheartedly. The one who's always late, but for whom you hold up the party because you need him—the charmer, the one who gives a great toast with no notice, cracks the perfect joke in a tense moment.

They have a practiced banter, a routine.

"Carole, do you know that Anthony hates children and old people?" He tells me a story about Anthony in line with his groceries *losing it* over a sweet old woman in front of him who couldn't seem to find her change in the bottom of her handbag.

"No, but that's great we have that in common," I say, smiling.

"John, tell Carole about the camping trip when you almost killed us."

John complains about the small bedroom. Anthony tells him it's what he gets for being late. In the evening, we grill steaks and fresh vegetables and drink vodka with grapefruit juice, and I listen to the two of them top their stories of each other all night. Watching them this weekend, I can see they can't stand too close to each other, and can't bear to be too far apart.

The following weekend I meet Anthony's mother at her house on Dune Lane. She invites us to lunch. It can hardly be avoided any longer. I have the feeling they aren't used to Anthony bringing a girl around. He is thirty-two, but there hasn't been a serious one. His mother has heard about me, I'm sure—Emilia has likely reported our winter weekends.

Lee and Anthony's stepfather, Herbert, are waiting for us in the library. They stand up to greet us when we walk in. His mother has a striking face: wide-set eyes and sharpened bone lines. I see Anthony in it. She is friendly, and when she opens her mouth to speak, a lyrical voice delivers the words, like a woodwind instrument, melodic and precise. Herbert is a tall, elegant man, who looks fit for a smoking jacket and pipe. He's professorial, with distinguished silver hair. A highly regarded Hollywood director disguised as an English gentleman.

We start with awkward handshakes, but Herbert is warm, if unsure how exactly to proceed, and Anthony's mother, I can see, is naturally curious. We move to the patio, where pitchers of iced tea are set out, a small pitcher of sugar water for sweetener, and a pile of big, beautiful Queen Anne cherries in a wicker basket. Emilia serves us salad—avocado, fresh green beans, and thick slices of peeled tomato drizzled with lemon—as we wander through formalities.

"So where did you grow up?" Herbert asks, and when I tell him, he makes a touching attempt to do something with it. "Suffern, yes, of course, I know it." He turns to Lee. "I staged a ballet near there, a *long* time ago. It's a charming little area." My knowledge of ballet is limited, so I stick to Suffern, spitting out names of towns he might know in the area. "There's an old hotel," he says. "Off of Route Seventeen, I think it is. A charming old hotel way up on the—"

"Yes, right. Motel on the Mountain!"

"Oh, yes. 'Motel on the Mountain.'"

"I don't know if that's the real name. My family took that road upstate when I was a kid. That's just what I called it."

He knows of this drive for some reason, the back way upstate, though he can't quite remember how, and he talks about this part of New York as if it's another country. We have little common ground, and it is obvious but maybe not hopeless.

I become a regular at his mother's lunches on Sunday afternoons, and this is how my relationship with Anthony's family unfolds, between tomato slices and endive salad. Between grilled salmon and sorbet. It trickles out through Evian and fresh lemon wedges over the rims of fine crystal. From our level playing field at ABC, I am suddenly thrust into class divide.

Function versus form—this is what separates us. This practice of lunch, for instance, is foreign to me. Lunch to me is what you eat—a quick sandwich or a yogurt grabbed on your way out the door. It is not this formal theater, this dance, this series of small acts: the salads, the drinks, the sequence of courses. The slow waving of forks in the air. The time stretching out between bites.

I am in the habit of eating standing up, out of the refrigerator, or manning a sandwich in the car. Eating is strictly functional, like sleeping. There was a different cadence to meals in the house I came from. The meals my grandmother laid out in her basement were mostly disposed of in silence. After she died, all trace of ceremony disappeared. Food appeared at random intervals. There might be a pot of pasta and sauce or a big tray of frozen fish sticks or chicken potpies at night, or there might not. We were never required to attend meals. If you were near the kitchen, and there was food, you consumed it. And when we were grown, out of high school but not quite settled elsewhere, and having Sunday dinners together, we would all sit down at once and spoon from an enormous platter of pasta. Chairs were squeezed in, assorted settings scattered around. All of us banging elbows, grabbing for Kraft parmesan cheese, bread, butter. Cans of soda slid across the table. If there was something to say, it was at once, never fewer than three conversations in play, with all of us jumping in and out.

But here in East Hampton, meals serve a different purpose. The lunches have a simple feel, but no detail is overlooked, and the seating is carefully planned. They would be interesting merely to watch, but you aren't allowed to. You are expected to bring something, a story, to the table. You are graded on participation. I met Hamilton on one of these Sundays, and Hamilton always had a good story. I doubt he's ever gone anywhere without one. He has, in fact, extras, in case anyone comes up short. Lee became good friends with him through her job at Giorgio Armani. They seem an odd match; he's barely grownup, a year younger than I. But they are close, spending weekends and vacations together. He and Anthony are close friends too.

There is a hierarchy at these lunches. Usually one person is more highly regarded, and he or she takes the lead role. The rest of the table maneuvers itself in this person's direction. Stories are saved for this guest. They are currency, after all, and get a higher price depending on who's listening. You don't want to waste them. For instance, no one, I notice, is bursting with a story to tell me. The person sitting next to me will offer polite small talk and wait for an opening with the more interesting person on the left or the wife of the mogul across the table. I haven't quite mastered this art, talking about nothing while waiting for a turn to tell my story.

But I have learned a little. I glance at Dominick Dunne's column in *Vanity Fair,* because no one seems to tire of social gossip. I begin to save up stories about work assignments. I start to look for them during the week, stories I think worthy of a Sunday lunch. I learn to say *Peter Jennings,* and then just *Peter,* with terrifying regularity.

Then, too, there is the pressure of knowing who people are. In my family, you are expected to be familiar with the Yankee infield, past and present. A newcomer would never recover from *Who is Don Mattingly?* From then on he or she would be politely endured.

I am new at Dune Lane, and everyone here already knows everyone else. Or they have friends or a place in common that instantly unites them. They are familiar with Larry Gagosian, the gallery owner, who comes here in his role as art expert, and with Chris Whittle, who recently made a killing in private education. They all know Mickey Schulhof, the chairman of Sony U.S.A., who, because he was holding a Pomeranian under his arm when I met him, I mistook for Lee's dog trainer.

I feel as though I'm being patiently tolerated at these lunches. Though they are all friendly, this is a tough crowd to break into. I don't have a backstory. Sometimes I sense the curiosity of the guests. *Who is this girl of Anthony's?* Like an extended family, they all have some amount of claim to him, and they wonder who has engaged his heart. Less frequently I recognize genuine interest. And after a while I notice that my trump cards aren't really interesting to anyone. I'm not a former model. I don't have a famous uncle or step-uncle or ex-lover. I can't speak in the shorthand of boarding schools. And in this way, I reveal myself. Opinions are sealed without my knowledge.

It doesn't matter that I've been to the Gulf War, filmed two documentaries, and it won't matter if I go to Angkor Wat, with or without an Emmy, because Jackie and Lee have already been there. I am either unable to deliver these stories properly, or I'm simply cursed by lineage.

6

It is said there are only two stories—a man goes on a journey, or a stranger comes to town; they are both here in mine. I took a journey, and Carolyn came to town.

We were at Sea Song. I was washing dishes, Anthony was running on the beach, and John was reading the paper when she walked out of the bedroom, blonde and ten stories high, in a white cotton night-gown with eyelet trim.

She walked across the living room and put a hand on my shoulder. She seemed to know me. "Hi, I'm Carolyn. You must be Carole. I forgot a toothbrush. Do you have one I can use?" Her eyes were as big as quarters and blue like a swimming pool and she spoke softly, almost whispering. I thought later, she didn't want to scare me away.

I was wearing red-denim shorts and a white T-shirt tucked in. I remember this because she teased me about it for years. "You should have seen Carole when I met her, this sweet little thing, with her belted shorts and tucked-in shirt." She told anyone who would listen. We had a story, like an old couple, about how we met, and she loved this part.

"What was wrong with wearing a belt?"

"Lamb, no one was wearing belted shorts, and red! I thought, 'Oh, my God, who is this little one?'" She made me believe I was captivating.

I was geeky, earnest, completely miscast. I can see it in pictures now, but I didn't know then. I was protected by naïveté—the certainty that I was getting along just fine. She was drawn to that. I wasn't whom people expected Anthony Radziwill to be with. But then, she wasn't whom people expected John to be with either.

When I close my eyes and think of her, I see her hands. She was completely unaware of them, but they were threaded through every word she said like melody lines, changing tempo and rhythm with her story. They were quick, jumpy but certain. "I don't think we'll be doing that," she would say when something was ridiculous. Her index finger would draw a line around her sentence and stop, stabbing a sort of punctuation in the air. She had long, strong fingers. She wasn't afraid to get them dirty. She wasn't afraid to touch. She held my hand while she talked to me, or when we walked down the street. She played with my hair, absentmindedly, when she was making a point. It took me some time to get used to all the touching. She dismissed the barriers, the walls of politeness, the invisible personal space we protect. There was no awkward embrace with her, no hesitation. She hugged you tight, as if she might never see you again.

That first day, I noticed light and movement and her hands.

"Do you mind if I come with you to the store?" she asked.

"Sure, if you'd like," I said. I was going to pick up steaks for dinner. Several of John's friends had come by and were on the deck. He had a group of guys going back to college, and they were always buzzing around him.

"I'm so glad you're here. I thought this was going to be all boys, all weekend."

By the end of the weekend I learned that she had grown up a half hour from Suffern, in the blue-collar town of Greenburgh. That her father left when she was two, and her mother raised her and her two sisters alone. That as teenagers we had both worked for Caldor, she behind the jewelry counter and I at the customer service desk. That she now worked for Calvin Klein. What were the odds that John would bring home a girl from Caldor? She left a note behind in my bedroom.

Carole, you must seriously get rid of those Gap sneakers. Our friendship cannot proceed in a growth oriented way until you realize how important this issue is to me. Nice to meet you. XO, Carolyn

I thought that if we spent any time together we would be great friends.

They broke up the next weekend, and I didn't see her for two years. John went back to his on-again, off-again relationship with an actress. She came a few times that summer with two girlfriends who barely spoke and three kittens. I kept locking the kittens in the laundry room because Anthony was allergic.

At the end of the summer Anthony and I take a vacation in the south of France. We fly to Nice and drive to St. Tropez, where his mother is renting a house. We spend a few days around Nice and then drive

through seaside resort towns, gracing the Mediterranean with our
romance. We stop at a small café in Cannes, and Anthony orders
lunch in perfect French.

"Je t'aime," he tells me.

"Je t'aime," I repeat.

"Keep practicing, Sweetie," he says, winking.

"What does it mean?"

"It means I like you, a lot."

At St. Paul de Vence we stop at La Colombe d'Or and watch the
old men play boccie, groups of them in the hot sun shouting at each
other in French, throwing wooden balls at patches of dirt. We watch
them for an hour or maybe two, there's no hurry, and then we're off
again.

At the post office of St. Tropez, we call his mother to tell her we're
here and then wander around the small town. We stop for chocolate
croissants at the patisserie, for gelato at the ice cream shop. In the
beginning all of it is so new. Along the French Riviera, I think I'm the
first to fall in love.

The house his mother is renting is on a cliff overlooking the
Mediterranean Sea. It is the guesthouse on a very large estate, so large
the guesthouse has a guesthouse, and that is where we stay—in separate bedrooms.

Our routine is a series of small entertainments, flowing sleepily
one to the next. We walk the stone path, cool in the morning shade,
to the motorboat at the dock. Mediterranean villas often come with a
boat and captain on call to ferry guests to beaches and coves. We have
a swim and then take off for another place. We lunch at Cinquant
Cinq at the height of the season. With the people who winter in St.
Barth's and have a corner table at Sette Mezzo in New York. Then
spend afternoons back in town, sipping iced tea in the cafés along the
port, watching the yachts maneuver in and out.

A procession of minor events leads to dinner: a late-day swim or
tennis, conversation on the patio with white wine and vodka tonics,
and then finally our meal, and the next day we start over again. The

third day here is my birthday. His mother gives me a sarong from her favorite shop, and that evening we toast with champagne, *à votre santé!* We are young and happy and have all the time in the world.

7

After Iraq invaded Kuwait, *PJR* produced a series of hour-long specials on the war. All this summer I have been working on the third one, called *A Line in the Sand*. I resumed the research when I returned from St. Tropez. Looking for stories for the piece, I find a small article one morning on an inside page of *The Washington Post*: "Iraqis Fire Shots Near U.S. Team." There is a picture below the article of a convoy of trucks leaving a military facility in Fallujah, purportedly moving nuclear weapons. It is blurry, taken with a long lens, but I think we can use it for the show. The article quotes a United Nations weapons inspector named David Kay.

Luck and resourcefulness and an endless succession of phone calls—they connect the dots. This is what makes a good reporter.

You make a phone call and then another and then another and someone gives up a little bit with each one. I call the number in Vienna for the International Atomic Energy Agency, David Kay's base, hoping to find someone who will help me get to someone else who can get in touch with him. It is 10 a.m. in New York, 4 a.m. in Vienna, and he happens to answer the phone. He is just back from Iraq. There is no price you can put on luck in this business.

He tells me he was with the inspectors at the Abu Ghraib military facility, that they took pictures of suspicious crates at the military base, and that after that the crates suddenly disappeared. Intelligence reports tracked the crates to a site in Fallujah, so the inspectors followed, and at Fallujah they were rebuffed.

"But the pictures," I ask him, "how did you get those pictures?"

"One of the guys climbed up the water tower," he says. "And then the Iraqis fired shots."

I ask him for copies of the pictures, and he offers me video. "Video?"

"Sure. I have video of the entire incident. The convoy, the water tower, the Iraqis shooting at us, six tapes."

"Yes, I want it," I say quickly, before he can change his mind. "How soon can you send it?"

"I'll be in New York in two days. I can give it to you then."

I meet him at a coffee shop, and he hands me the tapes. I make copies and messenger them over to him at the United Nations that afternoon. He needs to play them for the UN Security Council.

The footage is incredible. When the guards deny the inspectors entry to the facility, one of the inspectors in Kay's group turns on the video camera. "Okay, then I'll have to call New York," Kay tells the guards, and he proceeds to set up a satellite phone in the middle of the desert—a clunky contraption with a big round satellite dish. Then he sits down cross-legged in the sand, waiting to connect. A camel walks behind him, and you can hear gunshots in the background. To which Kay remarks, deadpan, "It's cops and robbers in the desert, ladies and gentlemen."

Peter Jennings records the narration track to give the background of the story, and I edit David Kay's tapes of Fallujah into a three-minute piece that leads off the show to earn my first producing credit.

8

Anthony adds *I love you* to the end of a Sunday night phone call. The summer of 1993 starts out otherwise uneventfully. It is our second year at Sea Song and we're sharing the house with Marc and Lori. We're back in the city on Sunday, and he calls my apartment to say good night, the way he does every night I'm not with him.

"Sweet dreams, I love you." And he hangs up. Or maybe it is me hanging up quickly, startled. *What?* He is in the habit of ending our phone calls with *big kiss*—I am used to *big kiss*. I'm not ready for something new just like that. Shouldn't we be drinking red wine, kissing softly in front of a fireplace? Isn't that when this should be said?

I once spent a hot afternoon at the University of Texas, in the cramped office of Dr. Devendra Singh, and Dr. Singh used a specific science to explain love—the waist-to-hip ratio. I was working on a piece called "The Biology of Love" for a new magazine show called *Day One*. Dr. Singh was considered a pioneer for his work in the study of the evolutionary significance of human physical attraction. "Love at first sight," he said, "all boils down to one thing—the proportion of a woman's waist to her hips." Men, he claimed, are biologically hardwired to favor an hourglass figure, and to prove his theory he conducted a study of *Playboy* Playmates over fifty years. He discovered that the Playmates had gotten thinner over the years, but their waist-to-hip ratio—that is, the waist measurement divided by the size of the hips—remained constant. The most desirable proportion, he discovered, was a 0.70. And here I thought love would feel like an Etta James song, with all those thrills and flutters—passion from the depth of the soul. But my waist-to-hip ratio is a 0.71, so I was encouraged.

I say it back one night, *I love you,* a month after he does, at Sea Song. We are in bed with the lights off, about to fall asleep, and I say it. He says it back. There. It's done. And now we spend another summer building sandcastles with Anthony's nieces and nephews and grilling fresh corn on the deck.

When you live in New York, life decisions, like moving in with your boyfriend, are for the most part made based on who has the better real estate deal. I am subletting an apartment on the West Side, and Anthony lives in a rent-controlled apartment on the East Side. My lease is up, and I have to move. This is how we wind up together in his bachelor pad on Seventy-Eighth Street. I have traveled light these first few years on my own, and I have little more than a suitcase. Anthony clears out a drawer and closet for me, but for a month I keep my clothes in the suitcase on the floor. I love the idea of spontaneity, of clothes flung over chairs, and yet I'm just too practical. I manage for the downside; if it doesn't work, why unpack?

We disagree immediately on his décor. He has a couch covered in tiger velvet fabric that doesn't quite seem to fit in the living room, and two mismatched chairs. There is an antique coffee table and a large, rectangular butcher-block table. It's covered with piles of papers, magazines, bills, and letters, none of which I am allowed to touch. The tiny kitchen is stocked with mismatched dishes and pots and a cutting board so warped it is split down the middle. Down the hall is the bedroom—small with a dresser and bed and a clumsy-looking rocker in the corner. The economy of space in Manhattan does not permit the odd bulk of a rocker. On top of that, it's homely—oak with a low rattan seat and wide armrests. Anthony has gym shorts and T-shirts spread flat over it to dry. The arms and back are padded and covered with vinyl. The sort of piece that works better on the porch of a big farmhouse than in a small apartment on Madison Avenue.

He lets me replace the shower curtain—plastic with a map of the world and stiff mold on the bottom—though he thinks it is wasteful.

"It's still good. It keeps the water in, doesn't it?"

"It's gross," I say. "I'm getting a new one."

The cutting board I dismiss without asking, and it is the source of an enormous fight. We never seem to fight about interesting things— always passionately about the trivial: our different manner of cutting tomatoes, driving techniques, the high frequency with which I wash clothes and how much detergent is appropriate to use. The chair, though, is not settled with a quick fight. Our disagreement continues on and off for months. I try to adapt to it, moving it around first, from one place to another. Then I try to change the look with a chenille throw, a pillow wedged first on this side, and then that.

"Maybe we could give it to your sister," I say. "She could just keep it until we have a bigger place."

But it isn't just any rocker. His aunt sent it when he moved in. "I thought you might like to have this," she wrote in the note. "It belonged to Jack."

"I'm not getting rid of it," he says. "It was my uncle's."

"But that's exactly why it shouldn't be here. You should donate it to the library!"

"No. I like it. It stays. Besides," he adds with a wink, "where would I dry my gym clothes?"

I have bumped up against history. It won't be the first time. Most things here, I am learning, have a story. The tiger couch, for instance, is not just a couch, but one his mother had custom-made at De Angelis. It has been photographed for fashion books. People in certain circles *know* this couch, just as people in other circles *know* this chair. There is a well-known picture of the president sitting in it in the Oval Office, where it looks much better.

In August, on my birthday, I feel the bump.

"Feel my stomach right here," Anthony says. We are on the beach. "It feels like a little bump or something."

"Oh, yeah. I feel it. There's a knot. That's weird."

"Yeah. It's little. It's nothing."

Cancer is like this in the beginning. It tiptoes in like a teenager past curfew.

Anthony's body is carved and knotted with muscle—he runs marathons, works out at the gym every day, some days twice. It is impossible that there can be something unhealthy in this body that ripples on morning runs and twenty-mile bike loops around Long Island. We are quiet for a few minutes, then I run my hand over it again.

"It's just a little bump," he says abruptly. "I'll have someone look at it when we get back."

It is all very casual, and Anthony dismisses it with a quick hand motion, and we both lie down on our towels with our eyes closed to the sun. I let thoughts of the wedding we are going to that night, a twinge of hunger, fill up my head like sand. They spill right over the bump, and just like that I have dismissed it, too.

Unless you know to look for it, it is unnoticeable. It isn't touching us. We go to the wedding that evening. We finish our vacation. We drive back to the city and carry on with our daily business. We let the bump lie there for a few months, and it grows.

In October I return to Cambodia to produce a piece for *Day One*. This is my first piece as an official producer.

This time I stay in Phnom Penh, at the Royal Cambodiana. It has changed considerably since our documentary aired. The hotel has electricity, phone service, and "western-style" breakfast in the dining room.

I am working on a profile of Bobby Muller, founder of the Vietnam Veterans of America Foundation, whom I first met at the live debate on the night *From the Killing Fields* aired. He is someone you meet once and never forget. He has a clinic in Phnom Penh that makes prosthetic limbs for land mine victims. I interview young amputees at the hospital. I interview survivors of the murder at the torture prison in Tuel Sleng. On a day off from filming, my cameraman, Mark, and I take a plane to Siem Reap, in the western part of the country. It's a wild town filled with guns, prostitutes, and illegal gems traders. It also lies in the shadow of Angkor Wat, the largest and most famous of the temples built in the ninth century at the height of the ancient Khmer Empire.

I pick up a card at the airport for "guide and driver" and hire the man who answers the phone to take us there. We drive through the jungle, and then our driver pulls over, and through the trees we can see the ancient temple. It is deserted except for a few monks in saffron robes burning incense. The jungle is overgrown, and the roots of the giant banyan trees are twisted around the enormous sandstone pillars, as though they are keeping the entire structure from collapse. The colossal lichen-covered Buddhas carved on each of the temple towers, scarred from years of warfare, stand watch. By late afternoon, armed Khmer Rouge soldiers in camouflage replace the saffron-robed monks. We stay for the sunset and then our guide, nervous, insists we head back to the hotel.

When I return to New York, I find that Anthony has seen several doctors, and each of them has a slightly different diagnosis for the bump. One performed a needle biopsy that was inconclusive. Two others told him to come back if the bump grew. Anthony seems to have whatever it is under control. We barely speak of it.

We fly off to St. Barth's for Christmas, untroubled, to join Lee and Herbert and Hamilton. Herbert puts together a script for a short movie and then films it for fun. *The Kakadopoulis Story*—a satirical Greek tragedy about a murder and a double cross. Herbert directs and the rest of us make up the cast. Anthony plays the reporter trying to crack the case. Hamilton is hilarious as a misguided hairdresser, and Lee turns in a riveting performance as his mother. Lee's friend Count Giovanni Volpe plays the murdered tycoon. I coproduce and take one of the leading roles, a rival reporter who seduces Anthony to get the story. Anthony and I have a love scene; we flub our lines and can't stop giggling. You can hear Herbert scolding us off camera, "Carole, Anthony, stop laughing!"

It's only when I watch the movie later that I see the bump as Anthony turns shirtless toward the ocean in the second scene.

9

Before January 1994, I have never heard of a hematoma. It's a swelling—a clot of blood swelling in soft tissue. A hematoma is what people get from car accidents, when a head hits the windshield. It's a nasty internal bruise that can be fatal if it swells in your brain. When we return from St. Barth's, Anthony goes to see Dr. Klein, a family physician, and this is the diagnosis: a hematoma. He looks at the bump and decides that it is a clot of blood. We are all relieved. *At least it isn't cancer.* They schedule surgery to take it out. A simple out-patient procedure at Lenox Hill Hospital.

The night before surgery, Anthony and Lee and I decide to go to a movie to take our minds off it. It is *Intersection,* with Richard Gere. Gere plays a married architect who falls in love with a redheaded artist. Sharon Stone plays his devoted wife, and though he appears to be happily married, Gere is fatally drawn to the artist. In a climactic musical buildup he drives too fast in his Mercedes on his way to tell her he's leaving his wife. There is a lot of back-and-forth, a struggle between loyalty and love, and then the moment he makes his decision, he slams into *fate* in the back of a semi. Hours later he dies in the hospital from a hematoma. "We're losing him!" the movie doctors say, and he floats away with eyes closed and a smile on his face. Snapshots of his movie life flash by; the doctors' voices get softer and softer.

Anthony clears his throat, and his mother leaves the theater. *We'll laugh about this later, next week,* I think. But we never have a chance.

We check into Lenox Hill Hospital early the next morning, and the doctor says it will be a few hours. "We'll call you when he's in recovery."

Lee and I walk back to her apartment a few blocks away. She asks her housekeeper, Teresa, to prepare a light lunch, and I start to leaf through a book. The phone rings. "Madame, it's the hospital."

Lee motions me toward the back bedroom, and I pick up the other phone. The surgeon is calling half an hour after they started. Half an hour into a three-hour surgery. When the phone rang, the thought flashed briefly, *Oh God, he's dead.*

"We just closed Anthony up. I think you should come back now. It's not a hematoma." He pauses, and we wait. "We did a frozen cross section of the mass in the OR." I am picturing his mother's face in the other room. She has the kind of face that absorbs news, tucks it away. It is both reassuring and elusive.

"The frozen cross section shows spindle-shaped cells. We can't be certain what it is right now." He does not say *cancer* over the phone. He is careful not to say *cancer.* Instead he says, "It looks like a malignancy."

"Let's be up," Lee says in the cab back to the hospital. "No long faces." And she is. She walks in light and elegant with a big smile. "Ants, darling." I force my own smile and speak, it seems, too loudly.

After the surgeon discovers it's a tumor, Dr. Klein changes his report to fibrosarcoma, as if he were fixing a typo. He adds *high-grade,* like premium oil or a fine Scotch. We would have preferred something milder—a *non-spreading* tumor, for instance. One that won't skip around impetuously but can be contained and removed. So that's how it goes. Anthony checks into Lenox Hill in the morning healthy, it seems, and I take him home that evening, sick. While I sit in the bathroom watching him brush his teeth, I look at the bump again. It seems to have grown, ballooned up all at once. It bulges awkwardly out of his stomach. There is no missing it, and I think, *Was it always that big? How did this happen? How did we not know?*

But I don't understand yet the dynamics of this illness—denial, avoidance, the easy manipulation of truth. You can find a doctor, if you're persistent, who will tell you whatever you want to hear.

This isn't Anthony's first brush with cancer. I stumbled across it accidentally in a conversation about sex when we started dating.

"It doesn't matter," he said in an awkward discussion about birth control, the responsibilities of love. We'd been taking chances, or so I thought. "It's okay, I can't have kids."

We were lying in bed, and this was a slow-moving dialogue. I didn't understand him. We were quiet, and I waited for him to add the "just kidding."

"I had stomach cancer a few years ago, and I can't have kids." It jarred me. I was disoriented. As if a stranger walked into the room and spoke in Anthony's voice. He said it plainly, but I couldn't digest it. And then it hung there. I was talking about sex, and he was talking about cancer. He showed me the small scar, but it wasn't on his stomach. It was much lower. And then I knew. It said what he couldn't say, what the seven thousand men who die from this each year can't say. I didn't ask questions; I let him keep the lie. But when medical histories became a piece of our lives, it was there in neat, typewritten letters—testicular cancer.

Anthony has had cancer before, yet we still ignored the bump on the beach. Our behavior, then, defied logic, you must think. We stayed at Sea Song through Labor Day weekend and then made the three-hour drive back home.

Anthony checks into Memorial Sloan-Kettering Cancer Center on a Monday in February, two weeks after the hematoma surgery. He doesn't care for Sloan-Kettering. It's where you go, he thinks, to die. Among the sick, there is a subtle hierarchy of hospitals. Lenox Hill is the "baby hospital," with a minor reputation for sports injuries. There are no dark diseases lurking in the corners. But now we're at Sloan-

Kettering, and we feel processed. The hallways are cluttered with patients—on gurneys and in wheelchairs, dangling IVs. You check in, you wait on line, you rush out—the twenty-four-hour diner of terminal illness.

"We got it all," says Dr. Daniel Coit. He has excised a tumor from the right rectus muscle in Anthony's abdomen. And now it is gone. He explains to us about the Mylar mesh he put in to hold everything together, to protect Anthony's organs and make his stomach smooth where the muscle had been.

"We won't get the pathology results until the end of the week," he says, "but from the looks of the frozen section we think we have negative margins." This business of margins. It means they took the tumor out, plus the healthy tissue around it, and that the healthy tissue—the margins—was negative for cancer cells. To say this is good news is to say nothing.

"You need to come in for a follow-up next month, and CT scans every three months after that," he adds.

"Okay." I am writing it down in my notebook.

"We need to do chest X-rays monthly to make sure it hasn't spread." He pauses. "You need to be diligent."

In the hall, where Anthony can't hear, I ask questions. Dr. Coit tells me the longer you go between the primary occurrence and the first recurrence, the better the survivability rate. This is a very rare cancer, he confirms, sometimes fatal, but if it doesn't metastasize, the survivability rate increases dramatically. "Metastatic" is a clean, unemotional word, but in layman's terms it means, *You're screwed.* It means the cancer is spreading from one organ to another and there is little you can do about it. It means you're always one step, one surgery, one chemotherapy treatment behind.

On our second day at Sloan-Kettering I find out how long Anthony will live. It is laid out very clearly in a thick, dusty medical book. His mother brings homemade consommé and a pile of magazines. We are, all of us, full of hope. His aunt talks to him about being brave, and the past and a future. I go to the basement library and look up *fibrosarcoma* in the American Cancer Society Atlas. Then I close the book and file the information away. It is impractical. It doesn't tell me what to do when we go home. It doesn't tell me how to recover from this tumor, or when he can go back to work. It doesn't say what to do when your boyfriend has cancer. It says that in the best possible scenario he will live five years.

We get the pathology results at the end of the week, and they confirm Dr. Coit's judgment that the margins are negative, a cancer patient's "A" report card. We check out of Sloan-Kettering and resume our lives.

I look back on this time with nostalgia. How smooth and clean his body was—free of the bright red scars like Pick up Sticks that marked him later. They were about to draw the first line, and I wish I had given more attention to it. Loved it, felt slowly along each centimeter, memorized the bumpy unevenness, kissed it gently. When we were still lovers and bigger than the cancer. We learned a different kind of intimacy as we went on. The intimacy of night sweats and blood counts and dialysis machines.

10

He proposes on Mother's Day.

We are at Lee's house, planning to head back to the city that night. I am twenty-nine, and my boyfriend has cancer, and I am always thinking about it. But for Anthony it's over. He has had the surgery, the margins were negative—he's beaten it. *Don't you see, Nut? Don't be sad. We did it!*

"Wake up, Peanut. Let's go for a walk on the beach." I am trying to take a nap in the small library, but he keeps at me. I push him away, but he's stubborn. It's windy and cold and getting late and we have the drive back still, work tomorrow.

"Just to the jetty, Nut. I promise." He has to promise because this is an old trick. At the jetty it's "Just to the flagpole, come on." And at the flagpole, "Just to the log on the beach," the one that only he can see. But he's true to his word, and at the jetty we turn around. I am focused on the walk, the big rocks that mark halfway and the distance back. I am not sure I want to be here, with him. It is a lot, this, and I'm not sure it's what I want. I love him, and yet I have asked myself, *Can you leave a man who is sick?* In *Butch Cassidy and the Sundance Kid,* Etta tells Sundance, "I'll do anything for you, but I won't watch you die," and true to her word she leaves him in Bolivia to die alone. I don't know if I am stronger than she is—whether I can watch Anthony die.

These thoughts are rumblings, faraway thunder, eclipsed by the lightning-bolt urgency of others. *You can't leave him. You love him. You're going to save his life.*

We are walking back to the house, and I am ahead of him, taking the stairs from the beach up to the house two at a time, and when I look back he is still at the bottom. I sit down and wait for him, . feeling guilty now because he's had surgery and it slows him down. And then he's right in front of me. With the little black box.

Real life is a flurry, even the still moments. The ones like this when I remember *sitting quietly* and *not talking.* In real life there is always something. A cough, a look away, the sound of other voices. A dog barks and we both turn to look, and there are people in the house and we think of them. It is never still. But all of these things are edited out in memory, to leave a stretch of time standing still.

This is a big moment. A man I love is asking to marry me, and it seems as though everything stops for a moment while my life flashes by. I am sitting on a high rock, and everyone I have known is scattered below me like figures in a wax museum. Anthony beside me is frozen in a pose, too, while I climb down tentatively and pick through my past. Grandma Millie, Grandma Binder, Linda, Maria. They are all smiling. *Where am I going from here?* I want to ask them, but I can't speak.

We sit out on the steps to the beach for some time; I know this. I am sure we are talking, holding hands; he is kissing my forehead. I am sure we hug, he makes a joke, I laugh. I say yes or something close and put the ring on, and we sit side by side on the steps. I don't want to go back in the house. I don't want to announce this. I'm not ready. His mother is inside. Does she know? Does Herbert? I stretch this time sitting here exactly up to the point at which it might be considered strange or odd, or *Is everything okay?* I push us up to this line but don't cross it. Instead I stand up and Anthony follows, and we go inside the house. From the beach, through the windows, you would see the four of us hugging and rotating and hugging someone else.

Moments later I'm back in the library, burrowed into the armchair. My future mother-in-law is on the sofa with a yellow legal pad. She is drawing columns for the guests, one for each of us: my family, his family, friends. She is talking about churches and dates. My life feels like it is happening to me, as if I haven't been paying attention. We are not so different, my mother and I. Before you know it, your choices are made for you.

We drive back to the city and call Marc and Lori from the car, then my mother. Anthony calls his aunt and she is thrilled. "I'll have an engagement party for you."

11

There were two people I knew to have cancer before Anthony, and both of them died. Grandma Millie died in Kingston in the fall of

1985. It was long after I had stopped spending summers upstate, so I wasn't entirely aware she was dying. There were second and third-hand accounts wedged between other pieces of news in routine telephone conversations. But when you're twenty, seventy-six seems old, and you understand that a grandmother will die, so you don't pay such close attention to how. It was a time before I was anxious about death. I didn't yet perk my ears up at "cancer." I was uninitiated, and the uninitiated still believe these things can be fixed. You only hear "cancer" if you're listening closely.

I went to visit her one weekend while she was sick. We were watching the Jerry Lewis telethon in the living room in Kingston. Suddenly she picked up the phone and dialed the number on the screen, her index finger bunched into the hole of the rotary dial. She made a ten-dollar pledge with tears falling down her face. She checked herself into the hospital the next day and died there a few weeks later. I came up again to see her in the hospital. She was bedridden and sallow, with cloudy eyes, but she held down the center of the room. She was surrounded by people, swirling around her as they had her whole life, and in that way she didn't seem to be dying. Her funeral was in the middle of Hurricane Gloria, and we huddled under a plastic sheet at the Mount Marion cemetery, peeking up at the ornery sky.

Anthony's aunt Jackie was the other. I had met her a year before she or Anthony or any of us were thinking about spindle-shaped cells or malignancies. We were thinking about Christmas and families, and I was wondering what to wear to dinner at her apartment. I chose a black-silk skirt, above-the-knee, with a black sweater and patent leather Mary Janes with a gold buckle. I picked it all out carefully, and she answered her door in tailored slacks and said, "Oh, you must be cold," before he introduced us.

She had the same wide eyes as Anthony's mother. The same breathy voice. A seemingly intense interest in anything someone was talking about. There was a fuss being made over a young cousin that night. Her mother had died young. The girl was thirteen and long and graceful. Poised, it seemed, for elegance. And I could see Jackie

was ceremoniously offering her wing. It was an intimate holiday dinner: John and his cousins the Rutherfords; Ed and Caroline and their
children; and Anthony, his sister Tina, and me. I felt as if I were
watching through a two-way mirror.

A year later everything had changed. She called the apartment
the night Anthony left Lenox Hill, the night we learned that the
hematoma was a malignancy. It was a short conversation. "Something's wrong," he said to me after he hung up. She called back again
later that night. "I have something I need to tell you," she said to him.
"So do I," he replied. "You go first."

After that they went for long walks in the park, the two of them,
as often as they could. I tagged along once or twice, walking behind
them. I tried to stay out of the way. They had so much to say to each
other. Every few yards I would spot the paparazzi, long black lenses
poking out from a bush or behind a tree. They were waiting for her
to trip or fall—waiting, I was certain, for the picture that said she was
dying.

In late May, Anthony calls as he's leaving his office. "Can you meet
me there tonight?" It's Thursday, and he has been going to his aunt's
apartment every night after work. She checked out of the hospital
three days earlier; there was nothing left to be done.

I don't want to see her. I'm his fiancée now and this is his family,
but I don't want to go. When I arrive, the streets are crowded with
strangers, and the apartment is filled with family; most I have never
met. There are awkward introductions. Stilted conversations, swinging between strained small talk and stifled tears.

Anthony is called into her bedroom, and minutes later he motions
me in. There is a small circle around her bed, where she is lying, a
bright-colored scarf wrapped around her head. Her eyes are closed
and her hands folded peacefully, and someone leads off the prayers.
Anthony speaks in an unsteady voice. I want to run from here, out of
the apartment, out into the street, as far away as I can.

"I hope I can face this disease with as much dignity and courage as
you," he says, kneeling beside me, hands folded, head down. *Now they*

know, I am thinking. He just announced he has cancer. I can hear people breathing in the room.

I am swallowed up by dread. Here it is, death. *Courage* is a word I will learn to say; it is part of the vocabulary of cancer—*courage, hope, bravery.* Before this it was something that a man in a lion's suit chased. Now it is a word about cancer.

Anthony is a pallbearer. He has to be at the church early, so I go to the funeral with his mother. I meet her at her apartment and she asks, "Pearl earrings or no earrings?" We decide no earrings, and then she puts them on and takes them off and we go out to the car.

12

It seems like the wrong time for a wedding. I am relieved, because I assume we'll delay it. But Lee is resolute, and we meet for lunch. She is perfectly composed and has already made inquiries about the availability of a church in East Hampton.

"We need something to celebrate this year," she says. "Jackie would want that."

The wedding will be a celebration of life. I find myself agreeing, *Yes, a celebration of life.*

We talk about dates, and I tell her I have been assigned to work on a documentary. I will be busy this summer, too busy to plan a wedding. I can see that she is determined. She doesn't need me to plan this wedding, and we both know it. I have the feeling she would prefer, in fact, if I let her arrange it all. She tells me she's always wanted to have a summer wedding under a tent in her backyard and not to worry, she'll pay for everything. "If you get me your guest list, I will take care of the rest." So it is settled. There will be a wedding in August, two and a half months away.

The documentary is on Haiti. Jean-Bertrand Aristide, the deposed Haitian president, is waiting in Washington to return to his country after being ousted in a coup a few years earlier. President Clinton is considering sending the military to force the generals running the country out of power. I am flying back and forth to Washington to interview policymakers and Aristide's lawyer.

In between there is the guest list to finish and my wedding gown to design. Lee has sent over sketches from her good friend the designer Giorgio Armani with a note attached. *I think these are beautiful.* There are fabric swatches pinned to each sketch: organza and chiffon, pale silk with white tulle. I can't help but notice that the sketches bear a striking resemblance to Lee. I thank her and politely tell her I will take care of the dress.

Anthony is in Los Angeles, doing a profile of Hollywood producer Robert Evans and covering the Nicole Brown Simpson murder. Three days after the murder, he finds Beverly Deteresa, an attendant on O. J. Simpson's flight to Chicago—a reporting coup. Everyone in news is in L.A. in a feeding frenzy, hunting down friends, waiters, and neighbors. Anthony finds Deteresa the old-fashioned way, through a persistent trail of phone calls, and then he gets her to talk.

No one can be more excited for him than I am. We understand this together, the adrenaline high of connecting these phone calls. Anthony appreciates the beauty of my David Kay, and I his Beverly Deteresa. He has what all great reporters have, ruthless empathy. He can get people to talk. They *want* to talk to him. From the Queen of England to a sheriff in Idaho. He is subtle and gracious, and no one knows the famous family he descended from unless he is trying to land an interview with Monaco's royals. He knows when to play his cards.

Judd Rose is the correspondent on the Robert Evans piece, and he solicits Evans's help to play a prank. Anthony's colleagues are secretly shooting a video of him preparing for his wedding, highlighting his obsession with working out. We play it the night before our wedding. In it there is a scene of Evans challenging Anthony to lift a stack of film reels, and then again, and then "Can you do it ten times, and with the other hand?" There is no trace, not the slightest, of an operation in January. He is strong and eager. It is boyish and charming, this desire of his to be challenged, lifting the stack of reels ten times, then twenty. Then "way up above your head," Evans taunts him. It is sweet and funny. It is also not so funny if you know what is going on—most in the room don't—which is that he has cancer and difficult odds. If you know that, you feel a pang of anxiety—brief because this is a wedding and no time for such thoughts. But I recognize the searching look on Anthony's face and the stuttered speech, the way he says to Evans, "Why would you think I couldn't do that?" I can see that he is thinking, *Can he tell? Do I look sick?*

Our wedding is in a white clapboard church in East Hampton. My sister Terri is maid of honor, John the best man. Ushers in white linen escort the guests to their seats. Flower girls drop rose petals. I hear Mendelssohn's "Wedding March," and that is my cue. My father holds out his arm, his hair pulled back in a ponytail, and he walks me down the aisle to the groom. Father Sam talks about love and commitment, and I catch John smirking at Anthony. The three of us barely contain giggles at the pomp and circumstance of it all. I keep my eyes straight ahead and bite my lip. I know Anthony will laugh if he looks at me.

Herbert reads a Bible verse, Sirach 51:13–17. John gets through a Shakespeare sonnet. I hear, I think, a collective sigh when Father Sam says, "I now pronounce you man and wife." And we head back up the aisle. It's all very quick, and everyone claps when it is over. We make our way without incident past the paparazzi and into the cars. A procession of black Mercedes drives ahead to the house, to the oceanfront reception.

Then we are on a plane to Australia, flying away.

I see a bump the last week of our honeymoon, in a cool sunset on the beach. I brush my fingers across the chest of my new husband, then down across the scar that cut through his smooth, tan skin, his tight, muscled stomach. And my fingers catch it, so slightly. "I'm sure it's nothing," he says. "Don't make a big deal out of it. They'll take it out when we get back."

So I don't make a big deal of it. I file it away so we can lie back on our tiki chairs on an empty beach in Lanai with palm trees shading our eyes.

We stop in Los Angeles for dinner with Herbert on the way home. He's directing a new movie, *Boys on the Side*.

"Don't say anything to him about the bump," Anthony says. "It will just worry Mummy." So I say nothing to Herbert about the bump. I tell him about the nurse shark we saw diving on the reef. I tell him about the fresh powder snow we skied on in the New Zealand Alps. I tell him about the white-water rafting. I don't once mention the pea-sized bump, and we leave the next morning.

Dandelion Wishes

I would indeed that love were longer-lived,
And vows were not so brittle as they are,
But so it is, and nature has contrived
To struggle on without a break thus far,
Whether or not we find what we are seeking
Is idle, biologically speaking.

—EDNA ST. VINCENT MILLAY,
A Few Figs from Thistles: Poems and Sonnets,
"Sonnet IV"

1

The dandelion is a gawky yellow flower that blooms and then collapses into a soft, clumsy down that little children blow wishes on.
There was a sea of dandelions in our back yard on Madison Hill, and
Grandma Binder, swinging her scythe, would mount a futile attack
on them in her housedress and apron. They grew into a clotted forest
of long, milky necks in the backyard, and the best she could hope for
was just to cut them down to stubs. It starts with one slouchy weed—
pluck it out and it's gone. You never quite remember, can't pinpoint
the time between when there was one weed and a sea of them. There
was a time when the thing seemed manageable, and then we were
looking backward over our shoulders, running away from it.

You never stop thinking you might have beaten it somehow, and
there were moments when we thought we had. Your husband can be
dead years, and you can't stop thinking how you might have beaten it.
Or how they could have left ten minutes earlier, or the next morning.
Or that damn lighthouse could have flickered through the fog.

After our honeymoon, but before we go to the doctor, we go to a
friend's house in Connecticut for the weekend.

"I'm in trouble," Anthony says, stepping from the shower. Now
we can both see a lump when he stretches his leg out under the towel
so his skin is taut. This is a different one. It is a little smaller than a
golf ball, and oblong. It looks like something has been left there, like
when you make the bed and there's a sock under the covers and you
try to smooth the sheets. There's something under his skin, a bump,
that shouldn't be.

We go into Sloan-Kettering, and doctors remove the tiny bump I felt on his scar in Lanai. They also remove the second bump in his groin, but this time the margins are positive. Now we have to talk. Now there are rounds of meetings with doctors—Dr. Antman, Dr. Casper, Dr. Coit, Dr. Fair.

"Metastasized," they say in a serious tone.

"Positive margins," they say. We are in the room with doctors now, and I am listening but not hearing. *But it's a local recurrence. It only spread to the groin. It didn't move very far.* I am blowing spires off of dandelions one by one, sending them out to grow miracles.

Anthony's cancer was in one place, and Dr. Coit took it out. We hold on to that until it isn't true anymore. Then we just adjust the markers. *Okay, now it has metastasized but only right near where the original tumor was—not far away like other people's, not like the people who are dying.* These are the games we learn to play in our heads.

"Do you understand what this means?" A man in a white lab coat is talking; his mouth is moving, but I can't hear him. He points to an X-ray, and now I can't see him in the glare of the light box. There are *suspicious areas* on his lung. They don't call the suspicious areas tumors—"pulmonary nodules," they say. Now is when we begin lowering the bar.

We sit through weeks of meetings, shuffle in and out of exam rooms with X-rays—white coats on one side, Lee and Anthony and I on the other. The heads of the oncology departments at Sloan-Kettering: surgical, radiation, chemotherapy. We learn the vocabulary of treatment: MAID chemotherapy, stereotactic radiation therapy, spiral CT scans, antiangiogenesis. We go to Columbia Presbyterian in search of better news, but it's the same.

If you were my brother meetings, I call them.

"If you were my brother, I would tell you to do chemo," one doctor says. "If you were my brother, I'd sign you up for five rounds." We go to New York Hospital, and the doctors say, "It's up to you, but if you were *my* brother . . ."

This is how it happens. I have been studying it. It recurs close to the primary site, and then it metastasizes farther away, sometimes to the groin, then on to the lungs or the liver. And there it is, as though his cancer has read the instruction manual and is following the directions.

It steals in the moment we feel invincible. It depended on our denial, our disbelief. Cancer is nothing if not discreet. *Look at me,* it whispers. *I dare you, say my name on this sunny day with your future spread wide.* You won't, of course. Cancer counts on it.

It happened so quickly. He had cancer in February, then they cut it out and he was declared "cancer-free." He was "cancer-free" at our wedding, "cancer-free" in September. But now it's October, and we are squeezed into exam rooms deciding just how we will fix this thing. Lee takes down the private phone numbers of the doctors. I have my reporter's notebook and write "wide excision" and underline it. I scribble down "positive margins."

When it comes back, everything changes. We are married now. It becomes something I speak of using *we,* the way men will announce *we* are pregnant, or *we* are having twins; this is now *ours. We* have cancer. *We* need a biopsy. *We* are researching treatment options.

I become a specialist. I can tell you anything you want to know. Sarcoma is a death sentence but very rare, though that's little comfort once you've got it. I learn that recurrence is influenced by the histologic type, size, and grade. I learn that low-grade is better than high-grade; that it metastasizes first to the nearby lymph nodes, then settles into the lungs; and that there are three treatments: radiation, chemotherapy, and surgery. I learn that they all have uncertain outcomes, but that surgery has the best survival rates. I bury myself in details—my own desperate religion, and I cling to it.

I produce Anthony's cancer story, line up interviews with doctors, book appointments, assemble the team. I make phone calls and take notes and research different treatments—experimental clinical trials, new drugs, surgeries with pig valves. I study his pathology reports, his CT scans, his MRIs. I handle it all brilliantly. Anthony believes this, and I believe it, too.

His family trusts me. I can save his life, I think, and they will gather around me and bestow their seal of approval. His mother will never say to Carolyn, "I just don't *understand* what it is they have in common. ABC can't be all that interesting." Instead she will tell her how proud she is of me.

I realize that I am being charged with this mission. I will have to take control, because I am his wife now. It's my job. This is when we begin our endless dance of compromises—of small lies, deceptions, and secrets. A complicated and intricate set of rules created on the fly that moves us forward. Anthony wants nothing to do with any of it— the doctors, the hospitals. It's all a nuisance. He doesn't ask the doctors questions. His illness doesn't interest him. We silently agree that he will have the cancer and I will take care of it. We begin a delicate waltz with denial.

2

National Institutes of Health, Bethesda, MD
November 1994 *(Inpatient Record)*
Admitted: 11/11/94
Discharged: 11/18/94

CLINICAL DIAGNOSIS: High-grade fibrosarcoma, metastatic, to right inguinal area.

REASON FOR HOSPITALIZATION: This is a thirty-four-year-old white male, otherwise healthy, with recurrent high-grade fibrosarcoma. A 1 cm subcutaneous nodule in right groin was involved with tumor with *positive margins.* The patient is admitted now for wide local excision. The patient will also undergo spiral CT scan for possible pulmonary nodules.

◆

It is looking very grim, because the doctors are all pushing chemo-therapy. Anthony listens silently. He knows that in chemo he'll lose his hair. This is all he needs to know.

Then John calls and says, "It's done. You meet with Dr. Rosen-berg next week. He's at the National Cancer Institute. He's the best there is."

John has a gift for big moments, and this is a very big one. He gets us a ticket to the National Cancer Institute, a branch of the National Institutes of Health, the place we come to know as the NIH, or simply "Washington." This is a government-funded research hospital, Memorial Sloan-Kettering's academic older sister, the Mayo Clinic's wise uncle. If there is a breakthrough in cancer it will likely happen here first, but you can't just *go* to the NIH. You have to have the right type of cancer, or be at a stage in the disease that will benefit a study, and there is an application form and nervous waiting for all of that. Or you have to be able to do what John did: pick up the phone and call a senator, your uncle, who is at the time sitting on the Health and Human Services Committee.

NIH doesn't look like a hospital or feel like one. From the outside it is an office building in a nameless industrial park set back on a wooded landscape in Bethesda, Maryland. The buildings are nestled in a leafy, oak-tree neighborhood, a half-hour drive from Washing-ton. And it's away from New York, from home, away from people who know us, who might see us going into and out of hospitals. To have our cancer in Washington is a luxury. The NIH with its empty halls, lingering doctors, sports chats in the halls, is a dramatic depar-ture from New York.

We are invited to tastefully subtle offices to meet a smiling, unremarkable-looking man with wire-rimmed glasses, Dr. Steven A. Rosenberg, the chief of the Cancer Institute's surgery branch. Aside from his responsibilities managing a research staff of seventy and the expectation that he will save people's lives, he is a straightforward, unassuming man who takes pride in his job. He has a soft voice and is careful to finish pronouncing a word before starting a new one. He gives his patients time to think between sentences padded with medical terms.

"I've had our top radiologist take a look at your scans. There are a few spots on the lung that appear suspicious," Dr. Rosenberg says, pointing to the scan clipped into the light box. "Here, here, and here. I suggest we follow you closely and see if we notice any changes in size or shape." He tells us about a new CT scan called a spiral CT scan. It's the prototype, and the NIH has the only one in the country. The picture it takes is more detailed—a hundred times more powerful than the existing technology.

"So what do we do now?" I ask. I need the next step.

"Well, we can't even be certain it's cancer," he says. "It could be scar tissue. If it turns out these are tumors, your best chance is to remove them surgically, because the success rate of patients who have chemotherapy for high-grade fibrosarcoma is very low."

No chemotherapy. This is all Anthony hears. I hear something slightly different: chemo doesn't work. But I file that away. We schedule an operation for a wide groin excision to take care of the positive margins, and we head back to New York.

On the plane I daydream about this man. The one who is saving our life. I make a lazy list in my notebook. *All the ways Dr. Rosenberg is just like everyone else: family photos on his desk, baseball games, drives a Buick.* I picture him unpacking Saran-wrapped sandwiches and eating them at his desk, listening to the Orioles on the radio. I'm both comforted and disappointed by this. What you find out too quickly about doctors if you see them on a regular basis is that they are *human* and that you'd prefer they weren't. I need someone who does magic.

We return to the NIH a week later. Dr. Rosenberg greets us with a smile that I will get used to seeing.

The NIH is our altered existence—our ordinary. It is a place, initially, of success, hope, love conquering all. Anthony is the star of the cancer ward, performing remarkable feats of recovery. Getting an A on all of their tests—the athlete, the honor student, *ambulatory* by the second day after surgery. It is a place of playful giggles, shared secrets, stealing out after curfew. The doctors indulge our stunts: Leaving the grounds without approval. Sneaking in hamburgers and beer. It is a place, in the beginning, of winks and pet names and knowing smiles. *See, it's not so bad, is it, Nut?* We are newlyweds here. These empty halls are our private getaway. Anthony is in command, has everyone charmed. We sneak off campus and he is smooth talking his way out when we get caught in the parking lot. And I, giddy with his invincibility, run along after him, ready to do whatever he asks. The NIH makes the afternoon in his mother's apartment—the day the phone rang and it was spindle cells instead of hematoma—seem so far away.

John comes down this first trip after Anthony is out of surgery. "Hey, Tonypro," he says, strolling in casually. Anthony is happy to see him. They make jokes about nurses and sponge baths. We get some food and watch the news, and then Anthony needs to sleep, so John and I take a blanket outside. We throw it down on the lush lawn in front of Clinical Building 10, and he starts questioning me about marriage. "What's it like, being married? I mean, what's it really like?" We talk about gardeners and flowers. A close friend of ours is famous for his flower-gardener theory. The very best relationship has one of each. The gardener nurtures, and the flower blooms. We decide that two gardeners might work together, but never two flowers.

"I think I'm a gardener," John says thoughtfully.

"I don't think so." I laugh. "You're definitely more flower. You and Anthony both. You two need gardeners."

"Are you comparing me with the principe?" he says, laughing.

I am drunk with the warm sun, the autumn smells. And I think

that we are talking about this because of Carolyn; there are whisper-
ings that she is back. We lie on the warm grass, and he talks about her
without ever saying her name.

"Is it what you thought it would be?" he asks.

I shake my head. "I don't know yet. My husband is in the hospital;
I'm not a good one to ask."

"So, what do you think is going to happen?" he asks, and now we
are talking about Anthony. I am optimistic with what the NIH
promises, and I tell him that. But I can see he's not. He doesn't respond,
and we see the sun is going down, so we get up and head back inside.

The groin operation is uneventful. Dr. Rosenberg removes the
remaining tumor, and pathology shows negative margins.

A week later we are back in New York and at Caroline's apartment for her birthday. John makes an entrance with Carolyn. This is
her official coming out. There have been rumors and sightings and
John puts them all to rest here. Relaxed and dressed in black, she
walks casually into the apartment beside him, holding his hand. They
have been back together for a few months. Caroline hugs her brother
warmly and hesitates for a brief moment before greeting his date, *So
nice to meet you.* Her friends smile politely and then shift their focus
to John.

I am sitting in the library, and the room, as it always does, shifts
when she walks in, even if nobody notices it but me.

It's an impenetrable circle, this room, it sometimes seems. I know
what she's walking into. There is a shared past here that is too intricate to explain. The kind of shared past that is communicated by
winks, by facial expressions, by half-sentences—the short-cuts of
intimacy. It is as if they stop talking when you walk in, and they do,
in a way, because they speak to most outsiders in a different manner.

I met Caroline my first summer at Sea Song, rollerblading to her
house bruised and out of breath, and fifteen minutes behind. *Nice,
Anthony,* she teased him for racing ahead, and we were conspirators
for a moment—two women who knew what men were like, who
knew what Anthony was like, rolling our eyes together. We'll be

friends, I thought. But our relationship stayed superficial in a way I never quite understood. But Anthony adored her. They had fun together, laughing at a long-running joke between the two of them that I was never going to get.

I am an outsider here but a quiet one. I watch and adapt, but not Carolyn, I can see. She walks into this guarded room radiant and stubbornly original. Impulsively affectionate.

She sees me immediately and smiles big. It's been two years, but we pick up as though our conversation had just been momentarily interrupted. *Oh, now where were we?* We skip all the formalities and plunge right back in.

We have been out of the hospital for six days, and though Anthony limps, no one mentions it. So the party is happy. Thanksgiving is the following week, and "Mummy," he says, "has invited us for the weekend. I said we'd go." She and Herbert are at their house in East Hampton and I wince. To me Long Island, even, is too far to go now, so soon. It is subtle, this struggle of ours. Anthony always pushing, me pulling back. Me wanting to stay home, to recuperate, to be close to doctors, and him on to the next trip.

"Pack a good outfit," he says, distracted. "There's a dinner one night with one of her friends." A clue that I miss. We are strictly casual at his mother's in winter—jeans and sneakers. Then a car service shows up at the apartment, and it's the second clue I miss. I'm pouting a little and feeling bullied. I fall asleep in the car, and when it stops, we're at Kennedy Airport. "We're going to Paris, Nut," Anthony says and hands me my passport. He climbs out of the car with his cane, wearing a sly grin. *I got you.*

He can't walk well, but he's defying the doctors, the ones who said, *No travel for six weeks and keep your leg elevated as much as possible.* We are on our way to Paris just ten days later. Our good friends Glenn and Eva live there, and Anthony plans this scheme to spend the holiday with them.

We stay in an apartment owned by Anthony's aunt, Countess Isabelle D'ornano, on the Seine. She has two apartments in Paris and keeps this one for guests. When we arrive, we find on the bed an invitation to dinner addressed to *Prince and Princess Radziwill*. Europeans use royal titles the way Americans use *Mr.* or *Ms.* I saved the invitation and framed it for the bathroom.

It is cold in Paris, but we march on, lighting candles at Notre Dame, standing in line to see the *Mona Lisa,* shopping along the Avenue Montaigne. We wander along narrow cobblestoned streets, stopping for espresso and chocolate croissants. We sightsee until Anthony's leg becomes so swollen he can no longer walk, and then we take a taxi to the American hospital. The doctors drain the fluid from his leg to relieve the pressure. When they are finished, we take another cab to Eva and Glenn's for an expat Thanksgiving dinner— turkey and foie gras.

When we're back in New York, Anthony still needs the cane, though he refuses to take it to work. It is painful for him to walk, and he cannot hide a limp, but he makes up an elaborate story about tripping on a Jetway getting off a plane. He feigns embarrassment at his clumsiness and comes home delighted with himself for fooling his coworkers. He is determined to keep his illness a secret. Only a few of our very close friends know he's had cancer at all. The next week he is back in the gym.

We spend Christmas in Mexico and celebrate the new year in New York. We go to Caroline and Ed's for dinner to usher it in. It's just the four of us. There is no trace of a surgery, except for the scar on Anthony's leg. He is healthy and strong and running five miles in the park every night. There is light banter back and forth. We trade resolutions and plans. We toast to a better year, and after dinner each of us makes a prediction. "I'll try to stay out of the hospital," jokes Anthony. At my turn I say, "I think John and Carolyn will get married." And suddenly the room is quiet.

"No, he won't," says Ed. "Caroline doesn't even know her."

I'm caught off guard by this—his tone, the quiet.

There is a neat change of subject; the three of them move on.

3

Anyone who knows cancer knows the checkup cycle, the rhythm—
the three-month ebb and flow. The prelude to the checkups, the
weeks or days before, can be worse than the surgeries. The *news* feels
worse than the treatment. Our checkups are a day-trip to Washington. We take an early shuttle to Reagan National, rent a car, and make
the thirty-minute drive to the NIH. Our checkup takes a couple of
hours, more or less. Enough time to draw blood, X-ray Anthony's
chest, drink the orange contrast solution for the CT scan, meet with
the radiologist, and then we fly back.

At our January checkup, the suspicious areas on Anthony's lung
can still be clearly seen on the CT scan. Dr. Rosenberg isn't convinced
the shadows are tumors and decides we can go one checkup longer.
We are still hoping that it is scar tissue.

Carolyn calls late one day in February and invites me to one of her
fashion shows at Calvin Klein. "Sure, I'll go," I say. I am sure I sound
much too eager, but she is genuinely happy, as if I am doing her a
favor. "I'll leave your name at the door. Just tell them who you are and
they'll let you in. Can't wait to see you!"

Carolyn came to New York, to Calvin Klein, around the same
time I started at ABC. She worked her way up from sales to public
relations, and one of her responsibilities at the shows is to manage the
models. They are constantly, it seems, in crisis. She is mother to them
all, calm and ready with answers. The group hysteria, the high-
pitched drone all seem to subside, just perceptibly, the moment her
hand rests on someone's arm. *It's all taken care of.*

The show is at Calvin Klein's showroom on Seventh Avenue, and
there is a crowd around the door when I get there.

"I'm looking for Carolyn Bessette," I say to someone who looks like a security guard. And then I see her behind the runway talking to one of the models. She lifts the girl's hair up, then puts it down, fingers it into curls around her face. Her own long hair is pulled up in a loose ponytail, and she is wearing a simple white button-down shirt and black pants. She looks up with a huge smile and leads me to a small room behind the runway where she is working. There is a table set up with individual makeup stations, and there are racks and racks of clothes, each of them pinned with a number. It's not as glamorous as I expect, backstage at a fashion show. It's chaotic and tense, and very messy. Before the show starts, she finds me a seat out front.

"What did you think?" she asks when it is over. I am flattered she thinks I'd have something to say. I tell her I loved it; then she kisses and hugs me good-bye, and I go back to my cubicle at work. It is all over in under an hour, my foray into the world of long-lashed fashionistas.

A couple weeks later we have dinner, just the two of us. I meet her at her office at Calvin Klein. It is dark, with scattered piles of paper, fabrics, and catalogs. She is on the phone, and she points to a note I had sent to her after I met her at Sea Song. It is a picture of her in *Vogue*, posed sitting on luggage in Grand Central Station. The caption read, "Perfect Friday Casual," and I had scribbled on top of it, "Everyone should look so good on Friday at 5 p.m.!" She had it pinned on the wall.

Discovering her again, I feel the way I did when I found a Starbucks at the airport in Dubai. I had been too far from home, for too long, and here was something I recognized. It's a particular kind of joy. Now I can't imagine a time without her.

In March, Anthony and I are back to Washington for a checkup. After the CT scan, Anthony gets dressed, and we wait in the cafeteria while Dr. Rosenberg and the radiologist analyze the scans, compare them with the previous scans, and determine whether the shadows have grown or multiplied. We meet him at the clinic, in a small exam room on the fourth floor. He tells us there is no doubt now that the suspicious areas are tumors.

The CT scan shows twenty-one small tumors, *pulmonary nodules,* in Anthony's lungs—fifteen in his right lung and six in his left. Five of the nodules have grown since the scan in January. This is how it goes. The cancer is in one place, his abdominal wall, and then it spreads to another, his lungs. Only you don't say *spread,* you say *metastasize*. Disease spreads. Cancer metastasizes.

But they are small, we tell ourselves, and easy to get to—at the edges of his lungs, not deep inside.

Dr. Rosenberg brings in Dr. Harvey Pass, the thoracic surgeon, to explain the operation. He tells us he'll make a six-inch cut down the breastbone and then spread the ribs apart with a chest retractor, a saw that separates the sternum muscle and bone. He will then deflate the lungs one at a time and with his fingers feel along the length of each one. When he feels a bump, he will cut a wedge and then staple the ends together. When he is confident he got everything, he says, he will put the lungs back in Anthony's chest and close him up. He uses words like *invasive* and *risk*. The surgical consent forms admit the possibility the operation can "result in death."

It will be a painful surgery. It will hurt him to breathe. A breath will expand his chest and spread the incision. It will feel like a knife. They will insert thin yellow tubes into holes in his chest afterward to drain the fluid from his lungs. This may take days.

We are sitting in the exam room looking at the X-rays. The surgeon uses his pen to point out the areas of tumor, blood vessels, bronchial tubes, the trachea. We are attentive and polite.

"What's the worst-case scenario?" I ask.

Dr. Rosenberg neither exaggerates the truth nor masks it. "The worst case is when you run your fingers across the lung and it feels like sandpaper. Because each piece of 'sand' is actually a tiny tumor, too small to see on a scan. At that point there is nothing we can do."

I take out my Filofax. "Well," Anthony says, "what's it look like, Nut?"

"I'm screening my piece on Wednesday. What about Thursday, is that good?"

"Thursday's good. I'll move my meeting."

A few days later I get the news that *Day One* has been canceled, and all of us scramble to other shows. It is my beginner's course on ratings and focus groups. *Day One* was a good news magazine show with an unfortunate time slot—Thursday nights at ten. A one-hour news show stacked up against a second-year hospital drama called *ER*, competing with the steamy bedside manner of Dr. Doug Ross. Viewers defected in clumps—consistently choosing the doctor—and our show was dumped without ceremony.

I land at *World News Tonight,* producing for the evening news. *Hard news,* we call it. It doesn't matter if you have won Emmys or worked in Peter Jennings' documentary unit once you get to hard news. If the magazine show producers are the cheerleaders and jocks of ABC, the hard-news producers are the burnouts, hanging around the smoking section ready to beat you up if you get in their way. But I think *World News* might be a good place to work, because producers aren't expected to be on the road for weeks at a time. I can stay in New York and manage our schedule in Washington.

4

National Institutes of Health, Bethesda, MD
April 1995 *(Inpatient Record)*
Admitted: 4/5/95
Discharged: 4/11/95

CLINICAL DIAGNOSIS: High-grade fibrosarcoma, metastatic, to lungs bilaterally.

REASON FOR HOSPITALIZATION: This patient is a thirty-five-year-old Caucasian male, otherwise healthy, with a history of high-grade sarcoma. He returned in November with metastatic and underwent a wide excision of groin with negative margins. Follow-up scan in January showed an increasing number and size of pulmonary nodules by chest CT scan. The patient now returns for a bilateral thoracotomy.

◆

One of the myths about cancer is that it triggers bravery and heroism and larger-than-life qualities amplified against the bleak backdrop. But bravery can be confused with denial. A patient can deny what is happening and then go on about his business—*live life to the fullest*—but that is not the same as being brave. A patient's wife can sit hours at a bedside, memorize lists of medicines, and spend countless nights on a hospital cot, but that is an entirely different thing from being staunch or devoted. It is what the bewildered do, stunned in the headlights, unable to come up with anything else.

Anthony and I fly down to Washington the day before the surgery and check into the Hyatt hotel on Wisconsin Avenue. We drive to the NIH and meet Dr. Pass in the clinic on the fourth floor. He explains the surgery to us again, adding that we have much more lung tissue than we actually need. He says Anthony's lungs are larger than average and ensures him he won't miss the offending tissue. But you don't want to do this any more than you have to, so you put it off as long as you can, because it's the same surgery whether there are twenty nodules or one. He says good-bye and tells us to be back in the morning by six-thirty.

Anthony's mother meets us at the Hyatt, and we drive to Positano's, a neighborhood restaurant a friend has recommended. It is dressed like a Tuscan villa—ivy hangs down the walls, garlic on the door. Frank Sinatra plays in the background. Wine bottles are stacked along one wall, and a mural of the Italian coastline covers the other— Positano, Ravello, Venice, the summers of Anthony's youth.

The three of us sit through an awkward meal, picking at salad and spaghetti pomodoro, his mother trying admirably to keep the conversation lively. She is practical. No sentiment or drooped heads when it can be taken care of with a thoughtful subject. She is certain this can all be resolved. It is just a matter of going to the best doctors, finding the newest treatment. Though she is not unfamiliar with Fortune. Anthony and I eat like petulant children. Still bitter at being cheated out of a hematoma.

The next morning we are up and at the hospital early, Lee in a light-blue sweater, a departure from her signature black pants and turtleneck. She never wears black to the hospital. "It's depressing," she tells me. "I don't want him to wake up and see black." When we get to his room, a nurse is checking his blood pressure; she fixes a patch to his arm for the IV, and gives him 10 mg of Valium before he gets on the gurney that will take him to the OR.

This scene, the patient going into surgery, is as heartbreaking as every television drama has ever shown it. I hold Anthony's hand, walking alongside the gurney. He is sedated, a bit groggy, clingier than usual, sweet. He holds my hand tight. Tighter the closer we get to the big double doors. "I love you, Nut," he mumbles.

"I love you more."

He smiles; this is our thing. "I love you mostly."

I am determined to be casual, smile, not say *good-bye*. "Okay, see you later, Sweetie." Never *good-bye*. Then he disappears. The big blue double doors swing shut behind him. It's quick, this whole scene. No lingering, no second or two longer. A brisk walk and *swoosh* and the doors swinging shut. Then it is completely quiet.

It's an awkward stretch after we see him into the OR. His mother and I, neither knowing what to do, sit in the dark, drab waiting room. Lee is debating: a museum or Dumbarton Oaks? "Why don't you join me? Get some fresh air?" But I don't join her for some reason, choosing instead to punish myself under the glare of fluorescent lights. "I think I'll head to the cafeteria and get a bite. I'll meet you back here." Instead, I find the closest empty room and go to sleep, a solid sleep that feels like sinking to the bottom of a pond.

By noon Anthony is out of surgery and in the ICU. They took the pieces of his lung out in wedges, twenty-one tumors, this first time.

Dr. Rosenberg comes in, and the first thing I see is his smile. He knows to smile; he knows we are looking for it. "We got it all," he announces. "Right now I can say Anthony is 'cancer-free.'" I'm encouraged. We don't have sand.

These are the halcyon days, when we think we can beat this. Anthony is up and walking six hours after surgery, is out of the hospital within a week. He is back in the gym the morning after we return to New York, back at the office two days after that. We resume our lives, *cancer-free*.

5

I live another life at ABC, or more accurately, in other places. But I have been deskbound now for months, and I discover it doesn't work. I grow frustrated with the day-to-dayness of the evening news, the three-minute stories. One day blurs into the next. A pool of producers, warm bodies plucked at random to download video from satellite feeds, fill in the black holes in pieces sent from the field. I spend hours on the phone doing interviews: lawyers, policy wonks, experts from the Brookings Institute or the Heritage Foundation. There are presidential elections this year, and we recite stump speeches by heart during the day to amuse ourselves. It's a true day job, producing the news:

low-end research and no travel. We are out the door as soon as Peter Jennings says, "Good night."

Then *World News Tonight* decides to do a ten-part series called *Listening to America*. The senior producers, or maybe the marketing department people, think we need more human-interest stories. The kind that appeal to the average American, ideally with a sympathetic underdog and a bully. I attach myself to a story in Montana about the American buffalo—an iconic symbol of the Wild West—being shot down in cold blood by greedy cattle ranchers.

I meet a camera crew in Bozeman and read the research on the three-hour drive to Yellowstone. The bison carry a virus called brucellosis that can be fatal for cattle, though it's almost impossible for them to become infected, and there are no documented cases of their dying from it. It's what's known as a stock story: an animal is deemed a nuisance, one group wants to kill it, one group is outraged—there is always a news show willing to cover it. The ranchers are organized, and they persuade the state livestock department to cull the bison herd without a dead cow in sight—preemptive slaughter.

It isn't hard to kill a buffalo. You walk right up to it and shoot it in the head. If there are others nearby, they might look up, but then they go back to grazing, so you can clip a bunch of them in a few minutes. I get footage of park officials in brown uniforms, Smokey Bear patches on their sleeves, shooting buffalo at point-blank range. It is excellent video for the evening news.

There is a small group of locals fighting the ranchers to stop the slaughter, and they are holding a town hall meeting one evening. I take the crew to film, and it dissolves into a shouting match between the groups. I interview a few ranchers and an official from the state livestock department. The next morning we shoot b-roll footage of elk and bison grazing, tourists on snowmobiles, and Old Faithful erupting. I've got it, basically, and I'm scheduled to fly back to New York, but I stall. I'm in no hurry to get back. I dread it, actually.

At breakfast I overhear a story about a hermit living in Idaho, a real one—brilliant, with questionable hygiene. "He lives in a cabin in the woods, in Last Chance, just over the border," the waitress tells me. I convince myself this guy could be a story, so I call the news desk and sell them on it. They let me check it out.

Last Chance is small, a bar and motel on the western boundary of the park, known primarily for its fly-fishing. My cameraman and I pull off at the motel advertising "reasonable rates 'n' COLOR TV" and ask at the A-Bar next door about the hermit. "Dave," the bartender says. The men on barstools eye us and then nod toward a stack of books by the door. *Passion Below Zero: Essays from Last Chance, Idaho,* by David Hays.

"He lives up the road—just keep going in that direction," the bartender says, pointing to his right. "There's a dirt road that turns off. He's at the end of it." I buy a book, grab a business card, and we head down the road in our rented blue Taurus until we see a cabin wedged among overgrown bushes. We pull up to the outhouse just as the sun is setting and get out of the car. The house looks deserted, but a man yells from the porch, "Can I help you?"

"Hi, we're from ABC News," I say, and show him my ID. "We're doing a story on the bison in Yellowstone." I hold up a copy of his book, and he smiles slightly.

"Oh, I saw the car and thought you were feds," Dave says, then waves his arm to motion us up.

"They were here last week asking lots of questions. They were looking for the Unabomber." Dave's remote cabin has a computer but no plumbing or heat. Books on technology and Eastern philosophy are stacked floor to ceiling. For a moment I think, *I've found him. It really is the Unabomber!* Visions of Peabody Awards dance through my head.

"So what exactly is it that you do out here?" I ask.

"Right now, I'm teaching myself Mandarin Chinese," he says. He shows us the books in Chinese and copies of *The Island Park Bugle,* the small newspaper he publishes. He writes the editorials under the name "Seldom Seen," and his book is a compilation of them. He signs my book before we leave. *Thank you, D. Hays.*

We decide Dave's not sending bombs through the mail, and we drive back out to the highway. I call the news desk from the A-Bar and tell them there isn't much of a story. The next day, I go home. Back to the news desk, back to hurricanes, and back to taking in satellite feeds. I start studying for the GMAT and collecting admissions forms for graduate school.

6

Carolyn calls me one afternoon in July. "What are you doing?" she asks in her secret-agent voice, low and loaded with plot.

"Working, why?"

"Come down right now." They are just back from the Fourth of July on the Vineyard. She has a story for me, too good for the phone.

Carolyn moved into John's loft in Tribeca a few months ago. It's the ultimate bachelor pad, with bad furniture, bad lighting, ill-placed bathrooms, and small closets. When John bought it, it was industrial space, so he hired an architect to design it: a kitchen, two baths, and one bedroom. A couple hundred thousand dollars later, it looked like industrial space with a bedroom at one end, an office at the other, and mismatched furniture from his mother's house scattered in between. We gave it nicknames: Home Depot, the Warehouse.

I take the No. 9 subway train to Franklin Street, then walk a block to North Moore, and she buzzes me in the outside door. Seven floors up in the cramped elevator and then left down the hall. The door is open for me.

"Well?" I take a banana from a bowl on the table. She's lying on the couch, grinning, and I sit down on the floor facing her.

She sticks out her left hand. "Look!"

"Wow," I say. It catches me off guard. *She's here for good now,* I think, and I'm thrilled. But I have a flash, too, of unease. I take a bite from my banana and swallow it. "Wow."

"Stop saying 'Wow'! You're scaring me. He gave it to me this weekend."

"Were you surprised?"

"Yes!"

The ring is nice, a band of diamonds and sapphires, but not something she'd pick out for herself.

"It's a copy of a ring his mother wore. He said she called it her 'swimming ring.'"

She didn't say yes or no, she tells me. They just understood it would happen. She loves him, but she isn't in a hurry to be his wife. "Don't tell anyone," she says. And I don't, not even Anthony. She would like to stay secretly engaged forever, I think.

Graduate school was my idea, though Anthony is thrilled. I know it's crazy, but we don't say that. I want something away from everyone I know, a place where I am just a student, a place away from cancer. To Anthony, I think it is a relief.

We are not ones to speak about death—as it relates to him, anyway. He never hints at his own death; he never admits he might die. Nothing is to be put *on hold,* which of course implies *on hold until after.* Instead we speak of futures that won't exist. With all of the earnestness of a gambler putting down a bet. We pretend to be two people who have every right to talk casually of places, for instance, where we might move someday, of projects we might start, of career moves we might make.

When I think about graduate school, I have in mind dreamy afternoon literature classes at Princeton, but Anthony is more practical. He pushes me toward NYU, the Stern School of Business. He doesn't say it, but I suspect he thinks an MBA will be useful for a future I might have without him. He is careful, in any event, to make sure I will be okay.

So I apply to Stern's Executive MBA program. My admissions interview goes well and my GMAT scores are respectable. I'm accepted for the fall.

I love school. The routine, the weekend classes, the study groups after work. School is my own thing—my escape. There are four men and a woman in my study group, all with their eyes on promotions and boardrooms. We meet once a week, sometimes twice. They know nothing about me except that I am a journalist, I have a last name they recognize, and I don't quite fit the profile of business school student.

They have families—children, wives, and husbands who need them. Sometimes if someone is sick, we cancel study group. Two people travel occasionally on business. And sometimes I am away, spending nights in a hospital.

7

National Institutes of Health, Bethesda, MD
October 1995 *(Inpatient Record)*
Admitted: 10/16/95
Discharged: 10/22/95

CLINICAL DIAGNOSIS: High-grade fibrosarcoma, metastatic, to lungs bilaterally.

REASON FOR HOSPITALIZATION: The patient has previously undergone a bilateral thoracotomy to remove 21 nodules in April 1995. He is

admitted now to undergo left thoracotomy for recurrent solitary lung
nodule.

◆

"Right here," Dr. Rosenberg says, pointing to the X-ray. I point to
an area that looks shadowy. *Here?* And he nods at me seriously. He
points out the scar tissue and the blood vessels. To me it all looks the
same. Tumors are small and make shadows on the film, and the doctors somehow know whether the shadow is scar tissue or blood ves-
sel or nothing at all. Anthony and I check our schedules, and we plan
the surgery for the following week.

We are hopeful. We are still saying things like *cancer-free.* It will
be the second operation in six months, but Anthony recovers easily. It
is nothing, we say. Hardly anyone even knows we go to Washington.

After this surgery, the doctors put two hoses in his chest, attach the
hoses to clear plastic buckets, the buckets to the wall. It means days of
lying in bed hooked up to the wall. Anthony can't stand it. "Hey, Nut,
get me my gym bag. It's in the locker."

Before *Nut,* I was *Peanut,* and before *Peanut,* I was *Bear.* I remember when I became *Peanut.* Anthony was standing in the living room
waiting for me at Sea Song. "The Peanut's here!" he yelled out when
I walked in, and it stuck. We get strange looks from the doctors
whenever he asks me about something. *Nut, what do you think?*

"Nut, get my gym bag," he's telling me now with a look on his face
I know well. He swings out of bed in his T-shirt and shorts. "Grab the
buckets and see if they fit."

"Sure," I say, as if he's asking me for a tissue or to turn up the volume on the television. I put the buckets in the bag.

"Can you zip it?"

"Um, yeah."

He pulls his jeans on, grinning. "Hurry up!" He throws the bag
over his shoulder and tucks the yellow-plastic tubes under his shirt,
and we are off. The two of us walk nonchalantly down the hall past

the nurses. "We're just going down to the second floor," he tells them. "Stretching my legs." He doesn't look like he's just walking down the hall, but they don't question us. He is the darling of the NIH. They are all rooting for him. The doctors all want a patient like Anthony. He isn't content to be the Very Satisfactory patient; he wants to be Excellent. So if they are looking for him to be up and walking on the second day, he makes it the first. If they expect recovery in five days, he does it in four. He is thrilling to watch. He is unstoppable, the unseeded player taking the tournament by storm. It is a shame there are only the few of us to see, because his accomplishments are stunning.

We drive to Hamburger Hamlet with the gym bag of hoses and sit at the bar eating hamburgers and fries, watching the football game on a big screen.

After the second time we sneak out, Dr. Michael Cooper pops his head in the room. "Carole, can I talk to you for a sec?"

"Sure," I say. He is a young doctor and one of our favorites.

"Listen, I saw you leaving. I'm not going to say I think it's a good idea. It's not. But if you're going to go out, you need to take these with you." He gives me a pair of clamps that look like long, thin scissors with flat ends. The ones they use in surgery to close off the arteries so patients don't bleed to death.

"I shouldn't be abetting, but this is important." He is all business. "If the tubes get weak they let air in, and if air is going in instead of coming out, that's not good. If a tube rips or falls out or gets loose and disconnects from the bucket, that's not good either." He has a firm grip on the clamps and squeezes them together to demonstrate. "You've got to clamp it immediately."

"You mean within a minute?" I ask him.

"I mean immediately."

I practice clamping so I will be ready if a tube pops out, and Anthony times me. "Okay, Nut. Go!" I grab the clamps from my bag and squeeze down on the yellow tube the way Dr. Cooper showed me. Anthony keeps timing me, like a fire drill. He grabs his chest suddenly at the bar of Hamburger Hamlet. "I'm taking in air!" he shouts, and then laughs while I fumble for the clamps. The bartender eyes us cautiously. By the second day of this I can get both tubes clamped in four seconds flat.

8

After the second thoracotomy, Anthony's mother arranges a trip for us to Cap Juluca, a fancy resort on the island of Anguilla. I'm feeling uneasy this trip. We are falling into a habit I am uncomfortable with—masking illness with storybook getaways. I lie on the beach unable to focus on a book, a magazine, a conversation.

My mother-in-law is a staunch believer in the curative powers of sun and sea, so we swim in the ocean, take long walks on the beach, and sprawl out lazily in the sun. On one of my walks around the resort, I hear Anthony's voice and stop to eavesdrop. I like these spontaneous moments to spy on him. He has withdrawn a bit. He has adopted a role, as have I. Our lives seem more scripted.

He's a few yards away, holding his tennis racket, talking to security guards. One is telling him a story, and then Anthony says something and they all laugh. I can see they're enjoying him. Then the Queen of England appears out of nowhere, in a cornflower-blue floral dress. She is carrying a white handbag and has a plaster cast on her arm. She is small but commanding, unmistakable. It is clear the way the slack is pulled in. The guards snap to immediately. Anthony changes his posture, too, and then asks her in a brisk British accent, splitting, not swallowing, his Ts and lilting in the right place, "Madame, what happened to your wrist?" She answers him quickly.

"I fell off my horse. Thank you for asking." She pauses to smile at him, then steps away in a cloud of security.

The moment catches me off guard; there he is, cute and funny. I run over giggling and kiss him on the neck. He puts his arm around me, mock-serious, still in accent, *What's gotten into you, Nut? You're off your rocker!*

When we get back from Anguilla, we start looking for a bigger apartment. I look at sixty and keep a log of every one of them sorted by type (classic six or classic eight), price, and description. I know what Anthony wants, and I don't bring him in until I find it—at 969 Park Avenue at Eighty-Second Street. Number 7F. "It's in the back and doesn't get much sun," Gary, our realtor, says cautiously in the elevator, and Anthony brightens. "That's fine. It'll be quiet."

We fall in love with its sixteen-foot ceilings and tumbled-marble bathrooms. Then the owners take it off the market. A month later, Gary calls to tell us that another apartment has become available at 969 Park. Number 5F. And we go straight from work to see it.

The apartment opens into a dark and narrow foyer painted a hospital-tone pea green and ends at what looks like a closet but turns out to be a converted kitchen. It is dark and shabby, a fixer-upper, and appears not to have been cleaned in years. Both of the bathrooms are filthy—worse than the annually scrubbed ones of my childhood. Gone is my naïve assumption that slovenliness is averted with money: 5F is just short of horrible. Still, we call the following day and put in a bid. Having seen the same apartment on the seventh floor, we know what it can be. We are fantasizing about our future—rolling our sleeves up, making a home together.

We close in January and then there are walls to rip out, floors to tear up. We are anxious about paying for the renovation until the Sotheby's auction of his aunt's estate in April. Anthony is listening in on the phone, and I am sitting across from him when our chair comes up—not ours, but one of them, the president's rocker. They seem to be everywhere. I have a naughty image of storage lockers stacked high with presidential rocking chairs—Jackie unloading them as discreetly as possible: a birthday here, a housewarming there.

The bidding starts at four thousand dollars and shoots up—it stops just over four hundred thousand dollars.

"Oh, my God." Anthony stares at me, astonished. "They have to be kidding." And then we start laughing, as the thought hits us both at the same time. "Good thing, Nut, I didn't listen to you and give it away!"

It takes a few phone calls to get our rocker on the block, but we do and it is sold to the runner-up bidder, Prince Albert of Monaco. The Sotheby's men come the next day with padding and rope to take it away, and then the knobby wooden chair is shipped to the royal palace in Monaco. We use what is left after taxes and commissions to start the work that turns the dark apartment at the back of the building on Park into paradise.

A few weeks later I fly to France with my MBA class. We are studying the airline industry, and we spend two days in Toulouse meeting Airbus officials and touring the factory. The night before I fly home I call Anthony. He is just back from dinner at Caroline's.

"I have bad news and good news," he says on the phone, and without waiting, "the checkup wasn't good."

We both know what this means, so there is nothing to discuss. We can handle surgery logistics when I get back.

"And the good news?" I ask.

"John and Carolyn are getting married!"

I call Carolyn right after we hang up. "Congratulations! How'd that come up?"

"I don't know—John just blurted it out. I was as surprised as everyone else."

It's been nine months since John proposed, and I know she's been in no hurry to set a date or even announce it to his family. But I'm not surprised. Anthony's news is more frequent now, and most often bad. John can't do anything about the next operation, but he can take our minds off of it by making a different announcement.

"Did you act surprised when he told you?" she asked.

"Of course," I said, laughing.

This is wonderful news, but I am apprehensive on the flight home. The bad checkup means surgery on his lungs, and this will be the third. I am starting to fade, to feel heavy, and Carolyn reaches in right here to pick me up. "Why don't I come with you this time," she says when I get back. She is not asking but telling me she will come.

9

National Institutes of Health, Bethesda, MD
May 1996 *(Inpatient Record)*
Admitted: 5/22/96
Discharged: 5/28/96

CLINICAL DIAGNOSIS: High-grade fibrosarcoma, metastatic, to lungs.

REASON FOR HOSPITALIZATION: The patient, a thirty-seven-year-old male, has undergone two previous thoracotomy operations. 21 pulmonary nodules were excised in April 1995 and one in his left lung, October 1995. He is admitted now to undergo a median sternotomy and metastasectomy of five bilateral pulmonary metastases.

◆

Everything changes when Carolyn comes to the NIH. I am in danger of losing my optimism, and she distracts Anthony and me both.

Anthony takes an earlier flight, and Carolyn and I fly down

together in the afternoon. I am excited to show her around: the Hertz rental lot, the Pontiac Sunbird I've reserved. It's all old hat to me now. I am proud, even, of the sure-handed way I zip up the Beltway from the airport.

"Here is the suite," I say, when we check in at the Hyatt. "This is my room and this is Lee's." She watches as I unpack—shirts all in one drawer, pants in another, pajamas and underwear separate. I have a strict procedure and a bag full of products that I carefully unpack and set on the bathroom counter. I group them by category—hair gel, face moisturizer, body lotions—then line them up by size. Then I pull out my flannel-lined jeans to change before going to the hospital. Carolyn studies me intently, then bursts out laughing.

"You're insane," she says. "And where did you get those jeans?"

"L.L.Bean."

"Oh, my God, you can't wear those. I can't even believe we're friends."

"Laugh, but you'll see," I say wisely. "It's cold in the hospital; you'll wish you had flannel."

She jumps up and fishes something out of her small travel case. "Here," she says, and hands me a lipstick. "Ruby Stain. It will look perfect on you. Keep it." She buys Ruby Stain because Ruby is the name of her black cat. A haughty ball of attitude that only she could love.

When we get to the hospital, we find Anthony in his room unpacking. Carolyn gives him a big kiss.

"Look what I brought for you!" She has a framed 8 x 10 glossy photo of her dog, Friday, backlit and paws crossed like a Vargas pinup.

"Just what I've always wanted," he says, grinning.

"Everyone needs a dog," she says, and hangs Friday on the wall. Anthony kisses us good-bye and heads to the clinic for pre-op lab tests.

"Oh no, how dreary," she says, after scanning the drab room. "We need to get flowers before he comes back." We get in the car and turn up the radio, roll the windows down so the air can rush in, and then we cruise down Rockville Pike. We stop at Bethesda Florist to buy bunches of yellow tulips for Anthony, and at the 7-Eleven for Spaghettios for us. We eat them cold right out of the can. Then we drive back to the Hyatt to wait for Lee. When she arrives, Carolyn gives her a double kiss and before we leave to pick up Anthony for dinner, they have plans for lunch in New York.

At Positano's we gossip about fashion designers. We pass around bruschetta and drink glasses of wine. It's easier when Carolyn is here. She fills in the gap of formality between Lee and me—mother-in-law and daughter-in-law.

But Carolyn is new here, engaged to John, not yet technically family. She does not have an official role, and she knows it. For her to fly down and stay with me, to comfort Anthony, is slightly out of order and regarded, we think, with suspicion. So she downplays it. "I'm the only one without a life," she jokes. She has recently left her job at Calvin Klein. "It's easy for me to go."

When Carolyn and I arrive at the hospital the second morning, Anthony's cousin Caroline and her husband, Ed, are seated in two of the blue chairs in the waiting room outside the ICU. I am startled by the unannounced visit. I am not used to seeing them here.

The four of us seem unnaturally large and quiet in the small room, and then there aren't enough chairs, so Carolyn waits in the larger room outside. I ask polite questions, and they answer them. *Are you staying over? No, we're leaving this afternoon.* We are stiff and awkward; small talk is scarce. Anthony is thrilled to see them. I am relieved when they leave.

Lee leaves, too, that afternoon, and Carolyn and I move into her bigger room. We stay up late watching *I Love Lucy*. The next day Carolyn catches an early shuttle back to New York.

When I check out of the Hyatt, there is a note at the front desk.

Lamb,

   Please know that I am always thinking about you and worrying about you. It is so lonely and scary to go through that

and I can't bear the thought that you ever had to do it alone. I
can't ever let you go again without me. It broke my heart.

XOXO, *Carolyn*

I drive to the NIH to pick up Anthony. The operation was
uneventful. Anthony is in perfect health, except for the cancer.

After the first operation that Carolyn comes down for, we have almost
a year of no cancer. A respite. She jokes that she is our lucky charm.
There are three-month checkups, and shadows, but they are either
too small or too few to act on. I look back and think *wow,* a *year.* A
long time, but only in retrospect. It's short while you're living it, when
you don't know if it ends today or tomorrow or next month. I am con-
ditioned. I am afraid to turn my back, breathe a sigh of relief. We are
on the lam. We have a year—a nervous year, yet there is promise in
the air.

We take a deep breath in June. We will not even talk about cancer
until the next checkup, in September.

Anthony interviews with Sheila Nevins for vice president of documentaries at HBO.

"I have cancer," he tells her.

"Well, I could get hit by a bus tomorrow," she replies, and hires him.

Chester, our contractor, starts the work on our apartment. He is
Polish; I know, because when Anthony introduces himself, Chester
repeats the last name and pronounces it the proper way, with the "w"
like a "v"—then he says it again. The recognition worries me. There
are greatly exaggerated tales of a Radziwill fortune, and I suspect that
on occasion we are charged according to it. So I call vendors for
estimates—once as Carole Radziwill and once as Carole DiFalco.
Mrs. Radziwill is consistently quoted more, so I am Carole DiFalco
for the renovation.

In the first few months, we walk over from our place on Madison
every night after dinner to look at all the new things. The entire

apartment is gutted: wires hang from the ceiling, walls have disappeared. It smells of sawdust and fresh lumber. One night, before the new walls go up, we take thick black Sharpies and write our names and draw a heart around them: "Carole + Anthony TLF" and "We were here on April 29, 1996, 11:30 p.m." The next day they close up the walls with our names forever inside.

Our friend Hamilton is working at Ralph Lauren, and he arranges a deal that allows us to buy furniture at cost if we let *Elle Decor* do a photo layout when the apartment is finished, highlighting the Ralph Lauren Home Collection. We order two leather armchairs and a dining room table and chairs. I go to De Angelis on Ninety-Fifth Street for our couches, because it's where Lee goes for hers. There are framed thank-you letters on the wall from assorted first ladies for furniture shipped to the White House.

I drive upstate to Hudson for antiques and buy anything that looks *English,* anything that might resemble Anthony's childhood home in London. I pick up a sheaf of good paper at the stationer's and a leather case and set it by the phone with razor-point felt-tip pens, because I noticed this in Lee's house. I put fabric on the walls of the TV room, like Lee, with a matching roman shade. They come out all wrong, but there isn't time to care. To finish is the thing. I furnish the apartment all at once, like a showroom.

I want to make a home for my husband, and I want it immediately. If the apartment is done, I reason, then we have a life together, for however long it lasts. I'm creating the illusion of time: *Here it is, everything we've collected over the years.* I am aware of the ticking clock.

I unpack all our wedding gifts: everyday dishes, the dinner party settings for eight, the silverware, the Baccarat vases, and the silver candelabras. I organize the crystal stemware and real silver for the dinner parties we will give, though it turns out we aren't the type.

I open accounts at Lobel's butcher and at the Korean deli on Lexington. I try to cook. Anthony has an old *New York Times* recipe book, and I thumb through it. I find a hundred-dollar bill on the page with the recipe for asparagus risotto. "Leave it in there," he says. "It's for luck."

So for luck I try the risotto; it looks my speed. I pull a stool into the kitchen and sit where I can see the television in the library and still reach the stove. Then I stir the rice and broth slowly for thirty minutes and watch the news. I love making this dish. When it is almost done, I add asparagus from the steamer. I make a green salad, with the skin peeled off the tomatoes the way Anthony likes, and lay it all out with our everyday plates and silver on our wooden TV trays.

Risotto or pasta with red sauce, this is my repertoire. Some nights we order steaks from Lobel's and I cook them—seven minutes on each side—and bake two potatoes until the skin is burnt crisp.

We have a normal life, with habits, and it is reassuring for both of us. We have regular days, weeks of them in a row. Anthony is up at six every morning. He sets the coffee machine timer so the coffee is made when he comes out of the shower. He has one cup with a toasted bagel, then walks to Crunch Gym. He is there by seven every morning, works out, and then walks to his office. Me, I take it slower. The offices at ABC fill in around ten.

At night we are back home at seven and Anthony has an Absolut, chilled and on the rocks, before dinner. We watch the news shows together—Larry King and CNN—until eleven. Then Anthony kisses me goodnight and I stay up late.

We are happy. I print up note cards when the apartment is done to send out with our new address. The design behind the print is a mock floor plan.

Finally!
The Radziwills
969 Park Avenue, Apt. 5F
New York, NY 10021
Carole and Anthony

10

Carolyn is planning her wedding. They have decided on September and picked Cumberland Island off Georgia, because John's close friend Gogo owns a bed-and-breakfast there. They are trying to keep the wedding secret, and they know they can confide in her.

John and Carolyn come to Sea Song for Anthony's birthday in August, but we say hardly a word about a wedding. It is all strictly classified. I barely see her over the summer, and when I do we don't talk about it—as if to talk about it will break the spell.

Carolyn flies to Paris with Narciso to work on her dress. They've been close friends since they worked together when he was a designer at Calvin Klein. Someone takes a picture of them sitting in a restaurant, and the papers report an affair. She is thrilled. The press is off the trail.

Gogo books a caterer and finds a deejay. Father Charles is pulled aside, because they know they can trust him. He met John ten years earlier when John was a law student at New York University. He has to get a dispensation from the diocesan bishop in Georgia, because the church is out of his jurisdiction. John and Carolyn select a small group of family and close friends, altogether around forty guests. Outside of the wedding party—Anthony is John's best man—no one is told in advance.

Anthony has a checkup just before, and we are all holding our breath. I am afraid to hope for too much, but he gets a pass.

The weekend before the wedding, John makes a phone call to each of the guests, inviting them to a party on Cumberland Island. He asks them to make plane reservations and not to say a word. A week later, we are all in Florida, catching a ferry to the deserted island.

Weddings are make-believe, and we believe this weekend that we aren't sick, and that it is a wedding like any other. We believe this weekend that love conquers all and that happiness is lasting. The ferry captain who takes us to the island confides in us that there's a wedding—"a big one," he says knowingly. "Nicole Miller, I heard." There is another rumor that Michael Jackson is coming for the weekend and has locked down the island. This second part is true. No one on the island—the caterers or the hotel staff—is allowed to leave. A security man meets us at the dock and hands each of us an Indian Head nickel. We are told to keep it with us at all times. It is the secret code, the passport that separates guests from intruders.

There is a general exuberance on the island, and we are all proud to be conspirators. They have pulled this off, and no one yet can believe it. We have dinner on the veranda and toast the future, the women in sundresses, the men in shirtsleeves, and after dinner we walk down for a bonfire on the beach.

The inn has a limited number of rooms and houses about half of the guests—Carolyn's parents, her grandmother, John's aunts and uncles—so the rest of us bunk up in the small cottages usually reserved for the staff. Anthony and I and another couple share one of the cottages, the "Chicken Coop," named for the chickens that were removed to convert it into a small bedroom and sitting area.

On Saturday we follow the long dirt road past thousand-year-old oak trees draped in Spanish moss to the beach. There are security guards along the way, but no one bothers to check for our secret nickel. After the first night it's apparent we are the only ones on the island. We swim and lie in the sun all day, and then head back in late afternoon to change for the ceremony.

Vans shuttle guests from the inn to the chapel on the other side of the island. John comes over to the Chicken Coop to take a shower, and then we take our wedding clothes to a small house near the chapel to get dressed. Gogo told the owners there was a wedding and asked if the bride and groom could use their house to change, and Carolyn is already there when Anthony and John and I arrive. There is an elderly maid at the house, and she almost faints when she sees John. He invites her to the wedding, and she comes and sits in the back pew.

We are running late to the chapel, because John can't find his shirt and Effie takes the Jeep back to the cottages to look for it. By the time we get to the church, the sun is setting and it's dark inside. There is no electricity, so Effie collects candles for light. The chapel is shabby, but the candles make it look elegant. There is a steady whine of mosquitoes outside, and we pick our way carefully through little piles of pig muck to get into the church. Somewhere along the way the flowers got lost, so Effie gathers fresh bunches of wildflowers for the flower girls.

It is a warm evening and we leave the door of the chapel open to catch a breeze. Father Charles takes his place at the altar, wearing a white deacon's stole. He reads from the Gospel, by flashlight. He speaks of the love that John and Carolyn share and how this small private ceremony reflects the space they have created for themselves and their family. We take open-topped Jeeps back to the inn for the reception. It starts to rain, and we laugh as we get soaked.

Anthony makes a toast at dinner. He had been working on it the entire week before, editing on the plane, with various funny anecdotes about John. In the end, he kept it simple.

> We all know why John would marry Carolyn. She is smart, beautiful, and charming. So what does she see in John? A person who over the years has taken pleasure in teasing me, playing nasty tricks, and in general torturing me. Well, some of the things that I guess might have attracted Carolyn to John are his caring, his charm, and his very big heart of gold. It might sound corny, but it is true love, and it has brought all of us who love John a great deal of happiness, knowing that he will have someone as special as Carolyn by his side for the rest of his life.

We dance to deejay music for the rest of the night under the small tent in front of the inn.

When we check out the next morning there is some confusion about payment arrangements, and we are presented with a bill for our room and meals. John is horrified and tries to straighten it out at the last minute, but it gives Anthony wonderful ammunition. *You made us pay to eat at your wedding, you cheap bastard!* We save the bill with the Indian nickel, and other mementos of the weekend.

Someone faxes a press release to the AP, and John and Carolyn leave on their honeymoon. It was a coup, unthinkable that they did it without the press. Not a single paparazzi photographer there. But they made up for it later. When John and Carolyn returned from their honeymoon, dozens of photographers were lying in wait outside their apartment, and they stayed put for the next six months.

11

Carolyn has great faith in the zodiac. She gives me a copy of *The Secret Language of Relationships* and refers me to it regularly. She can tell a person's sign after talking to him for ten minutes, and then how to fix his life, but I lack her intuitive skill, her propensity to solve. I lack her swift stroke.

The relationship book says my and Anthony's strengths are that we're "well-directed," and "compromising"; on the other hand we're also "secretive" and "struggle-oriented."

Nothing is ever as it seems. We hide our reality from the outside world and from each other. We float along on process, Anthony and I—*What will we have for dinner, did you call your mother, what time do you think you'll be home?* Phone calls and kisses and thank-you notes. You can lose a whole life on that.

The thing is, one of us is sick and the other sits by the bed, and some days it seems that's all we know. There was a hint of what we might

have had when we first met, but it was overshadowed. We might have
been the sort of couple who gave dinner parties. There might have been
children, or maybe a dog. We were both headstrong and stubborn, so
we might have fought a lot, or we might have been people other couples make fun of, sappy and giggly and always holding hands. But cancer showed up like an unplanned pregnancy and completely defined
who we were together.

We flash helpless smiles at the rest of the world when it pops in. It
is subtle, this performance. We show up at dinners with friends and
with family. Anthony handsome and charming, me by his side. The
truth is my husband is dying, and we are lonely together. There is the
disease and the person, and though I am living with both, one has
robbed me of the other. He is devoted to something else. It is in some
ways similar, I imagine, to an affair, only in an affair I could pack my
bags and storm out, slam the door shut, clearly wronged. There'd be
some satisfaction in that. This is a secret he won't talk to me about,
and I am not allowed to resent it. When he looks at me he sees his disease. I am managing it, too closely connected to it for intimacy. I
reflect it, and I suspect this angers him. After a point, the cancer, the
thing we both hate, is the only thing that we share.

It has been eleven months since his last operation. At school we are
studying businesses in emerging markets. It is the final spring semes-
ter, and China is emerging, so our class goes. It is an eight-day vacation
to me. We haven't had cancer this year, but I can't stop thinking about
it. I can't stop thinking about a future I cannot plan. We are in the second hour of a horror movie. The calm quiet to lull you before the last
fright. It appears peaceful, but you look at your watch, and you know
something bad is coming up because the movie is only half over. That's
how I feel this year. So I have eight days not to think about that. And
in China I fall in love with a different life for a moment.

We are America's future business leaders, touring factories and
sharing dinners with Chinese businessmen and politicians. We are the

voice of America that week, and after four days of tiresome lectures, we hear an interesting one by a journalist for *The New York Times*. Here, finally, is someone I can relate to. A welcome change from the drone of corporate titans. It is a glimpse of the passion I came into this business with—the girl watching the world unfold through a TV screen in her kitchen, the ABC internship, Cambodia—the big adventure that had opened up for me. I am back there for a moment.

He talks to us about the current political situation and America's history with China back to the Nixon-Kissinger years. At the end, I realize I am smiling. I linger and introduce myself afterward.

"Hi, I'm one of you. Carole Radziwill, ABC News."

"News? You're a journalist?"

"Yes. Producer, actually, with *World News Tonight*."

"So what's a nice producer like you doing with a group like this?"

He has the eyes, the laugh, the deep voice—the stuff that draws susceptible women in. This is whom you cast as war correspondent in the movie. The rogue, the one who seduces the unseduceable heroine, then goes off to chase Chechen rebels, leaving her behind with a note: *I'll catch you next time.* We chat for a bit, like you do when you're young and single in a foreign place and find you have something in common with the leading man.

He offers to show me around the *Times* office, which I know is just him. "That sounds nice," I say. "The ABC News bureau is in that compound. I wanted to stop by there anyway." It's true it had occurred to me to stop by, but more as a diversion from the lectures. Now it is less innocent.

"I'm not feeling well," I tell the dean. " I'll try to meet the group for dinner." And then I get a cab and give the driver the address I have written on a slip of paper.

The *Times* bureau is not much more than a couch and a desk stacked with books and old newspapers. There are crammed bookshelves on the walls. I have no professional reason to be here. He has no professional reason to invite me. It's like being in a strange man's apartment in the middle of a workday, and lying to get there.

We keep talking and walking, back and forth, circling. I pick up pictures, he tells me who they are. I pull books out, he tells me about the people who wrote them. He asks how I wound up in business school, and I sit down, rest a foot on his desk. It is an afternoon affair without the sex. And maybe that is worse. I have loosed myself from all the rules or guilt that might have pulled me back, might have stopped me from getting in that cab. I am handed a ruby red poison apple and am savoring it, polishing the shiny, smooth skin. I am careful not to bite only because I want to take this whole beautiful snapshot away with me, with all of its promise.

"You've been to Beijing before?"

"I was here for a piece a few years ago."

"What was the piece?"

"A documentary on U.S. foreign policy in Cambodia. Peter Jennings was here to interview Prince Sihanouk."

There are photos on his desk—sweet-faced young children, a pretty wife. I pick them up, smile, put them down. None of it applies to me. It is my afternoon, my invitation.

I offer him little about my life, a brief mention of a husband. I am teasing myself with a different story after all, not thinking of home. I am in his office like this for several hours—flirting, being clever. On the couch, on the edge of his desk. Our legs brushing and not flinching, our eyes meeting and not turning away.

It is obvious to me what we are doing—both considering scenarios—and then he says, "They might be looking for you. It's getting late." I am desperate then to stay, have him hold me in his arms, no one in the world knowing where I am.

Instead we walk out of the office together, and he gets me a cab. Walking slowly toward the front gate that leads to the road out of the compound, we linger, still, our hands touch briefly. It rained while we were inside; the air is damp, thick with mist. A cab pulls up to the curb, and I get in. "I'll look you up if I ever get to New York," he says. I know this is the polite thing to say, that I will never see him again. But this is okay. I have something. We say good-bye but don't move, and he bends down and kisses me on the lips. Not a long kiss, but a sweet kiss, knowing. Soft. A wistful kind of kiss. I touch his face and get in the car.

I hung on to that kiss, that afternoon. I hung on to it for a long time.

I call when I get back and sing into Carolyn's answering machine.

Who can turn the world on with her smile?
Who can take a nothing day and suddenly make it all seem
worthwhile?

I am tone deaf, and my singing always makes her laugh.

"Ha, ha. It's me. Call me."

"You're retarded!" she says when she calls back, and then she drops her voice down to secret-agent level. "What are you doin'?"

"Not a lot. Come by. We'll work on a story."

The first time Carolyn came by my office she surprised me. "I was in the neighborhood," she said on the phone from the lobby. "Can I come up?"

ABC News had moved into a new building above the Disney Store on the corner of Sixty-Seventh and Columbus, and every producer got an office. Mine was on the fourth floor, with a couch. I spent my first month scouring the building after hours until I found one in the basement where they shoot *One Life to Live*. Carlos, a friend in building services, helped me move it.

"Oh my God, are those *real?*" she said when she stepped into my office. "You have Emmys?" She grabbed me by the shoulder so I faced her. "Carole, why aren't you *telling* everyone?" She made me seem interesting.

Now she stretches across the couch, and we work on our plan for the rest of her life.

"I'm thinking about going back to school," she says, "to get a master's degree in psychology."

"I think that's a great idea. You could probably teach the class." We spend an hour discussing logistics. If she applied right away she could start in September. She wants to apply to NYU; it's close to her apartment. I suggest uptown, at Columbia University.

"I'll pick up an application for you next week," I tell her. We are always, it seems, making plans. She pulls out her date book—a mess of strike-outs, scribbles, in pencil and different-colored ink.

"When, again, is your graduation?" I tell her for the fifth time, and she traces over it once more, making it bold.

The next week I take the subway to Columbia and pick up the admissions forms, the course catalog, and the brochures and drop them off at her apartment, where they sit for months on the kitchen counter.

She is trying to imagine the life she is expected to lead, winging it just like me.

12

National Institutes of Health, Bethesda, MD
June 1997 *(Inpatient Record)*
Admitted: 6/17/97
Discharged: 6/26/97

CLINICAL DIAGNOSIS: High-grade fibrosarcoma, metastatic, to lungs bilaterally.

REASON FOR HOSPITALIZATION: The patient is a 38-year-old white male, otherwise healthy, who is well-known to this hospital. He has previously

undergone bilateral thoracotomies of 21 lung nodules in April 1995;
solitary nodule in his left lung in October 1995; five bilaterally in May
1996. Now CT scans show one 3 x 4 cm nodule in his lower right lobe.

◆

The cancer reprieve ends with a bang. There are shadows on
Anthony's CT scan at the checkup in May, and there is no mistaking
them. It is three weeks before graduation. Anthony has planned a
party and invited my entire class to the apartment for cocktails and
hors d'oeuvres. We schedule the operation for the week after.

Carolyn and I get off the plane at Reagan National, and it's as though
no time has passed at all. Anthony has come down before us; Lee is
just behind. We check into the hotel, wait for Lee, and then pick up
Anthony at the hospital. We drive to Positano's for an early dinner
and then take Anthony back; he stays overnight now. The doctors are
more cautious as these visits go on. There are more tests, more pre-op,
and they want to monitor him overnight.

In the morning when the alarm goes off, I drag myself out, and
Carolyn grumbles. She's sharing my room and stays in bed while I
start to get ready—my "Miss America" routine, she calls it.

I wash my hair and blow it dry with a round brush. I pull on the
flannel-lined jeans and a sweater.

"Lamb, it's June. Do you really have to wear those?" she says.

I go through the assorted products in the bathroom and carefully
apply face moisturizer and concealer under my eyes.

She gets up, brushes her teeth, pulls her hair back into a ponytail,
puts on her jeans and a T-shirt, and then freezes in the ICU.

Anthony does push-ups in his room while he waits for the gurney.
We are a picture of tranquillity—Lee in her light-blue sweater, me in
my flannel jeans. Carolyn kisses Friday and hangs him on the wall.
"Look at him, he's a movie star," she says.

"You have an unhealthy obsession with that dog," I tell her. "You can't have kids, you know, you'll drive them crazy."

"No, I won't. Just you."

Lying on the gurney, Anthony smiles at us. He is getting groggy. He grips my hand tight all the way to the double doors. And then he's gone.

Lee goes back to the hotel. Carolyn and I find an empty room to sleep. We all know what to do. None of us is surprised to be here again. It doesn't seem as though any time has passed at all.

There's a complication after the surgery, and when we arrive the next morning the nurse pulls me aside—there's been an air leak. *Subcutaneous emphysema,* she calls it. It's when air leaks out of the lungs during surgery. It seeps into the soft tissue under the skin and forms pockets. The doctors call it *Rice Krispies,* because when you poke the skin it crunches, like the cereal.

"I don't want you to be upset when you see him," she warns me. "It looks worse than it actually is." We have been doing this for too long for me to be upset or alarmed at anything I see. But it is very odd, and I flinch just slightly when I walk in.

"Hey there, good morning." I smile. His entire body is puffed up like a balloon, his skin stretched tight. His face is moon-shaped and swollen. All of his features are puffed out of proportion, and his skin crinkles when I touch it. "It's crunchy!" I poke him, trying to make light of it.

"Stop it, Carole."

"Listen to it, crunch, crunch."

He gives me a look.

He is not amused by this, my poking him, though he's not concerned either. It's another day, and he's trying to watch the news on the television behind me.

Anthony is on suction on the wall for over a week to get out all the air. There are no trips for him. No Hamburger Hamlet, no walks, even, down the hall.

Carolyn rubs his crunchy feet. She brings back a loofah and peppermint lotion from The Body Shop. I am here, but she does the work. She holds his hand while they watch TV. She takes out her pedicure kit and soaks his feet. When we leave the hospital for a break, she never fails to bring something back for him. Anthony, I know, is uncomfortable with this level of attention. He is not the sort for this, but I don't try to change anything. I don't step in for him, redirect her as I do the others, because I need her here, and he knows that.

He's in the ICU for four days, and when he sleeps we go out into the sun, into the air, where there are cars and traffic and people on lunch breaks and mothers pushing strollers.

I do not have a photograph of the two of us. As far as I know, such a thing does not exist. We did not, as a rule, take pictures, but if I could pick a scene to freeze, it might be this: Carolyn driving the rented white Sunbird on 495 South, our windows rolled down, with the radio turned up. Her left foot resting on the dashboard, her fingers tapping the wheel. The two of us throwing our heads back, shouting along to Tina Turner, "Oh, you better be good to me / because I don't have the time for your overloaded lies . . ."

We drive to Tysons Corner in search of Hush Puppies. "It's all about a Hush Puppy," she declares. "You aren't leaving this town without them." We stop at Bloomingdale's and give each other makeovers at the MAC counter. We order sticky rolls at Cinnabon. At a Clarks shoe store we try on every style of Hush Puppy they have until I settle on the black-suede slip-ons. While we are boxing up the shoes, I feel someone watching us. I look up and see an older black woman a few feet away, beaming toward us—shivering, it seems, with happiness, so much that I'm afraid for a moment she might cry.

She is completely overcome, and then Carolyn sees her and walks over. "Hi," she says, reaching for the woman's hand.

"Oh, my God." She says it softly, but we hear her and smile.

"Oh, my goodness. Are you Mrs. Kennedy?" She puts her hand to her mouth and then into her purse, searching for something. "I don't have anything to write on—an envelope, here. Would you please, can I have your autograph?"

"Oh, you don't want that. What would you do with it?" Carolyn puts her hand on the woman's arm and then grabs mine. "This is my cousin, Princess Radziwill," she says mischievously. She knows I will cringe. Then she adds, "She has three Emmys." The woman looks at me, still smiling, but confused. We ask her where she's from and talk to her for a few minutes. She has grandchildren, and she shows us their pictures.

"I can't believe I'm talking to you!" she says. "I can't believe you're just out here. All by yourself! Don't you have security?"

Carolyn holds the woman's hand and tells her it was nice talking with her. I take my Hush Puppies to the register to pay, and we drive back to the hospital.

The White House is screening a Tom Hanks film about the moon tonight. John has put him on the cover of his magazine, *George*, and he and Carolyn need to be there. He flies down in the afternoon and comes to the hospital to pick her up. Anthony is still in the ICU. The swelling has gone down, but he looks weaker and is hooked up to so many machines. It's a jarring sight. John is taken aback. Anthony knows this, and he knows to break the ice.

"Try not to embarrass yourself tonight," he says. John has a funny boyish way of eating, with his head bent down and one arm around the plate, as if he is guarding it, the other shoveling in the food. Anthony always teases him about it. "Try to keep your tie clean."

"I'm sorry I have to leave, Sweetie," Carolyn says to Anthony. It is ridiculous, she thinks, to go to the White House to see a movie while he's here in this room. Here is where she wants to be. But that is their life.

Before they leave, she takes a makeup bag into the small hospital bathroom. She combs her hair up in a bun, clips it into place, and applies MAC Studio Fix powder on her face. "Before . . . after," she says, as she dots the circles under her eyes. She finishes up with Ruby Stain.

"I'll come back in the morning," she says as she straightens the picture of Friday. She kisses Anthony good-bye, and then me. She grabs her black Yohji dress to change in the car. When she arrives at the dinner, photographers will be stacked on top of one another to take her picture.

Before we left New York for the NIH, Carolyn had given me an amethyst ring for my graduation to match hers, so when we get back we go to Tiffany's to get them inscribed.

"You're driving her crazy," she says to me at the counter. We've been standing here for fifteen minutes now, the saleswoman patiently waiting for us to make up our minds and leave the rings.

"I just want to make sure it looks right."

We decide on our initials and then "secret friends forever." It is important for me to make sure that the inscription is accurate, with "s.f.f." in lowercase and our initials in caps. I want to know what the font will look like and whether they can do italics on the "s.f.f." but not the initials.

I live in the details, Carolyn in the big picture.

When I order food, I always ask how they will prepare it. If I am getting takeout, I ask for the fries to be separate, because I don't like mushy fries. It is my clumsy way of explaining myself, I suppose. A need to define myself as something, the sort of person who prefers her fries to be crisp. If I was always this way or if I'm just controlling what I can during the cancer, I don't remember.

"Lambie, just tell her what you want!"

"I want our initials," I tell the saleswoman. "But it needs to be on the opposite side. Hers first on my ring and mine first on hers. Can you center it with the amethyst? So the 's.f.f.' lines up with the stone?"

And now I am simply stalling, because I don't want to leave. I want to stand here in the pretty store arguing about silly things forever. I don't want to walk out of the store, kiss her good-bye, take a cab back to my office. So I keep asking questions about the ring. I keep changing the font.

"Don't you have a job?" Carolyn teases me. "Don't you have to go to work?"

13

National Institutes of Health, Bethesda, MD
October 1997 *(Inpatient Record)*
Admitted: 10/29/97
Discharged: 11/5/97

CLINICAL DIAGNOSIS: High-grade fibrosarcoma, metastatic, to lungs
bilaterally.

REASON FOR HOSPITALIZATION: The patient is a 38-year-old Caucasian
male. He subsequently presented in October 1997 for follow-up spiral
CT scan which once again revealed a new lesion in the lower right lobe.
Patient denies shortness of breath, wheezing, or hemoptysis. He continues to run daily. He is admitted now for a right thoracotomy for
recurrent sarcoma of the right lower lobe.

◆

We all picked roles at the beginning. His mother picked one;
Anthony picked one. I was the good wife. This was my thing. I was
going to *do this, handle it. Leave it to me.* At first, I was emboldened
with the idea that I could, that if I managed it and researched it, I
could direct it. And by the time I realized it wasn't the role I wanted
to have, it was too late. I was too afraid of disappointing them. Hadn't
they trusted me, hadn't they said how courageous I was? Didn't I
know all the medical words, the latest clinical studies, and where to
find an extra blanket in the supply closet?

I had been hoping that someone would step in at some point and
grab the wheel. *Okay, that's enough now, Carole. We'll take it from here.*

I was waiting for someone to recognize how unsuited I was and take it away. It was a desperate and lonely feeling to realize that it was more or less up to me. Carolyn saw that and stepped in.

"You are completely screwed up." She is upset with me. "You can't do this every day, without help. Why aren't you seeing a therapist?"

I only think about it when Carolyn brings it up. "I don't have time," I tell her.

"That's bullshit. You don't go because you think you don't matter." She says this in a matter-of-fact tone.

"What am I going to tell a shrink?"

"You're kidding me, right? Your husband has cancer, you're taking care of him pretty much on your own, you married into the royal family, and you wonder what you'll have to talk about?"

It has never occurred to me to see a therapist. It's not that I think therapy is a sign of weakness. It never occurs to me that I am depressed. This is hard and overwhelming and too much to do alone, but I like it when people say that I am *amazing,* that I am *handling it all so well.* It makes me feel good for a moment. I don't want to let go of it.

I can say *Washington* now with enough cool nonchalance that nobody questions it. *I can't make it Saturday, I'm in Washington,* I say. Or, *Anthony's in Washington this week. Can we reschedule?* One thing about cancer is that it makes your priorities crystal clear. It trumps everything else. There is no worrying, *Where should I be in my life?* No wondering why there are no children yet. The hospital schedules are nonnegotiable. The focus is on cancer and all that goes with it. My hobbies? Cancer. My interests? Cancer. My specialties, education, concentration? Cancer.

This is our fifth thoracotomy. Al Gore's mother-in-law is in the ICU this time, in the room next to us. She doesn't have cancer, but she is here in this barely occupied ward of the National Cancer Institute. It's a good place to hide, which is why we love it. We are thankful for her, Carolyn and I, because we are here for long stretches of time with nothing to do and she lights the place up. She is old, with deep lines etched in her face like parentheses around her nose, her mouth. Her eyes are small and deep-set, but bright. She wears a fabulous cashmere floor-length coat over her hospital gown that reaches almost to her slippers, and she takes short shuffling steps down the hall searching for cigarettes. "Where are my cigarettes? Someone stole my cigarettes!"

"Oh, my God, I *love* her!" Carolyn whispers to me the first time we find her in the hall.

We are delighted when she mistakes us for private nurses and sends us on errands. We sneak Italian ices from the freezer in the staff lounge and take them to her room. We bring in extra blankets and check in on her throughout the night. We are secret comrades, the three of us, all tucked away where nobody knows. Carolyn and I know a little about the unique rhythm of this place, and we help initiate her.

Her daughter comes to visit on our third day and a man in a dark suit asks us to close our door. "No," I tell the man, annoyed. This is *our* hospital, I think. We're putting in more time here than anyone. No, we are not going to close the door.

There is some distress about this, some unpleasantness. The Secret Service, it seems, is concerned about our visitor—Sam Donaldson, a close friend and colleague. His voice is unmistakable from the other room. But he doesn't care about the mother of Tipper Gore. Sam is here to see a friend, his friend is confined to bed, and he struggles to give the impression he doesn't notice. He is not the least bit curious about our neighbor. It is a small battle and I lose. I quietly close the door.

The next morning, we move to the regular ward.

The operations are getting harder, the risk of infection is greater. We take Anthony for walks with the buckets of blood; Carolyn and I taking turns carrying the bag. But I'm a reluctant accomplice. Anxious, gripping the clamps in my pocket.

Anthony wants to leave the moment he can swing out of bed, to go for longer walks, drive farther away. I start to dread these trips, and I haven't said so but Anthony senses it. He recruits Hamilton when he comes down for the weekend, and they run off, sneaky, like men stealing off to happy hour. *Don't tell the wife.*

They drive to the mall because Anthony needs new shirts. He carries the Plexiglas box without the gym bag, bare. He carries it like a briefcase, because he knows Hamilton will think it is funny to set the box with blood swirling around in it on the counter at Neiman Marcus. He knows it will be funny to shock the saleswoman, when he politely asks for the blue pinstriped shirt in a size sixteen and a half, thirty-four, the blood at his elbow, the hoses visible under his shirt. By the time they get back, I am waiting in the room, angry. It is funny, hilarious to them in the retelling. Anthony prodding Hamilton along as if this is just a fun weekend away with friends.

14

When Carolyn became Mrs. Kennedy, the press camped outside their apartment. They shot her walking Friday, talking on the phone, going to the deli, drinking her coffee. They caught her in the doorway kissing John good-bye, getting into taxis, walking the steps down to the subway. They followed her in perimeter, just a few feet away. There was a steady hum of clicking the entire first year.

One afternoon when she was supposed to meet me uptown at my office, she called and was crying. She had been out, and they had tailed her the whole time, and she couldn't bear to go out again. I went down to see her. Photographers were sitting in parked cars, some with the engines running because it was cold, in twos and threes. They held cigarettes out the window. I could see them talking and laughing, on stakeout.

We came up with the idea that afternoon that she'd wear the same outfit every day—jeans and a white shirt, with her hair in a ponytail and sunglasses—and then the pictures would all look the same. And they'd stop taking them. We thought it was brilliant. But it didn't work. They just kept shooting. The same picture over and over.

I had fantasies about Carolyn after she died and in all of them I was saving her life. And it was always in a grand, theatrical way. There was a crazy woman who used to stalk her; she came with the family. At some point she had stalked all of them. Anthony, too. And in one of my fantasies this woman drew a gun as Carolyn and I were coming out of her apartment and I jumped in the way. Sometimes I changed the person or the place, but there was always danger, and I always saved her life. And there were always photographers standing by, taking pictures.

There was one fantasy where I just shot the stalker. I shot her outright, before she drew. There was a long trial and the paparazzi were demonized and we were allowed to testify on end, Carolyn and I. We had a captive audience. No one in the jury told her to *get over it*.

"It's not like they gave me a handbook," Carolyn says, laughing, standing in her closet a year after they were married. She pulls suits out—Prada suits in grays and browns—and throws them into a pile on the bed. "You take them—at least you have someplace to wear them." She had bought the suits after their wedding for lunches she supposed she'd be having, appointments she'd be making, things she thought "Mrs. Kennedy" would be doing. She had picked out pale-blue stationery with Tiffany liners. Stationery she thought another woman might use to write out long letters to confidants and friends.

And now a year later we're both laughing at the pile of someone else's clothes. She knew things would change when she became his wife, more than she could imagine. She tried to tuck herself in neatly that first year. But it wasn't so much about learning the rules as it was about learning they weren't for her.

The glass wall and you're constantly bumping into it.

I didn't have a handbook either. If there had been one, I doubt I would have left Suffern. It would have seemed too impossible. I would have stayed where I was, my nose pressed up to the windows, wishing I were somewhere else. There is a map, I am sure, in those handbooks, and "You Are Here" would have been a place way off to the side, with no roads to anywhere. *You can't get there from here.*

Carolyn is studying herself in the long mirror in her bedroom. "I'd never wear this anyway. You'll have to take it in," she tells me. "But take it. And this one, too. They go together."

"My butt is definitely smaller than yours," I say, laughing.

"That's because I'm six feet."

"No you're not. The press writes that because it sounds good— 'six-foot blonde.'"

"Don't worry about it," she says, "being short. You have nicer breasts."

We try on clothes and then get takeout from Bubby's and spend the rest of the evening talking; which of us would look better pregnant, what she will name her kids.

"What about Stas?" she says, looking at me sideways. She is lying across her bed with Ruby curled up under her arm.

"I like it," I tell her. "But is that a family-approved name? Besides, I think *I* get it."

"It's whoever has him first. Stanislas Kennedy," she pronounces. "It has a really nice ring!"

I start to laugh. "You would never get away with it. I have to bequeath it to you."

There are rules about these things, and being married now, she is aware of them. She makes me promise to be godmother.

I get a note a few days later on the pale-blue stationery engraved with her new name.

Dear C,

Never have I had a more irritating experience ushering one through a wardrobe metamorphosis. Good Lord, you are a nut! Who knew? Not me, poor unsuspecting, loving, devoted, loyal friend and cousin that I am. Thanks for keeping me company! And, remember, it's all about me.

XOXO CBK

15

National Institutes of Health, Bethesda, MD
March 1998 *(Inpatient Record)*
Admitted: 3/2/98
Discharged: 3/26/98

CLINICAL DIAGNOSIS: High-grade fibrosarcoma, metastatic to lungs and to chest wall.

REASON FOR HOSPITALIZATION: This patient is a 38-year-old male who is well known to the National Cancer Institute. In October the patient had a re-do right thoracotomy with metastasectomy. He is admitted now to undergo fiber-optic bronchoscopy with recurrent right thoracotomy, along with a chest wall reconstruction and possible diaphragm resection and reconstruction.

◆

Anthony is grinning wildly, watching the rearview mirror. We are at a stop sign when he shifts into reverse. "What are you doing?" I turn around and see the headlights of a car behind us coming closer. "Anthony, what are you doing?" I repeat, but he's not listening. He's chuckling to himself, backing up steadily until our bumper hits the car behind us with a jolt.

A door slams shut; an angry voice comes toward us. "What the hell are you—Jesus, Anthony, you bastard!" It's John, and Anthony can barely breathe he's laughing so hard. John marches back to his car, and Anthony, still laughing, puts the Jeep back in gear, and we drive off with them behind us. We're on our way to a birthday party in Bedford for John's cousin Bobby. We knew they were coming, but it is a coincidence they pulled up behind us. Anthony marvels at his fortune.

It's a family birthday. I'm having the conversations you have at these things, catching up. There are people here I see only once or twice a year, and we're working our way toward food, getting drinks through rooms crowded with people, eating standing up. But if I stepped aside, pulled myself back from this to watch, here is what I might see. Anthony and John, doing their show, dodging jabs like sparring partners—who's quickest. Anthony has the edge now because of the car, and because of the car, John will goad him on, introduce him as the Petit Prince all night. It's a particular art—one they've been honing for thirty-odd years. The imitations: Anthony does a perfect John, John a perfect Anthony. They will invariably have a complaint for Carolyn and me about each other on the drive home tonight. Each one keeps score and wants reassurance he came out ahead. One will think the other did something deplorable. *John didn't even bring a bottle of wine,* Anthony might say, a slave to manners. John will still be irked about the car and will be scheming his next practical joke. Here they are at their finest.

But then we are somber. There is a checkup at the end of the month, and then a surgery. We expect it now when we go in. There is, I know, only so much they can do here. I see it in Dr. Rosenberg's face.

I know there will be a time when we stop coming here, but I think we'll look back and see how good some of these days were. *We were crazy—how did we do all of that?* We've talked about this, Carolyn and I. *Some day so far from now, we'll come back here and everything will be different. You'll be in a different life and we won't even believe we were once here.*

It is a harder operation this time. Anthony's recovery just creeps along. Each week they tell us he needs to stay longer. He has an infection they can't seem to get rid of. The halcyon days, the skipping, the laughing, sneaking out with buckets of blood and tubes tucked into a gym bag—are all suddenly so long ago.

The day after surgery is Lee's birthday. "Oh, no," I say as it dawns on me.

Carolyn is driving the car. We're on our way to Building 10, and she stops in the middle of the road. "Are you kidding? We can't just ignore her birthday."

She turns the car around, and we go to the florist in Bethesda and pick out arrangements of Oriental lilies. Big, bright flowers. "These look like her," she says. We spend an hour with the florist getting them just right, and take them back to the hotel and put them in her room. Carolyn signs the card from the four of us.

I have to change my routine a bit this time. I can't stay during the week, because I'm in the middle of shooting a story, so I arrange for other people to visit, and fly back and forth as much as I can.

"Gustavo was here today," he tells me on the phone. "Provi made dinner." He doesn't say it, but I know it makes him happy. Provi is Gustavo's mother. They live in Georgetown, fifteen minutes from the NIH. She is one of the family almost. She worked for his aunt and uncle in the White House, and they took care of her after. *Provi*—you can say her name after thirty years, and she instantly becomes part of the present. She is older and doesn't come to the hospital but sends home-cooked food with her son, who is Anthony's age. With Gustavo, Anthony can bypass the last ten years. He comes almost every night while I'm away, bringing dinner and sneaking in beer.

Anthony is at the NIH for twenty-five days while I fly back and forth to Reno tracking a con man.

There is an infomercial on late-night cable for a company called National Affordable Housing Coalition. They promise low-interest mortgage rates, regardless of credit, income, or bankruptcy. Its founder, Craig M—, targets low-income people, most of them living in housing projects. He promises them a piece of the "American Dream," and they believe him.

Craig has a paper trail of failed businesses, disgruntled employees, and cheated clients. He is a reporter's dream. I track down his ex-employees and people he has ripped off. I call hundreds of his victims and listen to their stories. It is always the same: they went to Craig's seminar, gave him five hundred dollars, and never heard from the NAHC again. I take a camera crew to an Atlanta housing project and interview one family he scammed in their overcrowded, run-down apartment. I call the toll-free number from the infomercial and sign up for his ten-dollar seminar, which turns out to be nothing more than a long pep talk to persuade people to join the NAHC. At the end of each seminar, those who pay the five hundred dollars are promised that someone from the NAHC will walk them—people with little money and poor credit—into the home of their dreams. He is making millions, but no one is getting a home.

I'm working with the correspondent Arnold Diaz, who is well known for his "Shame on You!" series that used to run on the local news. Our plan is to confront Craig after we get all of our footage.

Carolyn loves this story. She wants to take this guy down. While I'm staking him out, she calls me hourly for updates. "What are you doing now?" she says, when I answer the phone.

"Nothing. I'm in the parking lot, waiting."

"Call me back as soon as you see him!"

I wait in the parking lot for almost six hours, and when I spot him, I call her.

"He just left the office. He's getting into his car," I tell her. She wants all the details.

"What does he look like?" she asks.

"He's short, and his gut is hanging over his khakis, and he's wearing a Ralph Lauren button-down shirt. I can see the logo."

"How close are you?"

"He's walking to his car. It's a Mercedes. Oh, perfect—his license plate reads 'Idea Guy.'"

Carolyn groans. "What a loser!" she says.

I slide down in the front seat and whisper into the phone, "He just walked by my car."

"Holy shit, did he spot you? Let me come out there!"

"Yeah, I'll really be undercover then with you in tow."

I don't have a crew in Reno, but we catch him in New Jersey. This time he's giving a seminar, and we film it with the hidden-camera glasses—black, chunky glasses with a tiny camera embedded in the bridge. After the seminar Arnold comes out and approaches Craig in the hallway with the camera crew for a "spontaneous interview." He tries to talk to us walking backward, but then turns around and starts to run. We chase him to the elevator, and Arnold and the camera guy squeeze in with him, the video still rolling.

Craig calls me a week later to schedule an interview. He wants to explain himself, he says. He's afraid we have the wrong idea about his company, and he wants to set the record straight. I set up an interview at a hotel in San Francisco because he says he will be there on business, but he doesn't show up. I have the cameraman film the room with his empty chair and Arnold Diaz with his arms crossed, tapping his fingers and watching the clock. I couldn't have planned a better ending. The NAHC goes out of business the week after our piece airs. A class-action lawsuit is filed in Reno.

Anthony's planning a trip the minute he gets back from Washington. We flee New York to escape cancer whenever we can, however briefly. It seems to collect in New York. We go to places that don't have hospitals, so I travel with the number of MedEvac SOS International in my wallet. It is how I am able to sleep at night, with the number for MedEvac under my pillow. The assurance that regardless of how far away we go, there is a phone somewhere with a helicopter on the other end that can come and get him and take him somewhere safe.

Anthony wants to go to Alaska. "Enjoy your trip," Dr. Rosenberg says. There is a shadow on an X-ray, but he says, "We'll take a look at it when you get back." We don't see the shadow, we hear *Enjoy your trip,* and think, *How bad can it be if he's letting us go away?* So Anthony organizes an eight-day guided kayaking trip through the Tongass National Park, down the Bering Strait, to watch the whales. We fly to Juneau and spend the night in a bed-and-breakfast with a small group of people and Kelly, our guide. The next morning she hands us life jackets, head nets to keep the bugs out of our eyes, and plastic ponchos in case of rain. Our kayaks and camping gear are packed on a boat, and we travel up the strait to a small island forty miles from anywhere. It's a dream vacation, life-changing even, in different circumstances. It will take us five days to kayak back down the strait. We are with twelve strangers. Anthony is strong and laughing. Nobody knows he is dying.

We set up our tents under the spruce trees that line the pristine shoreline. There are breathtaking views in every direction, and then it starts to rain. We have a small two-man pup tent, and everything is wet, and the rain leaks into the tent through the seams. This I am not prepared for. The rain does not let up for three days. The morning of day three is the moment, if there was one, when I am ready to walk out. The rain has tapped my reserve, and Anthony must suspect this, that I am approaching a critical border, because he is doing his best to relieve it.

"Wake up, Peanut. I have a surprise." He is tapping on the outside of the tent. It's 7 a.m., and the other campers have already been up for an hour. He let me sleep in this morning, in the rain, while the rest of them made breakfast by the fire under a plastic tarp.

"Hmmm?" I mumble. I don't want to move. I want to stay buried in my damp sleeping bag for the rest of the trip. I'm sure he's going to make me get up, sing camper songs, traipse somewhere in the rain. I will not come out, I decide in my half-sleep, there is nothing they can do to make me.

"Come on, Nut, wake up!" I peek out, and he's on his knees, smiling at me, holding a bowl of hot oatmeal with sliced bananas on top. Offering gifts. The sweetest man in the world, my husband getting up early to make me breakfast by the fire, but then he unzips the tent. It caves in from the weight of the water, collapses on me, and now I'm drenched. Everything that was just damp is now soaked—our sleeping bags, our clothes, our rain gear. Anthony slowly backs up with the oatmeal still in his hand, and I sit there for a minute, rain pouring down on me. I can choose to laugh or cry. But I'm afraid if I start to cry I won't stop, so I get up quietly and pack up the tent.

The rain lets up by the afternoon and the sun comes out, and it is magical. We paddle out in the kayaks in search of the whales. A few hours pass, and suddenly we are surrounded by them. They are huge and graceful and seem to be showing off for us. They throw themselves straight up into the air and smash back down, slap their massive tails on the surface of the water and create swells that rock our kayaks. The first time they do this we all look up at the sky. We think there might be a storm. It's like paddling up to thunder. "Hit the sides of the kayak hard with your oar if they come too close," Kelly instructs us. "They'll move away."

At night we sleep in the tents under the stars and listen to them "sing." "They sing long love songs," Kelly tells us. "It's part of their mating behavior." It goes on for hours. They are enormous and indestructible and gentle. Everything else in the world seems so much smaller right now.

On our fifth night there is a commotion. One of the campers has a night terror and wakes up screaming. Everyone runs out of the tents,

Kelly with her gun, thinking there's a bear, and Anthony right behind her. When Kelly calms the man down, she determines there is no bear, no beast, no danger, and they file back to their tents. I sleep through all of it, so Anthony recaps it for me the next morning over coffee by the campfire.

He's so excited telling me that I am completely caught up in the story, watching him and the way he tells it. It's the way he told me about the space shuttle taking off at the beach in Florida. He can't wait to get back to tell his girl.

"Wow, so you just ran out of our tent?" I smile as it finally occurs to me. "While I slept through the whole thing."

"Yeah."

"You ran out."

"Yep."

"You thought it was a bear."

"Uh-huh."

I pause to let him save himself, and he doesn't. "Were you going to come back and get me?"

He takes a long sip of coffee and then winks. "We're in Alaska, Nut. When there's a bear in the camp it's every man for himself."

On the last day of the trip we take a walk through a beautiful field of grasses and wildflowers. I pick a dandelion. I make a wish, because I always make a wish, and for five years it has been the same thing. *We will live happily ever after.* Then I take a deep breath and blow.

Year Five

Turning and turning in the widening gyre
The falcon cannot hear the falconer;
Things fall apart; the centre cannot hold.

—WILLIAM BUTLER YEATS, "The Second Coming"

1

I call from the bar of the Delta Shuttle at Reagan National and schedule a meeting of what I've named the "Knights of the Round Table." The shadow we saw on the X-ray before we left for Alaska is clearly cancer. A new CT scan shows that the tumor has spilled out of Anthony's lungs and is now filling up the free space of his chest so that it can't simply be cut out. "Call Karen Antman," Dr. Rosenberg said to me as we left the NIH. He gave me Dr. Antman's number, but there was no need. I already had it. I let him give it to me. I want to think this is a new thing. That we are not simply retracing our steps. That we are moving on, not back.

So here we are again in these meetings, the heads of the heads in a half-circle around a table in a stark conference room. Anthony sits with John on one side of him, me on the other. His mother and Hamilton on my left. We are here to decide what to do next. Dr. Antman introduces Dr. Mears, the head of hematology at Columbia, and Dr. Jerry Groopman, famous for experimental DNA therapy, is on the speakerphone from Boston. It's the war room. This is the cabinet.

Diane is here, too. She has been in the wings all along, ready to help when we need her, and now I have asked. Anthony worked with her at ABC for ten years, and she adores him. She has been making calls to doctors around the world to find experimental treatments, and hired a research assistant to follow up and read the studies. She helps me balance all of this with work. And sitting here in this room, as Diane Sawyer, she adds gravitas. *We are serious about this,* we hope we are saying.

Dr. Mears lays proposals out in front of us like someone pitching time-shares in Miami Beach. At appropriate intervals we nod. I am sitting by the window and Anthony is to my right. He trusts I know what I am doing. I ask a serious question about Decadron and side effects, but I don't write anything down. I have my notebook, still, with me everywhere, but today I doodle in the margins. *CD + AR.* I write in loopy letters, *Carole A. DiFalco, Carole D. Radziwill, Anthony Stanislas Albert Radziwill.* I draw hearts around our names. I look out at the windows of other buildings. There is nothing in this room to hear. No one is going to say, *We know how to fix this,* so I focus on the cars driving over the bridge that I can see from the window.

"And what, exactly, is your level of expertise?" Dr. Antman asks, and it snaps me back. She is looking straight at Hamilton. He has asked a question about chemotherapy cycles. We are desperate. We are defensive. We want someone to blame.

This is Year Five. It has been four years since the cancer metastasized. According to the medical book in the basement of Sloan-Kettering this is Anthony's last year. The cancer has performed brilliantly. It is exactly on schedule. It has played out exactly the way the book said it would. Anthony's tumor has moved outside of his lungs to the mediastinum. It is wedged around his trachea, through his bronchial tubes, near where his heart sits. I am in awe of his cancer.

In Year Five there are five rounds of chemo and two surgeries. There are six radiation treatments and four trips to emergency rooms. There is dialysis three times a week. I am still working, but the stories I produce are a blur. There is a profile of George Stephanopoulos, of Julia Roberts. Anthony still goes to his office, though he is now just filling in time between hospital stints. There is the stale smell of overbleached hospital sheets and white-cotton thermal blankets. I am with Anthony around the clock, it seems, or else I'm on the phone with doctors. I'm researching clinical trials at M.D. Anderson and the Mayo Clinic. I type up his medical history and start handing it out, like a flyer, to anyone who I think can help.

In Year Five we find antiangiogenesis, the cure for cancer, it says, on the front page of *The New York Times.* Antiangiogenesis drugs work by cutting off the blood supply to the tumor. So Anthony starts taking thalidomide—the sleeping pill that produced babies with club feet and webbed fingers, scientists find, will also starve growing tumors. The FDA took it off the market after the babies were born deformed and are carefully doling it out as a last-hope treatment to cancer patients. I file the necessary paperwork, and a few weeks later ten bottles arrive.

In Year Five someone suggests experimental surgery, and Diane comes with me to meet the head of oncology at Mount Sinai. We take Anthony's CT scans with us—I am shopping them around now— and the doctor explains to us a procedure using a pig valve that reroutes the trachea out of the patient's back. "There's really nothing we can do for him," he says, holding the scans up to the light. He tells us the tumor will likely rupture an artery and he'll bleed to death, or it will squeeze his bronchial tubes and he'll suffocate. "He's going to die a horrible death." Diane stands perfectly still. I keep my head down and jot notes about the pig valve.

In Year Five, a friend arranges for Anthony to see a healer, and a woman comes to our apartment to teach us to meditate. She works with Deepak Chopra. She writes down our mantras and instructs us to repeat them with our eyes closed. My mind wanders, and I make a mental note to call Dr. Saal at New York Presbyterian and check on the dialysis machine we are getting installed in the apartment. If our eyes were open, I'm certain we'd catch each other rolling them. We are incapable of meditating; there is too much to think about. If there are moments when I am not thinking about cancer, they happen in Carolyn's apartment, or in the upstairs room at her gym when I meet her there.

In Year Five things are not as they were at the NIH. We left possibility behind in Bethesda, with the pasta pomodoro from Positano's and the tree-lined streets and Hamburger Hamlet. We are back in New York, and it's a business again. Anthony isn't the star patient anymore. We have been here before, and everyone at the Round Table knows his record, and they must have their own guesses at how much time is left. That we are back in New York is a defeat in itself. We thumbed our noses at New York and chemotherapy, radiation. But surgery didn't work, so we are back, heads down.

The Round Table recommends chemotherapy, and we sign up for five cycles, five separate sessions of seventy-two-hour drips. We have Dr. Best of the Best. *You're in good hands. He's the best there is,* people say, because there is nothing else left to say.

If Dr. Rosenberg was hope and sincerity and a devout professionalism, Dr. Best of the Best is slick and self-assured, tasseled Gucci loafers and rented yachts. Meeting him is instantly repellent, like lifting the lid of a garbage Dumpster. I imagine Dr. Best of the Best clinking ice in his Scotch at the country club, rocking back just a little on his feet—the other men asking him, *So what's the latest on cancer?* And Dr. Best of the Best clearing his throat, careful to speak softly, frame his thoughts, move his free hand now and then in a certain way to brandish his words. Careful to reflect his Ivy League articulation. His friends, titans of business, are wide-eyed at how smart and serious the doctor is—how good to have him in their circle.

But there are not a lot of places for us to go at this point. At this point he is all we have.

When we step through the doors of Columbia-Presbyterian's gilded McKeen Pavilion, with its concierge and four o'clock tea, I lose my breath. Disease clings to us like wet clothes. I hate how Anthony is marked. The hospital is crowded with residents and interns and nurses, people who don't know him. People who don't know there is more to him than this.

Anthony's treatment is called MAID—a cocktail of four different drugs: mesna, Adriamycin, ifosfamide, and Decadron. Mesna's sole purpose is to ease the side effects of ifosfamide, to help prevent ifosfamide from destroying his bladder and his kidneys.

The anticancer drugs kill the cancer cells, but they also kill healthy cells. There are no *possible* side effects; they are certain: vomiting, loss of appetite, hair loss, mouth sores, increased chance of infection, excessive bruising, excessive bleeding from minor cuts, excessive fatigue.

Maybe in ten or twenty years we'll look back on chemotherapy and gasp. Another generation may be appalled that we ever did this, dripped poison through a needle into a person's body to make him well.

We start the first round two days after a surgeon puts a port in Anthony's chest for the chemo drip. A Wednesday in August, and I have it carefully scheduled:

> 7 a.m.: Check in
> 9 a.m.: Yoga
> 10 a.m.: Sheila and Richard
> Lunch: Lee and Herbert
> 4 p.m.: High tea in the Pavilion, Marc
> Dinner: Carolyn and Hamilton (KFC)
> 8 p.m.: John

The nurse comes in to do a blood test and takes it down to the lab before she starts the chemo drip. The lab checks for liver function, potassium levels, and creatinine levels to monitor kidney function. Then they send the drugs up in bottles, one at a time, starting with ifosfamide. The nurse sticks a needle into the port in his chest, attaches the plastic sack to the IV pole, and weaves the tubing through a machine that controls the flow. Anthony watches television until the yoga instructor comes; then he wheels the IV pole to the center of the room and follows her through warrior poses and breathing and down dogs until he's suddenly nauseated. I send her away. The nurse gives him a shot of Compazine for the nausea, and by the time Sheila, his boss, arrives with our friend Richard, he's feeling better but not okay. They bring him a Chinese fish painting, a symbol of good luck, and chat about new projects and office gossip. It lifts his spirits, but they do not stay long. In spite of Anthony's valiant performance they can see he is not feeling well and say their good-byes quickly.

Lee and Herbert bring homemade consommé and wrap sand-

wiches from William Poll. He drinks the consommé and nibbles on
the sandwich. In the afternoon the nurse comes back to start the second drug. This one, Adriamycin, comes in a thick glass brown bottle.
She explains, when I ask, that it is so toxic it would burn through a
plastic sack. The nurse wears rubber gloves and places a dark bag over
the bottle before hooking it up to the pole. Any exposure to light and
the poison will decompose.

When our friend Marc arrives, he spends most of the visit with me
in the McKeen Pavilion, listening to the piano and picking at rasp-
berry squares. Anthony rests for the afternoon, and then Carolyn and
Hamilton come with dinner. They bring Anthony takeout from Il
Cantinori and a bucket of chicken with mashed potatoes and biscuits
for us. John stops by after work and eats the leftovers.

The second round is three weeks later. We check in on Friday morning, and the nurses take his blood and start the drip. I go to my office
for a few hours. I'm working on a profile of Julia Roberts with Diane
and researching other stories that go nowhere. I can't focus on anything. Carolyn and John are in Italy this weekend for our friends
Kissy and Jamie's wedding. We would be there, too, but there is this.
Months ago, we were planning this trip together, trying to decide
whether to go early and spend some days in Capri and then head to
Lake Bracciano outside Rome. Or stay after the wedding for a few
days of fun, just the four of us.

I have abandoned the visiting schedule. In fact, now I am discour-
aging anyone from coming. My mother wants to visit, and I push
back. Anthony is sick from the moment they start the drugs until they
stop them. He doesn't have the strength, only good manners, to make
polite conversation.

I spend the weekend bunched up in the armchair next to his bed,
getting up periodically to make sure the chemo lines aren't blocked—
the warning beep and the flashing red word, *occluded*. If the nurses
aren't here, I do what I have seen them do: open the door to the Med-

Vac, check for kinks in the plastic tubing, then press stop, pause, reset, and the poison flows again.

I wait for Anthony to sleep before I close my eyes. I miss Bethesda. I miss Carolyn, and our drives to nowhere down the Beltway. We are in New York, where people have their lives to live, and my life is happening in the McKeen Pavilion. I am certain I will die here, with him. My system, too, is slowly shutting down.

After the second round his hair falls out. We wake up one morning and there is a fine layer on his pillow. I brush it off quickly into a wastebasket. For three weeks the hair dusts his pillow every morning. We go to see Roy, who comes recommended by a friend. He does hair and makeup for Meryl Streep.

Roy makes a plaster cast of Anthony's head. He takes almost three hours to finish, measuring his head carefully, taking hair samples to match the color. He is serious about his work, but it is fun, like getting fitted for a costume party. There are props all over his apartment, a collection of Barbie dolls in perfect miniature replications of Bob Mackie gowns. He makes two wigs so that while one is cleaned and re-shaped, Anthony can wear the other. He makes them with a special double-sided adhesive that is strong enough to shower with or for swimming in the ocean. You don't take them off for anything until it is time to swap, and then Roy will come to our apartment or to Anthony's office to remove one wig carefully and affix the other. If we are in the hospital, he comes to the hospital.

The wigs are perfect, but this is a setback, losing his hair. The scars on his chest could be from anything—Anthony is fond of telling people "shark attack" and watching their faces recoil in horror. But the hair loss is swift and brutal. It marks him undeniably. It's the thing more than anything else that makes you look like you have cancer.

The third round is in September and Carolyn is back, and while Anthony drifts in and out of sleep we sneak off to Wendy's for a junk-food fix.

I order a number two—a Classic Double, no cheese. "Biggie the fries, biggie Diet Coke," I tell the cashier, and she punches it in.

It's a little Wendy's in Washington Heights packed with moody teenagers and sleepy-looking residents.

Carolyn sighs dramatically after I order. "Can you please stop saying 'biggie' every time we come here?" She rolls her eyes at the girl behind the register and jerks her head toward me.

"No, and you want biggie fries, too."

She rolls her eyes again.

"Say 'biggie,'" I tease her.

"I'm not saying 'biggie.' I want a number two and a Frosty."

I turn to the cashier. "One more number two with a Frosty," I tell her, "and biggie the fries."

If there is anything certain in our lives at this point, it is that I will biggie the fries and she will roll her eyes at me. I drag out our Wendy's lunch as long as I can. I eat every single fry, dipping each one carefully in ketchup. I talk nonstop, pulling out every single piece of office gossip I can think of. *Don't get up,* I am silently willing her. *I don't want to go back.* But we do stand up, clear our table, empty our trays in the orange garbage containers, and walk back to the hospital.

Weekend chemotherapy is lonely. People have weekend plans and so won't be stopping by. We don't want anyone to come but can't stand to be alone. Hospitals on the weekend are smothered with emptiness. There is no sense of movement, of change, of seasons. We start the same day over and over. The same false lighting glares down at you everywhere, no matter the time of day, and it is always cold. Somewhere in New York there are people warm and surrounded, and none of them know of this, that we are here.

Sundays are completely dead. We try to schedule the cycles to finish on Sunday, so Anthony can be at work the next day. After our first Sunday, spent searching for someone to check us out, we learned to get his discharge papers signed earlier, before his doctor leaves for the weekend.

By the fourth cycle things are going wrong, and we deal with them the best we can. Anthony can't walk. He is leaning on me. I have to reach my arm around him and hold him up under his arm. No one remarks on this as we leave. No one says, *Hey, are you okay there? Are you sure you're ready to go?* Had they asked, Anthony would have answered angrily, a steely *Yes!* We would still have checked out. But I would feel better if someone noticed: *Yes, you see it, too! I'm not crazy. I need help.* But no one says anything, and I begin to think I'm imagining it all. His entire body shaking, unable to walk without my help. I consider mentioning this to the resident when he hands us the discharge papers, but I know Anthony will regard it as a betrayal. I smile and take the papers.

We are referred to a neurologist, who diagnoses Anthony with polyneuropathy. Another diagnosis. They barely register now. The nerve endings in his legs are dying. There is nothing to do about it. I buy him a cane at Zitomer's on Madison.

On a Friday in October I go to the hospital as usual after work. It's our last cycle. The tumor hasn't shrunk, but it hasn't grown either, so Dr. Best of the Best has encouraged us to go ahead with the last treatment. When I walk into Anthony's room, there is no equipment, no Med-Vac to drip the chemo. The lights are off, and Anthony is sitting hunched on the edge of the bed.

It's six at night, and my thoughts are panicky. *Has something gone wrong? Did we forget to check in this morning?*

"Where's the doctor?" I ask him. I force myself to sound calm.

"I don't know. I think he left."

He is alone, thin and pale. I am struck by how helpless he looks, the empty room. I take it in cautiously. "I'm confused. Have you been sitting here all afternoon?"

"The nurses are waiting on something from the lab." He is anxious. He tells me no one has checked on him.

"Where the hell *is* everyone?" I am trying to keep my voice steady.

"They're waiting on my blood work."

"When did they take it?"

"A while ago, I guess. Don't make a scene, Carole. They're just busy."

I know when I hear him call me by my name to be careful. He has said this before, *Don't make a scene*. As a patient, he does not want attention called to him. He thinks there must be patients who are worse off, and they are getting treated first. After all, he thinks, he's going to get better, and these other sicker patients might not. But it's no longer true. Now he is sometimes the sickest patient in the unit. I am not the sort of person to make scenes, I think, though it turns out I just need the right set of circumstances.

This is my *Terms of Endearment*–Shirley MacLaine moment. It's in all the movies in which someone dies—the moment when you understand, when you get it. This is all just a charade. The doctors have moved on to other patients and you're left screaming for help at the nurses' station. Anthony is not so much a patient anymore but a guest who has overstayed his welcome.

"I just got to my husband's room, and he's been sitting here all day waiting for the chemo," I say on the phone to the lab. "I left this morning, and he's been sitting here *all day*—why is he still sitting here?" The last three words are tight, clenched.

"I'm sorry, Mrs. Radziwill. Someone should have called. We're waiting to hear from his doctor. We need a dispensation from his doctor before we can release the drugs."

"Why? His doctor already ordered the treatment."

"His blood work came back, and his creatinine level is a little high."

The creatinine level indicates how the kidneys are functioning; it is monitored closely because kidney damage is a possible side effect of ifosfamide. A healthy creatinine level is 1. One is perfect. It means you're walking, eating, drinking, and everything is running smoothly. Ten, on the other hand, is total kidney failure.

Anthony's creatinine level is approaching 2, they tell me, and yes, they have called Dr. Best of the Best. He has okayed the chemo but asked for a modified version: slightly reducing the ifosfamide to compensate for the kidney concern. But the lab hasn't sent up the drugs yet. "We have another call in to the doctor. We're waiting to hear back."

His doctor ordered it, I think. *If he says give it to him, then give it to him!* His creatinine level is elevated, but still it's only at 2, and kidneys don't fail until 10. Or so I thought.

"What is going on?" I ask the doctor when I reach him on his home phone. "Anthony's been waiting in his room all day."

"What are you talking about? I ordered the drugs," he says. When I repeat what the lab has told me about the creatinine level, he answers me testily. He's aware of the problem, he says, and has already addressed it.

Dr. Best of the Best sounds impatient. I'm sure I am not welcome, calling him here. "I ordered the fucking drugs. I told them to send up the drugs this morning. Hours ago."

The *fucking* startles me. I have not heard a doctor curse. Best of the Best is angry with the lab.

I switch the phone to my other ear and glance at Anthony. He is staring at a wall. His arms look thin but heavy. As if they have dropped there at his sides and he can't lift them back up. I look past him out the window at the commuters—people leaving offices to drive to houses in the suburbs. Warm food and garlic smells hugging them as they walk through familiar doors.

I don't know whom to turn to. I need to trust the doctor, to put my faith in him completely. I'm lost if I can't. He's my compass. I need to trust that he is right and that the lab is responsible for the delay. A simple miscommunication. This is not the time, in the fifth round of chemo, almost at the end, that I am eager to question Anthony's doctor.

In the early rounds I did the research. I combed the Internet for new drugs, new treatments, and studied their side effects. I brought it all to Best of the Best's office. He listened quietly while I read from articles and *World News Tonight* transcripts and then gave me his opinion. After the third round he didn't respond. I named the drug, and he wrote the prescription without even looking up. He gave me a triplicate prescription for Marinol, the "pot" drug, which I filled and then took myself to get to sleep. When Anthony asked how long he would live if he didn't finish the five cycles, Best of the Best replied, without missing a beat, "Oh, I hate it when my patients ask me that." In the beginning, yes, I would question, but now I don't have that kind of time.

Twenty minutes after we hang up, the lab brings up the drugs.

I am pleased with myself, a little. I have taken charge and taken care of something, I think. I help Anthony get comfortable; then I find a supply room and go inside and shut the door. I sit down on a step stool, next to boxes of surgical masks and bedpans and a stack of white blankets, and cry.

He does the chemo drip for three days around the clock, and after seventy-two hours I have forgotten about the lab and the cursing. We are back on course, pushing ahead. I move it away from everything else on my mind.

2

It is two weeks after the fifth cycle of chemo, and Anthony has not regained his strength. Best of the Best told us it might take a little longer to recover; the last cycle is always the most difficult. He has been home but unable to go to work.

No one knows what goes on in our secret lives. We guzzle NyQuil to sleep. We get up in the night to change the sheets, which are soaked in perspiration. Anthony sleeps upright so he can breathe easier. If I hear him struggling, I nudge him to wake him up. He is always, it seems, up during the night. I take his temperature every hour. I cry in the shower so he cannot hear me.

He has had a fever for days, and we are biding it. But this night seems worse. It is four in the morning, and he is running a 103-degree fever and is filling the crescent moon–shaped bowls they gave us at the hospital with bile, so we agree on the cab.

"Columbia Presbyterian, emergency room," I tell the driver calmly.

We are used to going to hospitals in cabs. In New York this is what you do.

There are things I know how to do, regardless of how crazy it all seems. I am serious, efficient. Following my own made-up directions. I am unable, still, to say *I can't do this by myself.* And no one suggests that I get help. There is such a fuzzy line between sick and rush to the hospital, and we keep moving it. Hailing cabs at four in the morning. *Keep moving. It will be worse if you stop.*

This is the second trip to the ER in as many weeks. But this time, before I finish checking him into the hospital the emergency room doctor says, "I think you should call his mother," as he puts an oxygen mask on Anthony and hooks up a saline IV.

We have been in hospitals for years, but now I am worried. It is the expression on the doctor's face. The stark change, it seems, in Anthony from the door of our apartment to here. I have a fleeting thought of him dying right here in the ER, but that can't be possible. Can it?

The ER doctor is serious and direct. He is disheveled, sweaty, and he's talking fast. He has no time for careful meetings. He tells me Anthony is fighting a massive infection. They won't be sure what it is until the blood tests and cultures come back from the lab. The doctor starts an IV for Vancomycin, the antibiotic of last resort. "It's not good," he is saying. "His immune system is so compromised from the chemo, he's having difficulty fighting back. There is very little we can do except wait." I don't respond. "The first twenty-four hours are the most important. If his condition doesn't improve, well, that's not good either." *Mrs. Radziwill,* he is trying to tell me, *I think your husband is going to die.*

Carolyn comes in the morning. Lee arrives with Hamilton. Herbert calls from Los Angeles. Friends start showing up in the afternoon. There are people who haven't seen Anthony in the hospital before, who don't know what this is like, and Carolyn won't let me reassure them. She is worried about me. She grabs my hand in the waiting room and makes it clear she will take care of me, and the others will have to manage this on their own.

After Anthony is situated in the ICU, I book one of the McKeen Pavilion's guest rooms, and Carolyn and I spend the night. She is afraid to leave me now. Afraid that if Anthony dies during the night, I will be here all alone. I wake up early the next morning and call the ICU.

"How is he?"

"He's the same," the voice says flatly. "Unchanged." The nurse says it slowly, without inflection, like a recording.

"What does that mean?"

"We were hoping for some progress."

Carolyn is sitting on the bed next to me, and I won't talk to her. I put the phone down and cry. She brings me juice and a muffin and runs the shower for me. When I get out, I see that she has laid out the clothes she brought for me. I get dressed and sit down in the bathroom and she blow-dries my hair.

I suddenly realize I'm not prepared for him to die. I'm not ready for this. Not yet.

I'll just sleep, I think. I'll wake up and he'll be coming out of it. *Close one,* I will tell him. He'll smile and squeeze my hand. But I wake up and his condition is the same and I can't look at anyone.

Carolyn and I walk silently to the ICU. John is there already. Caroline comes in with Ed, Holly with Pete and Joan. Marc and Lori are sitting in the waiting room outside. Anthony's sister Tina, here with her boyfriend, is visibly shaken. It looks as if Anthony is hooked to every machine they have. His resistance is breaking down, his kidneys are failing, his circulation system is going, his white blood cell count is skyrocketing, his red blood count is too low, his respiratory system is shutting down—it appears to be irreversible.

John comes back late that night in his tuxedo, straight from an event. It is nearly midnight, and Carolyn and I are waiting for him. He is the one who can save us somehow. The one we count on. The one who brings magic dust and sparkle, and we hold our breath each time, hoping he can still do it. We are hoping, Carolyn and I, that he can somehow pull this off.

He kisses her, gives me a quick hug, and walks over to Anthony's bed. We have been standing here for hours, watching him drift in and out of consciousness.

"Tonypro," he says quietly and grabs Anthony's hand. John's shoes are black and shiny. His bow tie is undone. His tuxedo looks comical in the yellow lights of the ICU.

He begins humming, and then there are words. We can barely hear him, but Anthony does, and he smiles. His eyes are still closed, but they seem more relaxed when he smiles, and then his mouth starts to move along with John's.

If you go down to the woods today,
You're sure of a big surprise.
If you go down to the woods today,
You'd better go in disguise.
For every bear that ever there was
Will gather there for certain because
Today's the day the teddy bears have their picnic.

They sing together softly, this children's song, with their hands clasped like little boys. They sing it over and over, John holding tightly on to Anthony's hand. They are in a place that no one else has ever been or could ever go, singing a song that John's mother used to sing to the two of them. The boys who laughed and played and sang silly songs are all grown up now—John in a tuxedo, Anthony in a hospital gown.

The doctors think Anthony will die tonight, and John takes him to the safest place he knows.

3

It's day four in the ICU. Anthony's immune system is helpless. He is at the mercy of every kind of infection, vulnerable to everything. His body has a septic infection and his organs are systematically shutting down, one by one. Each day that he holds on increases his chances of surviving. Each day they can keep him stable increases the likelihood he will pull through. But some systems won't be able to recover.

As if the ICU isn't gloomy enough by itself, there is a run of spinal meningitis while we're here. Bodies are wheeled by under white sheets. The first time I see this, the white sheet draped over a stretcher, I don't know what it is. By the second time it is clear.

None of us says anything to Anthony. No one talks about death in a hospital; it seems like bad luck.

I am following his creatinine level, because I think this is something I know about. It is rising steadily each day—four to five to six. It stops around six and a half, and I am relieved. *Thank God,* I think, *it's not kidney failure.*

The interns make their rounds every morning with their charts—clipboards with the numbers of Anthony's life: blood pressure, cell counts, hematocrit levels, culture reports, and creatinine levels. The ER doctor stops by to check on his patient. He is amazed that Anthony has survived. He looks at the chart and takes the time to explain it.

"This is what's going on with his kidneys," he tells me, showing me the charts and reports from the chemo. He shows me the creatinine levels rising: 1.5 after the third round, 1.9 after the fourth. Anthony's kidneys were beginning to fail long before our 4 a.m. cab ride to the ER, and the doctor is explaining to me how it happened, and that we can't do anything about it. He stops and waits for me to catch up, to understand that Anthony's kidneys will never recover.

What I don't understand before talking to the doctor is that at a creatinine level of 2 his kidneys are functioning at 50 percent. He essentially has one working kidney. You would think, or at least I thought, that 5 is 50 percent, not 2. The range is *1* to *10*. And because I thought this, I didn't panic when his level was 2. I thought we had room. *Even if it gets to 5,* I thought, *5 is okay. You can live at 50 percent,* I thought, *on one kidney.* But I'm wrong. This doctor is telling me that a level of 2 is as far, really, as he can go.

I can't believe what I'm hearing. I feel a quick and dizzying whirl of emotions: fury, devastation, hatred, as if I'm a windup toy and he has just pulled the string. And then I stop. I am too stunned to feel anything.

Later that day Dr. Best of the Best stops by in his pressed white lab coat. He is standing at the nurses' station checking Anthony's chart and I ask him what happened. Cancer patients, he says, are always at risk for infections after having chemo. "As for the kidneys," he adds, "there's no way to know exactly what caused it. It could well have been the thalidomide." It is the last time I ever see him.

When I get home that night I find a copy of *Elle Decor* in our mailbox. The cover reads, "Big Ideas for Small Spaces." Anthony and I are on page 198, "Paradise on Park." There is a full-page photo, taken eight months ago, before his last thoracotomy in March. We're walking arm in arm on the sidewalk in front of our apartment, Anthony, in a grey cashmere sweater and slacks, gazing down at me. Both of us smiling, a portrait of carefree lives. We look as if we have it all. There is a three-page photo spread of the apartment packed with the antiques, the furnishings, the subtle reincarnations of Anthony's history that I raced to put together. A past and a future assembled from our precarious present.

Diane's husband, Mike, comes to the ICU every day at 1 p.m. with a bag of cookies and sandwiches that he passes out to all the nurses. He is an old family friend of Anthony's and John's. We're all friends—he was at our wedding, we see each other at get-togethers, and I work with Diane—but I haven't really gotten to know him well until now.

He sits with me in the ICU, and if Anthony is awake, the three of us talk. If he is asleep, Mike and I talk, or sometimes we don't. He understands the awkward rhythm of hospital days, of having to entertain in a strange place, of feeling obligated to host. He comes in and sits down in the chair without hesitation, as if he's been coming here for ten years and is just now running into us. Mike distrusts doctors, so when the interns come around and discuss Anthony's condition among themselves as though he is deaf or dead, I have someone to look at across the room. While they tick off the succession of things that are going wrong, I have someone to hate them with.

It is very stressful, this stay, because we are in New York, and Anthony is narrowly cheating death. Word spreads quickly, and soon everyone comes, and I don't know what to say. I don't want to see anyone, but I feel guilty turning them away. I don't want this to seem like a viewing, a stream of people parading in to pay respects. The phone rings all day. *You tell me, when do you think I can come see him?* I don't want these calls. I don't want to schedule. I don't want them to come, but when they do sometimes it's nice. I don't want to be involved in it. Mike never calls. He shows up. He doesn't make me decide. He is a comfort to me during this stay.

After seven days in the ICU Anthony is stable enough to move to a room. We get the Sunny von Bülow room, informally named after the heiress who lived here in a coma for so many years.

She haunts the room, the penthouse suite at Columbia Presbyterian. There is a story told that she started whistling one day while an intern was changing her feeding tube. Whistling, out of nowhere, after years of lying mute. Of all the hospital rooms, this is my favorite.

It has full-length windows and a beautiful view. The picture window looks as if it was framed right around the George Washington Bridge. It is bigger than the ones in other rooms and has cream-colored curtains with a pattern of light-blue flowers. A city hospital room done in country chic. The bedspread and the shower curtain are made from the same fabric, and on a hook behind the door is a small table that unfolds to hold dinner for two. I sleep on a cot I make up with crisp white hospital sheets. I set it up between Anthony's bed and the window so I can stare out at the lights. The magic dots moving on the bridge. People coming and going with their stories—to the theater, in cocktail dresses, to apartments, to concerts, to dinners, to celebrate. It's enchanting, this view. The first thing people notice when they come. This is nice for Anthony, because it makes him the second thing. Most of the people who visit us are shocked. They don't realize we are this far along. We have managed a good front until now, and I can see it in their stretched smiles, their round eyes. *Oh, my God, what happened?*

Our world is beginning to narrow drastically. There are few people Anthony wants to see. This is his secret, this disease. I carefully filter the information I give to my family, to colleagues at work. There is no one we can talk to about it, because he still wants to pretend it is all fine. It certainly isn't.

4

In Year Five Carolyn and I make up a game we call The Townhouse: a conversation, really, that she humors me with when I'm down. There are days I call her and say, "Let's talk about the townhouse," and then she knows it's bad but doesn't ask. We play it in the hospitals or on the phone late at night in New York.

The townhouse as we know it is straight from Edith Wharton—a tottering mansion in Gramercy Park sitting remote and dreamy on an empty lot, towering over the neighborhood. There are four floors and sixteen-foot ceilings and a wrought-iron gate. Heavy velvet drapes cross the windows, and we sometimes peek out from them.

"*Grey Gardens* in Manhattan!" I dub it, and she shrieks at this, delighted.

"I'll be Big Edie," she says. "No, Little Edie, with a sun hat and halter, reading *The National Enquirer.*" Her smile spreads out, and her eyes become huge. "Oh, my God, that will be us. The Beales! People will say, 'Whatever happened to Carole and Carolyn? They had so much promise.' And we'll be locked up behind our gate, ordering takeout and dressed in vintage Dior gowns."

It is a house well-suited for dinner parties, so that's what we do, plan them over and over, or more specifically, plan who will come. They are the sorts of parties that cause heads of state to postpone summits. Such is the grandeur we assign.

Everyone wants to be here, and because of this we spend hours deciding on our guests. Carolyn has a schoolgirl crush on Steven Tyler, the singer from Aerosmith, so he is given a seat. I've just seen *The English Patient,* so I put Ralph Fiennes on the list. "We have to be selective about whom we have over," I say. "It will be *very* exclusive. No reporters. No interviews. And they have to be able to soft shoe and tell a good joke."

We expect there to be cameras clumped in the hedges at all times, waiting for us to appear—it suits us fine, since in the tradition of *Grey Gardens* we will rarely step outside. We imagine that everyone will want to talk to us, and we also imagine it quiet. We are wanted, yet left alone—the clamor entirely at our disposal.

"I'll be the eccentric, aged beauty," Carolyn says. "We'll have all these pictures of me—the young me—around and I'll bring them out for visitors."

The floors are dark wood, "very shiny," she says. "Walnut." And the closets are an acre wide filled with gowns and bejeweled shoes that we will change for every meal.

Our guests are completely enthralled with us, spellbound by our stories. They will stay until dawn, we imagine, and listen to us breathlessly, humbled and grateful for our splendor.

We are always dressed in our townhouse—fashionable spinsters with nowhere to go. "You, the 'Widow Radziwill,'" Carolyn says. "Who's going to date you?"

"Oh, *really*, look who's talking," I shoot back. "Mrs. John F. Kennedy Jr."

We are Lucy and Ethel, Ginger and Mary Ann, the tortoise and the hare. Pick a twosome—one dazzle and charisma, the other flannel-lined jeans. In the townhouse she lets me shine. She lets me have an *after*—in a grand, gothic style. It is a place where my husband isn't dying and she isn't expected to embody Camelot. Just a glittery room set apart from our world, where we live trouble-free, whiling our days away on guest lists.

5

In Year Five, Anthony almost dies three times.

Christmas is precarious. We make appearances. We haven't seen my family in a long time. They are aware of his cancer, but I keep them at a distance, making excuses for missed birthday parties. But Christmas is hard to avoid, so we go to my parents' house and exchange presents with my brothers and sisters. It's awkward. They haven't seen him like this. The house fills up and I flit around, work the room. I am louder and happier in hopes that no one will notice him. I try to be present enough for the both of us while zealously guarding his position on the couch. He barely moves from it. He is thinner now than anyone in my family has ever seen him. There is no hiding anything today, and no one knows what to say.

I am glad when we leave and drive back to the city for Christmas dinner with Carolyn and John. There is nervous energy around all of us. We plan a trip to Cuba and Greece. We are trying to ramp a lifetime into a few short years.

The next day Anthony and I fly down to Florida to spend New Year's with Holly. We stay with her father and stepmother, Pete and Joan, in their guesthouse in Vero Beach. Anthony is still very weak, but he wants to go, to be with Holly and her family, to swim in the pool and enjoy the beach. I feel guilty because I don't want to be here. At work people were talking about ski trips and vacations; couples were doing this and that. I was sick of death, sick of blood, sick of bile and walking with canes. I am tired, and I want only to sleep. I sleep on a chaise by the pool and dream about a beach in Cuba. But Anthony isn't there in my dream. I can't imagine how we can possibly get him there. I don't say it to anyone. It terrifies me when a little voice whispers it to me. *I want to be free.*

"It's not good. I think I'm in trouble."

I look at the clock; it is six in the morning. Anthony's standing over the sink. I jump out of bed and run to the bathroom.

"Oh. Wow. Okay. Okay, I need to call. We need to get to a hospital." He has been throwing up in the dark so he won't wake me, and when I flip on the light the sink looks as if it's filled with bright-red paint.

I call Joan and Pete in the main house and tell them I need an ambulance. Florida, it seems, is organized for medical emergencies. Joan pushes a button in the house, a direct line to the ambulance service, and four minutes later two men arrive at the front door.

Pete walks out of the main house when the ambulance pulls up. "Are you okay? Anthony?"

"We're fine, Pete. I'm okay." Anthony is sitting up on the stretcher, and I get in the ambulance beside him. We ride away watching Pete standing in the driveway.

At the hospital, the ER staff sees it is bad, and we go to the consent forms fast. I give them the background on his sarcoma and his surgical history.

"We need to do a bronchoscopy."

"Okay," I say. "What is that? What will you be doing?"

"It's obvious he's bleeding somewhere; there could be a rupture in his lungs. We have to put a tube down his throat with a camera on it, and we'll be able to see what's going on."

"Is it painful?" I ask. "Is it complicated? How long does it take?"

It doesn't take long, and they can do it in the ER, the doctor tells me. I sign the consent forms, and it all happens so fast. I am running down the list in my head of the drugs he was treated with in chemo, of allergies, of operations.

They give him Versed to knock him out, and he will have no memory of the procedure. I am standing next to his bed while he waits for it to kick in, the doctors anxious to begin the procedure. *This is it,* I think. Still, I know not to say good-bye. "I love you—I'll see you soon. I'll be right outside." He looks up at me and whispers, "Don't kiss any other boys." And then he falls unconscious.

I have been hoarding, like a squirrel for winter, all my acorns of hysteria. Nudging them as they come to a little place in my head for later. There hasn't been time to fall apart—Anthony won't tolerate it. Worry, panic, fear simply serve no useful purpose. The important thing is to keep them apart from one another, because I am afraid if they touch, these tight little balls of suppressed heartache, they will explode, and I am trying my best to save this for some fuzzy uncertain point in the future. When everything is over. When there is no more bad news and nothing to be afraid of and nothing left to worry about. *There will be a time,* I tell myself. *It will be clear, and I will have some period of time to look out above the clouds.* A period of time, long enough to let it all out like the air in a balloon.

Joan and Holly have followed us here, and they have been standing speechless, listening to me recite medical histories and medications.

"I have to go outside," I tell them. "I'll be right back." Carolyn and John are in Sun Valley for the holiday. I have my phone in my hand to call her, but before I call I sit on the curb between two cars in the parking lot of the Vero Beach hospital. I'm wearing pajama pants I grabbed from the floor before we left, and I let my body shake with sobs. I indulge myself. The kind of crying you can do when there's no one around to see.

Anthony didn't bleed to death. The doctors did the bronchoscopy, put the tube down his throat with the camera, and saw nothing. The bleeding had stopped, and they couldn't see where it had been coming from. "As if it simply healed itself," they tell me.

"You cleaned up the room!" Holly tells me the next day when we get back to the house. She looks at me as though I'm crazy. "I went to the room to see what happened, and there was a pile of towels in the hamper. You cleaned it all up before the ambulance came." I don't remember actually doing this, but I am relieved when she tells me. I knew Anthony would not have wanted anyone to see the blood. We have an early dinner with champagne and make a toast. *To a better year.*

6

We go to Suffern for dinner in January to watch the Super Bowl at my parents' house, and Carolyn insists she come along. "I can't believe you've never invited me there," she says, indignant. "I want to see where you grew up. I'm coming."

Tonight, my brother Anthony is here with his wife. My sister Terri is here with her husband. My father makes a big pot of pasta, and we eat at the table, passing sodas around.

After dinner Carolyn looks through all of the wedding albums. "You look like Cary Grant!" she says to my brother. She has all of them tell her their stories. Jeff, my brother-in-law, just got his pilot's license, and they talk about John's plane. "I don't know if I'll want him to fly when we have kids," she says.

"I know exactly what you mean," Terri tells her.

My sister-in-law is pregnant, and Carolyn dishes up her plate, makes her a cup of hot chocolate. She adds a pillow under her feet, then scolds my brother for not doing all this himself.

Driving back to the city, she sits in back leaning over the front seat, her head between us. She makes me tell her stories. My crush on Paul Merrick across the street; the gay guys who lived down the block; Linda and I lip-synching to Captain and Tennille in the Suffern Junior High talent show.

"Oh, my God," she says. "Is there videotape?"

Then we sing along with the radio, loudly, until we cross the bridge and Anthony begs us to stop.

A week later the hospital delivers the dialysis machine and sets it up in our home office. I buy a black-suede recliner at Bloomingdale's, a comfortable, stylish-looking chair that gives not the slightest indication of *function*—the sort of chair we might have bought anyway. I bring in a television. The office is small, so we move out my desk to make room for the recliner, the machine, the television, and a chair for the dialysis nurses who come three times a week.

On Presidents' Day weekend we fly to London. Anthony has the urge to revisit his childhood—the schools, the house on Buckingham Place where he grew up, the church his father built, and the country home in Henley. The house in Henley still has the wooden benches around the oak tree and the covered gypsy wagon on the lawn. He tells me it was a Christmas present from his mother to his sister and him when they were kids. He can't believe it is still here.

It is a great comfort to him to find it all the same. We pull into the drive at Henley, and the caretaker rushes out. But then Anthony introduces himself, and he walks us around the grounds. He offers to show us inside, but Anthony says no. He is content just to see it the way he remembers. We go to the small church that his father built on the property of the Polish school. We go inside to the crypt where his father lies and say a prayer by his coffin. We drive to the Old Stoner Pub for lunch, and he tells me about the day his mother and sister were driving on the winding roads from the pub back to their house and had an accident, and he and his father were called panicked to the hospital. He remembers the damaged car, the spattered blood, hairs stuck in the wispy threads of a smashed windshield. The horrible feeling of driving to the hospital with his father, of not knowing.

Then we go to the house on Buckingham Place—a redbrick townhouse, in the shadow of Buckingham Palace. We walk down the road and stand across the street and talk about ringing the doorbell, but he decides against it. He goes to William and Mary's hospital for dialysis the next day by himself, as he prefers, and I wander around the city. It is a bittersweet visit.

In March we go to the Oscars to root for *Swear to Tell the Truth,* a documentary on the life of Lenny Bruce. It is the last project Anthony produced for HBO, and it has been nominated for best documentary.

We stay at the Peninsula Hotel, and we watch the ceremony on a big television in the hotel room with our friend Mark, an editorial producer at *Primetime,* who books all the big interviews.

There is a picture of Lenny Bruce that HBO used for marketing the film. He is looking back over his shoulder, with his eyebrow cocked. His right hand carelessly dangles a cigarette, like a man who holds one longer than he smokes it. The left side of his mouth is tipped just slightly into a smile. It looks exactly like Anthony. It's the eyebrow, I think. The reflex of a man who is on to everyone and everything—death, life, pain, taxes. He's on to polite conversations, carefully chosen words, and finds it all a bit ridiculous. The smirk of a man who knows he gets it more than the person taking the picture. It's not arrogant, this smirk, not mean or sneering, just the look of a man who has seen some things. He is handsome and suave in this picture, like Anthony. He's confident, dapper, smart.

HBO wrapped the film when Anthony was still going to the office on a regular schedule. He is excited about the Academy Awards. The film doesn't win the Oscar, but we go to the after party at Morton's and squeeze into a banquette. They are parading Monica Lewinsky. She sits in the center of the room near Gwyneth Paltrow. Anthony is in a tuxedo that doesn't quite fit; it's big on him now. He wears his father's cuff links, inscribed in antique gold. One with *Luck* and one with *Love*. We're at the Oscar party. We will enjoy this. I can't help myself, though, from briefly hating the other people in the room.

In Year Five we entertain. We bring out the good silver, the Baccarat crystal, and the Limoges china plates. It isn't like us, and we get caught up in it, something different. It's sort of fun.

Marta has started coming to cook a few nights a week. She has worked for John's family for thirty years. We have no formal arrangement; nothing was ever said, but Anthony is sick, and food is more difficult for him. She has known Anthony, taken care of him, since he could crawl; it's almost a reflex. She purees the vegetables; she steams the fish. She brings home fresh, fat strawberries from Marche Madison. And some nights when we know she's coming, we invite friends.

We have my brother and his wife, some friends from work, but mostly John and Carolyn. John is making a point, I notice, of coming over more, or getting together. He calls more with plans. He is taking a stab, I think, at slowing this whole thing down.

John is given to musing in Year Five. "Who would have thought," he asks Anthony in our apartment one night, "we'd both end up with these girls? Two girls from, what was the name of that store?"

"Caldor," we remind him.

"Yeah, Caldor. Don't you think it's a little odd, Anthony?"

Anthony has no patience for this. For searching conversations, anything that eats up time.

"We were wearing yellow smocks while you water-skied off the *Christina*," Carolyn says, and the three of us laugh. We compare their yacht, with the waterslide from the top deck into the Mediterranean, the jet boats at their disposal, to the stale air of the department store, the sticky heat when you walked out after a shift to the asphalt parking lot.

Anthony says little. He is losing patience, I think, with all of us. We are going through much different things.

On another night Anthony recaps the Oscar party for John and Carolyn. He describes it much differently than I remember. His anecdotes are off slightly. "Carole," he says, teasing, "was starstruck." He looks over at me, inviting me to join in. He describes a night I didn't see. One in which we mingled and worked the room, watched Madonna dance. I sit quietly, not sure what to add. The truth is we barely spoke at the party and hardly moved from our table. It was loud, and Anthony was too weak to work through the crush of people. It's disconcerting, his retelling. But then John breaks in and saves us with a story about the night he had dinner with Madonna, and she barked at him suddenly to eat, and he wolfed down his food, terrified. We all laugh, and I am grateful to be on to something else.

The next week Carolyn and John come with Hamilton. We are sitting down to dinner when John says, "Let's have some wine." We have a few bottles in a rack, and I pick one out and open it. Anthony's reaction is instant and startling. "God, Carole! That's an eighty-dollar bottle of wine! What the hell are you doing?" The anger comes, it seems, out of nowhere, but I have lived enough to know now that is never the case. It was red wine, and John had asked for red; my selection had been arbitrary. I set the wine on the table, and Anthony keeps his frown, sitting down quiet and angry, but John jumps right up. "Don't yell at her! Leave her alone, you're smothering her!"

It is quiet for a few long moments, and then Hamilton changes the subject. We dampen it with simple small talk, safe things about family and food—*Marta, the halibut is perfect. What has Tina been up to?*—until the food is eaten, the dishes cleared, and it is an acceptable time for them to leave. Emotions are spilling over. We've crossed a line that we'd all prefer not to have crossed.

Endings

Maybe all one can do is hope to end up with the right regrets.

— Arthur Miller

1

Tragedy, when you look back on it, is not sudden so much as a series of small rumbles. Something had to happen; it was inevitable. The perpetual dying was taking its toll.

When Carolyn and I imagine the Townhouse this summer, sometimes it's a house in Snedens Landing, with dogs and kids running in the backyard. *Carolyn's* townhouse. We are both playing with a future that for now is on hold.

We are on the Vineyard. I am reading *Lady Chatterley's Lover* and wearing see-through dresses on afternoon trips alone into town. John's business is failing. He is keeping up appearances publicly, and privately meeting with bankers. Carolyn smiles and says everything will be okay. It all screams of dramatic flair.

Anthony goes to see Dr. Wong at the Strang Clinic, and I spend nights boiling tree bark and dried mushroom stems. He chokes down the broth. John starts traveling more, flying around the world now at the whim of advertisers and investors. Selling his face and hers to keep his business going.

We spend Easter together at the Vineyard. Anthony, John, and Carolyn go to church, and we meet back at Mike and Diane's house for an Easter egg hunt. Diane has hidden colored plastic eggs with gifts inside—press-on earrings, peel-off tattoos, fake eyelashes—and we run around the house, shrieking, to collect them. We have dinner and play parlor games until late in the evening. These moments of calm delude me.

A week later Carolyn calls from London. She sounds tired. She doesn't want to be there, at a store opening for Ralph Lauren, a business trip for John. She does not want to be traveling, and neither does he, and the whole trip goes badly.

"What is Runnymede?" she asks me.

I know Runnymede because we have a leather-bound book about it given to us by Anthony's aunt. Runnymede is the memorial garden for John's father in England.

"He wants to go to Runnymede and I want to come home. I think he was mad because I didn't know what Runnymede was." History bumping up on us, like the rocker and the framed sheet music of the Marine Band's "General Radziwill" march, which hangs on my living room wall.

Nothing slows when they return. There are more events: the White House Correspondents' Dinner, the Profile in Courage Award at the Kennedy Library, the *George* magazine awards. I try to distract myself with work but sit in my office staring out the window.

In May we are back at the NIH for elective surgery to remove a rib. Of all of the operations, this is the most painful. It is not encouraged by Dr. Rosenberg. *Why would you,* he must be thinking, *so close to the end?* But the tumor is pressing against Anthony's rib on the right side, and he can't get comfortable sleeping or sitting down or standing up for very long because of it. He is in pain, but he won't take painkillers. Unless he is in the hospital, on an IV drip, he takes nothing for pain. I keep it all anyway, fill all the prescriptions. I have dozens of bottles of Percocet, Vicodin, and Demerol. They are neatly grouped in our bathroom—sorted by drug, labels facing forward.

Two days after the operation, Anthony checks out of the NIH with a walker. The doctors would like for him to stay longer, but he won't. "Stay in the area," the on-duty nurse warns me. "Change the bandage every four hours or before if needed. Here is the number for after-hours care." She hands me a card with the bag of bandages. "Call if he develops a temperature."

It is sunny and quiet when we leave, the beginning of a three-day weekend. I give the nurse at the station the number to the Four Seasons in Georgetown. There is no question of staying at the Hyatt in Bethesda; it is too closely associated with his illness. He wants to believe, when we leave, that we are on holiday in Georgetown, not waiting to be officially discharged from the NIH.

I drive to the hotel, and we make our way up to the desk. Anthony is moving slowly with the walker. I can see he is trying not to grimace. We stand out in the glistening marble of the lobby.

"Room 1405," the pretty desk clerk says. "It's in building two. Go to the end of that hallway and you'll see the elevators." To the left of the desk, where she is pointing, there is a long, glass-domed hallway that connects to another building. "Enjoy your stay," she says, smiling.

I ask if there is something in building one, but there isn't.

It is endless, this hallway. It is heartbreaking. But Anthony will be horrified if I keep standing here. If I insist on a different room, if I say what I want to say. *Look at my husband, you fucking idiot! Do you think he can walk to building two?* He is watching me now, eyes narrowed. *Don't make a scene, Carole.* The clerk hands me the room key tucked into a card. "This one is for the minibar."

We take a few steps and stop. A few steps more, then stop. And this is how we wordlessly get to the elevators at the end of the hall. The porters passing by us stare. Hotel guests walking by us stare. If I fantasize about saving Carolyn's life, I also dream of rescuing Anthony from this hallway. In a way in which I am funny and strong, and he does not feel embarrassed.

We have a nice room, a suite, and I turn on the television to cover the silence. It is nerve-racking in this room all alone. He feels warm, so I check his temperature. It reads normal, and I am sure it must be wrong. There is a risk of infection, they told us, so I keep checking. I try to space it out so he won't think I'm worried. Bloody gauze bandages fill up the short, boxy trash containers.

"It's still bleeding," I tell the night nurse when I call at midnight. "Are you changing the bandages?"

"Yes," I say.

"Well, keep changing them and come back in if it gets worse."

When she says, *Come back in,* all I can think of is the hallway. We will never make it twice in one day.

The night goes on like this. I wake up to change bandages. I am relieved the next morning when we check out and drive back to Bethesda for dialysis. They examine him quickly and sign his discharge papers.

Mike and Diane have sent a small plane to take us to the Vineyard. It is waiting for us at Dulles Airport. There are two steps to get on to it from the ground, and it might as well be a hundred—the Four Seasons hallway all over. It takes everything he has left to take a step, to walk, to climb up these two stairs.

2

We will spend the summer here in the Vineyard, we have decided. Anthony confides in Diane. He tells her he is taking a leave of absence from HBO. His work, he says, is now sapping too much of his energy. It is a huge defeat, another benchmark of his normal life eroded. Diane suggests we move into their guesthouse, where he can concentrate on regaining his strength for the next treatment, whatever that might be. I take an official leave of absence from ABC.

I feel as if we are coming to the Vineyard to die, but Anthony calls it a vacation. "This is a *once-in-a-lifetime* opportunity," he says. "We'll have the summer off, I can recoup." He is upset with me for hesitating when he first brings it up. I don't want to move into an empty house on an island at the end of a long dirt road.

"I don't understand why you can't stay with us," John says when I call him with the news.

"Their house is closer to the hospital," I tell him. "Besides, we don't even know how long we'll be here."

We are not staying at John's house, not yet, because Anthony has his superstitions. You visit your *friends*. You are taken care of by *family*. He is not ready to go to his family. He is not ready to concede. It is all very difficult for me to navigate. There is a lot left to interpretation, and that means a lot of room for error.

The other reason not to stay there is more obvious but even less likely to be said: *Because you are healthy, John. You can swim and water-ski and kayak*. I don't say either of these things to him. I say, "It's closer to the hospital."

We are just visiting here this summer. Taking a leave of absence to recuperate. This is what I tell people who ask. Anthony is playing a complicated game in his mind. To stay alive, not to break down at the end, to be *brave*, to have *dignity*, *grace*, and *courage*. It is all that he knows to do, to be *brave*, and I wish he didn't have to be.

When we get to Diane's I call the hospital and give them detailed directions to the house. The ambulance driver tapes them to the dashboard. I get an oxygen tank and read the instruction booklet attached to the valve, and then I hide it in the closet of our bedroom.

We have been here three days when John breaks his ankle. He is up in the "flying lawn mower"—I call it this because it looks like a sit-down mower with a parachute attached, but it can fly as high as ten thousand feet. He has had it for a few years and never had an accident, but then today he comes down too fast and hits a rock on the makeshift runway he has constructed on their property.

Carolyn calls me from the hospital, and she is crying. "I don't know if we can survive a broken ankle. It's such a goddamn bad time for this." She is angry, exhausted. We can't afford to be careless now. We simply can't manage anything else.

"It's okay, it's—an operation?" I glance over at Anthony sitting at the table in the kitchen, squeezing a ball in his fist.

"Six *weeks* in a cast!" she says. "No kayaking, no waterskiing, no swimming. No physical activity of any kind."

I hang up the phone and look at Anthony. "John broke his ankle."

It is the last thing we need in what we know is an ill-fitting summer, another hospital.

When John checks into Lenox Hill they stare at him, even here whispering, trying to peek at the American prince on the stretcher. They gawk at him, rehearsing the stories they'll tell at home tonight, or to strangers on the subway, or when they get down the hall. "Haven't you seen a broken ankle before?" Carolyn snaps. "Stop staring! Please!" Furious now at the endless scrutiny. She is not comfortable yet with this part of the life they have together, and it frustrates her.

I'm starting to figure it out. I take Carolyn's advice at last and see a therapist. *You have to think about yourself,* she always tells me, and so I do. But there is a precedent for me; husbands have died before. There are books, even, on this. I have degrees and trophies, and now I have stood by my husband's side. However meaningless it may be now, I get his family's approval. They have told me as much.

On the other hand, she has stopped seeing her therapist this summer—even as she is thrilled that now I have one. She has stopped going to the gym. She has given up, for the time, the idea of going back to school. We talk about making documentary films, but she seems to have lost her footing. I want to tell her it will be okay, but I think it can wait.

The weekend after John's surgery they come to see us at Mike and Diane's. John and Anthony, both convalescing, are on level ground now. Anthony is propped up on the bed, and John is on two chairs pulled together next to him. Carolyn and I carry lunch to them on trays, and we all laugh about it, our helpless husbands. "Can you run the old chap a bath?" John yells out to us in a British accent for

Anthony's benefit, and Carolyn goes in to run water. Cold, with no bubbles.

We go out to the beach the next day, and Anthony takes off his shirt to go into the water. The ribs poke out of his skin. The lines of scars are messy across his chest, as if someone has scribbled on him, and John drops his head and sobs. He's standing several feet behind Anthony, and the sound of the waves drowns everything out.

"Hey," Anthony yells out. "Where'd you go?" He's making his way to the water smiling, oblivious, and John shakes his shoulders, takes a breath, and pulls himself together. He limps down in his cast, and Mark, who is here for the weekend, helps them both into the water, holding John's leg up with one arm so the cast won't get wet.

It is summer at the beach, and Carolyn and I plan parties: Anthony's fortieth birthday, Tina's bridal shower. We address invitations and send them out. We call caterers and discuss finger foods as if it were any other summer. As if this year were something to celebrate.

At the end of June, I fly back to the city alone for Tina's engagement party, because Anthony is too weak to travel. Holly offers to spend the night with him on the Vineyard. The party is at Caroline and Ed's apartment, and Carolyn comes by early to pick me up. She calls from the taxi on her way uptown.

"Should I wear a sundress with strappy sandals or something with flats?" I ask.

"Strappy sandals, of course."

When she arrives at the apartment, she hands me a small Cartier box. "Here, this is for you. Open it now."

The box holds a thin gold band. A toe ring, to match hers. "Put it on!" she orders me, her face lit up in excitement. "Uh, Lamb, what's up with the dress?"

"What?" I have on a thin, silky red sundress, gathered in the front and off the shoulder.

"It's a little *Postman Rings Twice.*"

"Really?" I'm happy to be away, on my own for one night. A girl, a summer night in the city, a pretty dress.

"Sweetie, your husband has cancer. It's a family gathering—you need to rein it in a little."

"Oh, come on, it's fine," I say, giggling now.

"Okay, Lana Turner."

I try to respond, but can't get it out because I start laughing, twirling around in my strappy sandals in front of the mirror.

"You are a complete kook," she says, and then hugs me.

We walk to Caroline's, and John is already there. Carolyn is always anxious coming here, and we are both usually eager to leave. Tonight they make it easy—after an hour they announce they have tickets to a Knicks game. "You can stay if you need to," they say. "Marta will be here."

The three of us take a cab back to North Moore and order takeout from Bubby's and watch TV until we fall asleep. The next morning John hobbles into the kitchen and makes us oatmeal with blueberries. After breakfast he and I share a cab uptown. I drop him off at an appointment and go into my office for a few hours. I fly back to the Vineyard that evening.

That night Anthony's breathing is more labored than usual. He wakes up struggling for air, taking long, shallow breaths. In the morning I call Dr. Ruggerio in New York. He makes an appointment for us in Hyannis.

We take the fifteen-minute flight to Hyannis, and then a cab to Cape Cod Hospital. The doctors do an echocardiogram. They point at the scans, shaking their heads. His heart is three times its normal size. The cancer has created fluid around his heart, and he needs an operation to relieve the pressure. The sooner the better, they say.

While Anthony has dialysis across the street, I schedule an

appointment with Dr. Girardi, a cardiologist at New York Presbyterian, for emergency surgery the next day. We return to the Vineyard, then take an early morning flight back to New York.

After the surgery, I catch Dr. Girardi in the hall. "How did it go?" I ask. "Is everything okay?" He's a young-looking doctor, Anthony's age.

"It went fine. Very well."

"What did you do?" I ask him.

"We cut a 'window,' they call it, in the pericardium. It's a sac that surrounds the heart like a cushion. We cut a hole in that to release some of the fluid caused by the cancer."

I am listening carefully. He is calm and matter-of-fact. "It should relieve his symptoms."

"The breathing?" I ask.

"Yes, it will certainly help him breathe easier."

We stand there for a moment. There is something not right. The way he looks at me or answers. Or there is something I am forgetting to ask. I lay a hand on his arm when I see he is starting to turn away.

"Wait. Where did the fluid go?" I remember. The cancer cells are what filled up the sac. "What did you do with the fluid?"

He hesitates, and I wait. "When we cut the hole," he explains, "the fluid drained into his body cavity."

"But then aren't you spreading the cancer everywhere?"

His look changes immediately, and he seems to understand. But I don't like the look. Pity, maybe, or disbelief, I can't be sure. "Carole, he's not going to recover from this. I'm very sorry. I assumed you knew. Your husband is dying. He has a few weeks left at best."

I take my hand off his arm, and he walks away. He says it so matter-of-factly, a little surprised, I'm sure, that he has to say it at all, that I might have been entertaining other options. The moment before a thing is said out loud. This moment has been five years for me. In five years no one has said this to me, that Anthony is going to die.

This morning, as sick as Anthony is, I thought, as he did, that they would cut the hole, and he would be okay. We have been going along like this. We'll go to the NIH, and then he'll be fine. We'll do chemo, and then he'll be fine. *Just a few weeks of radiation, Nut, and I'll be fine. I'll get a new kidney, and this will all be fine. We'll just take time off this summer to rest, and then I'll be fine.*

I let out a long, deep breath after Dr. Girardi leaves, and then it comes up on me fast. I start sobbing so hard my body shakes in the middle of a busy hospital. Embarrassed, I sit down on a bench at the end of the hall, and the elevator doors open and Diane walks out. She sits down beside me and puts her arm over my shoulder. We don't say a word; we sit there until I stop crying, and then we walk down the hall to see Anthony.

John calls me at the apartment the next morning early, while Anthony is still in the hospital.

"Hey, sorry to wake you. I need to talk."

"Is everything okay?" I ask. Wondering what he possibly has to talk about that can't wait until seven.

"We need to talk about Anthony. He's in denial, and he needs to come to terms with this."

He starts reading to me from a book, Elisabeth Kübler-Ross's *On Death and Dying.* He thinks, suddenly, he has an answer. To get Anthony through the "Five Stages of Death." He reads them to me: *anger, denial, fear, acceptance, peace.*

He is oddly formal with me, rehearsed. "I wanted Carolyn to talk to you about it, but she was afraid to. She was afraid you'd get angry. But, Carole, he can't go on like he is. He needs to accept that he is going to die." His voice cracks.

It's too early in the morning for this conversation, and I take a deep breath. "I'm not telling him."

"He thinks you're holding on to hope," he says. "You have to tell him it's okay."

"Don't you think that's a conversation I've wanted to have with him for months? Years?"

He is silent for a moment, and then says quietly, "No, I don't."

This stings, because I know he's right. I made my pact with Anthony long ago. I never wanted a husband with cancer. And I don't want to be the one to tell him he's dying.

It is too late at this point to talk about death. To shake Anthony by the shoulders until we are convinced he knows. It is too late to have everyone start saying it out loud. John is desperate and mad and trying to handle this, to pull us out. He knows this is his role, and he is stumbling. We are all a little frantic and too aware of the clock and looking at each other terrified.

It's a terrible thing to watch someone die. We are angry and desolate, consumed with hate for this disease. It doesn't help that we have silently sworn to keep up appearances. Things are about to change and never be the same, and it isn't a quick flick of fate's wrist but a slow, wrenching turn, as if the power steering has gone out.

Carolyn does talk to me about it later that morning in a cab on the way to the hospital. "We had an argument," she says, "because I told him I wouldn't talk to you about it. I couldn't."

"I know it's over. I know that he's going to die," I tell her. "Please don't worry about me." She starts to cry in the back of the cab. I know what she is feeling. The ambiguous space between saying it and then accepting it and thinking that maybe you'll be able to go on, yet not wanting to.

Sitting beside me in the back of the yellow cab with her face in her hands. Crying enough that the driver glances into his mirror, curious about the beautiful, white-haired girl. I shut the divider.

When we pull up to the hospital, she doesn't get out. "I forgot something at the apartment," she says. "I'll meet you back here." I know she is lying. There is nothing to forget at the apartment. She can't face this anymore. She can't see Anthony. "Okay," I say, and watch the cab pull away.

You can see the cracks, but not until after. She doesn't come back to the hospital. She comes to my apartment late that night. The doorman calls up and I buzz her in. "I'm sorry, Lamb. I locked myself out." I know this, too, is a lie.

It is three in the morning. She takes off her black dress without a word, crawls into bed, and falls asleep.

3

When we return to the Vineyard after the heart surgery there are glimpses of the Anthony I knew, the one I fell in love with. And there are glimpses of a future. There is a shift, a lightness, undetectable to everyone but me. As though by saying it out loud Dr. Girardi has given me permission to think beyond the present.

On the third of July we move from Mike and Diane's house to John and Carolyn's. John wants to spend more time with Anthony. I make no more excuses. He has put a bed in a downstairs room off the patio so Anthony won't have to climb the stairs. He has arranged to have Effie stay on to cook and manage the house. Anthony seems happy about the move. He finds a trainer from the gym in Vineyard Haven who will come to the house.

Later that week I am in line at the post office, daydreaming of an afternoon three weeks earlier. Anthony had gone for a swim in the ocean and come back to the house full of energy. He was playful, winking, making fun of his own skinny legs, their weakened state. He believes the ocean restores him. "Look, Nut!" he called to me, marching around the kitchen on his beautiful, clumsy legs. We watched the sunset and had a cocktail, and I sat on his lap with my arms around his neck. For a few hours he was my husband, the one I feel sometimes I've barely begun to know. For a few hours he was someone from my past—handsome and strong with a sly smile, a cocked eyebrow. He was looking out toward the water, at the sunset.

I burrowed a little closer, into his neck. He was holding me, and everything was going to be fine.

I replay this—the sunset and the marching—and I take a long, deep breath. I have finished the invitations for Anthony's birthday party on August 7 and Tina's bridal shower August 10, and I'm waiting in line to buy stamps. I feel *fortunate*. I have an unexpected rush of happiness. The kind of rush you feel when the sun is out and someone loves you and the grass is freshly cut and you can smell clean air. It's why we struggle to live, I suppose, for these fleeting and unpredictable moments.

I have a husband who loves me. We've gone through all of this, and there are still days like this one. *I did it,* I am thinking; *I did this.* I didn't do all the right things, and I was selfish sometimes, but I did the best I could. For a brief, elusive second, with Anthony waiting for me at the house and the sun shining in here through the glass doors, with the party invitations in my hand, I feel proud.

"That's a lot of mail," the man behind me says, nodding his head toward the bundle in my arms. He has a key chain in one hand, a package in the other. He is wearing shorts and a casual buttoned shirt, sunglasses pushed back on his head.

"Invitations," I say. "For a bridal shower."

"Not yours, I hope," he says, smiling. I am a little startled. I hear myself say, "No, just a friend's." The sun is out, and I'm running errands around town like any other young woman, flirting with the man in line behind me.

Once we're settled at John and Carolyn's, we pick up our routine. We go to the hospital three times a week for dialysis. Sometimes I drive him; sometimes he drives himself. There is a house we pass on the way, a Cape Cod with a long gravel driveway and a gold Mustang convertible parked out in front. It has a "For Sale" sign in the window. A 1965, like the one my father used to own. The car that pulled into the driveway when I was nine.

When I go to the pharmacy to pick up prescriptions, I pass by it. I pass by it on my way to Bunch of Grapes Bookstore. I become obsessed with this car.

I look for excuses to drive into town, to drive past it. I have flashes, and I feel guilty for them, of driving away in it. On an unfamiliar road, and I don't know where it goes. Driving with the top down, the radio blaring, far away from everyone. I steal glances, every time we go by, and it feels like a lover, this car.

"Wait," I say to Carolyn one afternoon. We are on our way to Midnight Farm, a general store, and we pass the car. I back up the road. "What are you doing?" she asks. I pull into the driveway and walk over to the car. What *am* I doing?

No one is home, but there's a phone number and I write it down.

"We'll drive cross-country, take a road trip," I tell her, giggling, when I get back in the car. "How much fun would that be?"

"It's very *Thelma and Louise,*" she says, smiling. "Okay," she agrees, "but I'm Louise, the one in charge."

"I knew you were going to say that. Fine, be in charge. I get to sleep with Brad Pitt." I'm grinning big, and she's trying not to but can't help herself. She gets caught up in it.

"Oh, I have an idea. We'll pick up hitchhikers along the way and interview them," she says, excited. "We'll get them to tell us all their weird stories."

"We'll make our first documentary, *Hitching Across America.*"

"We'll stop at every Wendy's." She looks dead serious, and I start laughing, and then she starts laughing, too. "We can bring Friday for protection!"

"Fine," I groan, "but he sits in back."

I call the number after Anthony has gone to bed. The man on the phone tells me he has just rebuilt the engine and most of the detail is original. "It purrs like a kitty," he says. "I'm selling it for ten grand. It needs some minor body work, but a friend of mine works at the Pit Stop and he can do it real cheap."

"I want it," I tell him. "Finish the work and I'll come by next week with a check."

Kissy and Jamie fly up on Friday. It is a welcome distraction, guests on the weekend to divert our attention. We spend the day on the beach and go waterskiing. John and Carolyn go with them into town after dinner, and I stay behind with Anthony. I like them here with their different stories, temporarily putting everything else aside. On Sunday everyone scatters separate ways. Jamie and Kissy fly back to New York, and John sets out early on a business trip to Canada.

The following morning Carolyn is getting ready to leave. She'd rather stay, but there are things she needs to do in New York. She and Holly and I are in the bathroom upstairs, and she is blow-drying her hair. I am sitting on the edge of the bathtub, looking up at her, and she turns the blow-dryer off suddenly.

"Here, try this on," she says, grabbing a pale-green sari out of her closet. "You'll look great in it." I put it on and sit back on the edge of the tub. "It looks fantastic," she says, pleased with herself.

She turns to Holly, who is waiting to drive her to the airport. "Okay, listen, Sweetie, let me just tell you straight-out. You need a major fashion overhaul." We all start laughing. Holly, I know, is thrilled with this sudden attention. "You need to sex it up a little." Carolyn hands her a leopard-print sarong. "Here, this too." She gives her a gold ankle bracelet from the vanity.

"And that straw hat with the blue ribbon—out," she says, laughing, "or I'll have to ban you from the house."

Then Holly takes Carolyn's bag to the car, and Carolyn grabs two more sarongs out of a drawer. "They look so good on you. Keep them." She looks quickly around the room and then gives me a hug.

The car horn beeps. *You can't leave yet!* I think. We run downstairs. She says good-bye and kisses me at the door. Friday is lying on the porch, and she scoops him up in her arms like a baby, kisses him on the mouth, puts him down, and runs toward the car. She stops suddenly, then turns around and runs back. "Here, take this, it gets cold at night. I love you." She takes the peach pashmina scarf she is wearing and wraps it around me and squeezes me tight. "I'll call you later. Remember, it's all about me."

I watch the car disappear down the dirt driveway. I whistle for Friday and walk back into the house, shutting the door behind me. And then the terrifying quiet.

4

Friday, July 16, 1999

I had prepared for an approaching sorrow, but not, as it turned out, for the one that was nearest.

There is an imperceptible shift of a life in the moment of time between the event and the knowing. After the thing has happened, but before someone has said it.

It's the moment before you pick up the phone and something is announced. *They're not here yet and I was just wondering, are they there? With you?* When the thing is still yours to lose. It's not real until you say it out loud. This is what it feels like, the click between one life and another. This is the blink of time between the way things are, and then never the same again. Like changing the channel on a television. It's this way—click—and now it's this. This, and then this. Fate. Fortune.

John has been calling me late at night all week, and it is annoying Anthony. He knows we are talking about him, and he doesn't want anyone doing anything out of the ordinary. John calling so late every night is not ordinary.

The calls are all the same. About life and love and how to manage it all. "I'm really proud of you," he says in one. "Everything you've done—ABC and then going to school and then all of this." He is quiet and sad, all winking humor gone. And he is trying to make a point about careers, accomplishments, and respect. "Carole, you've been amaz—"

"No, don't. Don't say that, please. I'm really not."

I don't want to be amazing. I am trying to figure it out. I am weak. I am scared. I am suffocating. I want it to be over.

We are having the types of grand conversations you have around endings. He is searching and reflecting and trying to find the thing that means something, to mark this moment in our lives. He tells me he has started to write Anthony's eulogy. I know it is breaking his heart.

Carolyn and John are both in the city today, Friday. They're coming up tonight for a cousin's wedding in Hyannis—a ten-minute flight from the Vineyard. We plan to see them tomorrow night.

Anthony wakes up early and goes for dialysis. When he gets back, Effie packs a basket with sandwiches and fruit, and we head to the beach in the Jeep. We get stuck in the sand dunes on the way and have to radio on the walkie-talkie for help. Effie is a quiet man, but I can tell by his look he's not happy with me, taking Anthony to the beach, having him sit here in the hot sun. He wedges wooden planks under the back wheels, and I gun the engine to get enough traction to move forward. We zigzag up over the dune.

When we get back, I have a phone appointment with my therapist. I consider not calling, but he charges me either way. So I call, and I talk about nothing for forty-five minutes and am glad when it's over.

I call my sister-in-law to tell her we won't make the christening for my nephew. I give her my sound bite, that we're away, relaxing for the summer. Anthony has had a difficult surgery, and we're just trying to recoup, you understand.

I call the man who is selling the Mustang to remind him I'm bringing the check in the morning. Then I sit out on the patio and watch Anthony and Stephan, his trainer, work with the large blue medicine ball until I fall asleep on the chaise.

Effie makes an early dinner, and we eat quietly. The only sound in the house is the dishwasher running in the kitchen. We take a short walk after dinner down to the pond, turn around before we reach it, go back to the house, and settle in. Anthony turns on the television; I pick up my book. We are watching a movie in the living room, *Papillon,* with Steve McQueen, when Carolyn calls from the airport. "We're getting a late start," she says. "I'll call you in the morning."

The phone rings at midnight, and I'm sleeping so soundly I think it's in my dream.

Anthony picks it up and hands it to me without a word. I had meant to move it that afternoon so it wouldn't wake him. I take the phone into the bathroom and shut the door before I put it to my ear.

"Hi," I whisper. I think it's John. "Is everything okay?"

"Oh, hi, Carole. I'm sorry to wake you. It's Pinky."

Pinky is a friend of John's. He is calling from Hyannis.

"Listen, I was supposed to pick John up at the airport, and they're not here yet and I was just wondering, are they there? With you?"

A simple question, *Are they there?* A door slamming shut on your life.

I feel my heart beating when I hear this voice. It is midnight, past the time when people call. It is the wrong voice, and I know everything now. I want to hang up before the noises form words. Before sounds and then words can push their way out of my throat. I want to hang up on this voice that's all wrong, go back to bed next to my husband, have a few more hours of my life.

"Pinky, what are you talking about?"

"I know, it's late. I'm really sorry. Maybe I'm confused, but I think

I was supposed to pick John up at the airport at ten o'clock, and he's not here yet."

Maybe a few seconds pass, or a minute, when I don't say anything.

Pinky forces a nervous laugh. "I'm sure it's nothing. You know John, he probably just changed his plans and didn't call anyone."

"They're in Hyannis, Pinky," I tell him. "Carolyn called me before they left. You must be mistaken."

"I know. You're right. I thought maybe he changed his mind and stayed in the Vineyard after dropping Lauren off."

I try to picture Pinky—is he in his car outside the airport? Is he watching the sky? Is there anyone on the tarmac? Are there any planes at all coming in? "No. No, Pinky, John's not here."

I hang up the phone and walk quietly out of the bathroom, but Anthony hears me. The way you hear panic, no matter how low it's whispered.

"What's wrong?"

"Nothing," I tell him. "That was Pinky, looking for John. They didn't get to Hyannis yet."

"Oh. Well, you know John."

"I know. I'm just going to make a few calls and make sure everything is okay. Go back to sleep. Everything's fine."

I walk down the long hall carefully, afraid to disturb anything. It is dark and still. Friday was sleeping under a chair, and he trots behind me through the dining room where we sat for dinner only a few hours ago. I flip on the lights in the kitchen and they startle me. I wonder, briefly, if I might prevent a horrible thing from happening, if it is in my power to stop it if I simply do not move.

I have walked through this kitchen, past the wall of photos, a hundred times. A wet suit is still on the chair in the corner where Carolyn left it last weekend when Kissy and Jamie were here. There is a small wooden table by the window and a butcher block in the center of the room, and this is where I put the pieces together. I write the information I collect onto yellow Post-it notes and stick them to the wall, above the black phone and the faded list of emergency numbers written carefully in elegant script: the pediatrician, Burt the caretaker who lives at the end of the long driveway, the movie theater in Vineyard Haven. There is nothing in the faded handwriting that can help me now.

I detach myself. This is a story I've been assigned, and now I have to figure it out. When working on a story, you start with what you know, and I know this: they left Caldwell after eight o'clock. Or was it seven o'clock? *Think, think, when did she call you?* No, it was after eight; I had already watched the news. They were dropping her sister Lauren off on the Vineyard and then flying to Hyannis. That was over four hours ago, so he must have landed in Hyannis. Pinky was wrong. He just didn't see them.

I call Hyannis airport, and Nick, the overnight maintenance man, answers. He is the only person there.

"My cousin was supposed to land there around ten," I tell him. "Has a plane landed?"

"I just got on duty. What's the name?" he asks me. "Maybe it's in the logs."

I hesitate because when I say the name everything will change, and I'm not ready for that. "It's John Kennedy's plane."

There is a familiar pause, the silent double take, and I know Nick won't hang up the phone and go back to watching TV.

"Oh, sure, I know John's plane. They were expecting him earlier. He parks at the far end so it's probably there. Let me check and call you back."

I wait in the quiet kitchen while the seconds tick off the clock. I wait for Nick to call back and say, *Yes, the plane is here.* They landed early, that's what happened. Pinky wasn't there, so they took a cab to the house. He probably passed them on the road. Of course this is what happened. Pinky's back at the house by now, I'm sure, and they're all making a joke of it, John teasing him for being late. They're all sitting in the kitchen, laughing at Pinky for waking me up. Pinky might even call first, before Nick. *Sorry, Carole. I screwed up. They're here. Sorry I woke you.*

But when the phone rings, it's Nick again. "Carole? Hey, I don't see his plane. I checked the logbook, and he hasn't checked in yet. Maybe he landed somewhere else. Are you sure he took off?"

His voice sounds distorted, like a record playing on the wrong speed, and I am trying to think of something else. "Wait, are you sure it's not there? It's a new plane. Can you look again? Please?"

"Uh, I'm sorry, but John definitely did not land here tonight."

I call the airport in Caldwell, where they took off, and the phone rings and rings. It stops and I call again. Someone named Matt picks up, and I have the same careful conversation—*my cousin, John Kennedy, I'm trying to find his plane*—speaking slowly because I don't want the answers to come too fast.

"His car is here," says Matt. I picture the white Hyundai parked in a far corner of the lot, where he can get in and out without too much attention. "But he keeps his plane in a hangar, and the hangar's locked."

"Is there a window? Can you look under the crack of the door? Can you just please go and look?"

I hear footsteps as he walks with the phone to the hangar that I know, before he tells me, will be empty.

"Okay, I need some information," I say calmly. There is silence.

"Um, tell me who you are again?"

I tell him who I am and what I know. I make him understand this is serious, that I'm not kidding around.

"Matt, I need his tail number and his flight plan."

He tells me there might not be a flight plan. That it was visual flight rules, so he wasn't required to file one. He gives me the number of Bridgeport Flight Service, and I write it down on a yellow Post-it. "They track all flights in and out of the area and they might be able to help you."

The man who answers at Bridgeport confirms there is no flight plan. "Radar shows a plane leaving Caldwell at eight fifty-nine p.m., heading east," he says. This is all they know. He tells me the tower at Logan won't have any more information, but I ask for the number anyway and I call. There are hundreds of planes in the air, they tell

me; if a pilot doesn't check in there's no way to track his plane. I call
LaGuardia, and they say the same thing.

No, I tell myself, *don't panic. This is just a story, getting information,
reporting, that's all. What's next? You've done this a million times.*

Of course, they were dropping off Lauren first, so either there is
someone on the island wondering where she is, or she is here and can
straighten it all out.

There's no answer at the Martha's Vineyard airport, but I leave a
message, and a few minutes later a man calls back. He tells me there
was someone waiting there for a plane that never arrived. There is a
note, and he reads it to me. "Lauren, waited for you for a while, then
went home. Call when you get in. I'll come get you. Daniel." He gives
me Daniel's number.

I recognize Daniel's confusion, waking in the middle of the night
to a strange voice.

"Daniel, I'm sorry to bother you. I'm Carolyn's cousin Carole
Radziwill, and I was wondering if you've heard from Lauren."

"No, I haven't," he says. "Actually, I thought this might be her. It's
not like her not to call. Is everything okay?"

Every other call I make is to Pinky. He's trying to reach Senator
Kennedy in the main house on the compound, where he is staying.
He will know, we think, exactly what to do, but no one is answering
the phone.

"Keep calling," I tell him. "We have to find him, Pinky. Are you
sure he's in the house? Can you get inside?"

The wall by my phone is covered with yellow Post-it notes: Tis-
bury police in Martha's Vineyard, Martha's Vineyard airport, Hyannis airport, tail number, local coast guard office in Menemsha.

Maybe they turned back, I think, *landed at a different airport, Teter-
boro, went back to the city.* I call their apartment and yell into the
answering machine. "Hey, are you *there? Please* pick up!" I call Carolyn's cell phone and leave a message.

I run back to the bedroom and shuffle through papers for the
number of John's flight instructor, Jay. It wakes Anthony.

WHAT REMAINS   239

"Everything's fine, go back to sleep," I tell him. I leave the room quickly, before he has a chance to ask anything.

John's been flying with an instructor all summer because of his cast. *If Jay was with him,* I think, *everything will be fine.* I run the scenario through my head: Jay's wife will answer the phone and tell me she just heard from him. *Emergency landing,* she'll tell me, *but everyone is okay, thank God.*

But Jay answers the phone, and I feel sick. I tell him John never landed at Hyannis. He is quiet. "Don't worry," he says. "He knows the area. He's made that trip so many times. He'll be fine."

I can tell from his voice he doesn't believe it.

It's after two in the morning now, and Pinky hasn't reached the senator. I have to make a decision. I have to call someone who can help. I place a phone call to the United States Coast Guard to file an official report. *They are missing.*

I am very calm on the phone, but when I hang up I am terrified. What if they didn't believe me? What if they did, but this is really a big misunderstanding, and I have panicked and jumped to conclusions?

The coast guard lieutenant gives me another number to call, and I speak next to Lieutenant Porter with the United States Air Force. I tell him everything I know except what I'm not saying yet—that it is too late—and then I call Pinky. "I just reported John missing with the coast guard, Pinky! And the air force. We have to find someone over there, anyone!"

Anthony is in the kitchen now. He is hunched over like an old man. He sits down at the wooden table by the window and scans the Post-it notes while I'm on the phone.

Boston Air Traffic Control: reviewing radar tape
Coast Guard District 1: sending out vessels
NE Air Defense Sector: reviewing radar tape
NY Civil Air Patrol: sending plane

He puts his hands over his face and cries. I hang up. And then I start to cry so hard I can't breathe. We can't look at each other.

Effie is sleeping in his bedroom off the kitchen, and I knock on his door. He gets up and looks at us and takes in the room, and then his body goes slack, and he just shakes his head. His hands hang at his sides; none of us know quite what to do with our bodies—they seem so insignificant now. He stares at the ground; he knows what I know, that this can't be fixed. And I am crying now, hysterical. A wall of grief, frustration, anger that I've kept dammed for five years has just been punctured hard. There is nothing to hold on to.

Between phone calls I rehearse the conversation we will have when they show up. *It wasn't funny!* I will scream. *Don't ever do that again. You can't do that, you fucking asshole.* I won't talk to them. I veer between hating them and being sick, all night, waiting for them to call.

Joe Kennedy is the first one to call from Hyannis. He is cool and efficient. On a cell phone, I can tell, probably walking across the yard at the compound. I can't put a face to his voice, his name so late at night. I can't remember if we have met. I am struggling to remember, in fact, which cousin or brother or nephew he is to this one, son to that.

"Did you call Marta?" he asks me. For him this is just beginning; there must be some mistake.

"Marta? No, I didn't call Marta. I called the coast guard and the air force."

Then there is an avalanche of calls from Hyannis: Senator Kennedy, his wife. They ask me for phone numbers and tail numbers and flight plans. They are calm, their voices even. It's reassuring to me; someone will fix everything now. It is just beginning for all of them—their certain advice: *Let's not panic yet, let's just stay calm. I'm sure everything is fine. You know John, I'm sure he just forgot to tell someone where he was.* They start making the same phone calls, asking the same questions. *Did you call the airports, whom did you speak to at Langley, did you contact the police in Caldwell, could they have landed*

somewhere else, did he file a flight plan? Are you sure they were coming
tonight? Did you try their apartment? Maybe they just wanted to get away
for a few hours.

We are in the kitchen not talking. Anthony and I are not looking
at each other. It makes me sick, in fact, to look at someone who
knows. I am horrible. I am thinking, *It was supposed to be you.* The
phone rings constantly.

I call her cell phone to hear her voice. "Hi, it's Carolyn, leave a
message." *Beep.*

She can't be gone. Not now. This is not, cannot be, happening. And
then I call again, and again. Talking and hanging up and then calling
back. "Hi, it's Carolyn, leave a message." *Beep.*

I have a vague sense of slipping. Of time closing in. Of everything
I have vanishing—like a fire sweeping through a house, losing everything. I have a sense of having nothing left of her at all.

I try to withdraw—hide in my mind somewhere, in an imagined
place. Where we played on the beach, dressed for dinner. Kissed our
husbands.

It's four in the morning now. The sun will be coming up. The
press may already have heard, and no one has spoken to Caroline.
She's in Idaho with her family, and we don't have a number. I call Ed's
secretary at her home in Queens, and she gets out of bed and rides the
subway to the office. When she gets there she calls me with the number of their hotel. She does not ask any questions.

"I'm sorry," the hotel clerk says, "but there's no one staying here
with that name."

I'm sure the clerk is simply protecting their identity.

"Maybe she checked in under another name," I tell her. "I know
she's there. This is an emergency."

"I'm sorry," she says, "but I can't help you."

And then Anthony takes over and tracks down the sheriff of Stan-
ley, Idaho. He finds his home phone and gets him out of bed. "I'm
sorry to wake you, sir, but it's an emergency. I need to get in touch
with my cousin at the lodge. It's important, and the phones don't seem

to be working. Can you go there and tell her to call Anthony at this number?" His polished, gracious manner kicks in, and in the insanity of this moment, here we are, the two of us. I look across the kitchen and see the reporter I met in Beverly Hills. The one who always knew how to find people, knew to call the local sheriff, knew exactly what to say.

In another circumstance we would have cheered each other. *Nice work, huh, Nut?* He might have winked. But this is a different story, and when Caroline calls, I pick up the phone and pass it to Anthony. Then I leave the room so I won't hear him talk about it. So I won't hear him choke, won't see his body shake. So I won't hear him trying to sound calm, both of us trying to sound so calm to everyone. Not wanting to be the ones to say *it*.

There is another call to make, the one I am dreading the most, to Ann Freeman, Carolyn's mother. Her husband answers the phone, and I am momentarily relieved. "I'm sorry to call so late," I tell him. "It's just that John and Carolyn haven't arrived, and there's a search out, and I'm sure it's fine, but I didn't want you to hear it on the news." I have barely hung up the phone with him when it rings again.

"Carole? It's Ann, what's going on?"

I have a little speech prepared by now about mixed signals and misunderstandings, and when I give it to her she is quiet. I have met her a handful of times: at the wedding, at the apartment. She is a strong woman, not easily impressed. I have always liked her.

"Oh, my God. Well, everything's okay, right?" And then, before I can say anything, she asks, "Was anyone else on the plane with them?"

I had assumed she knew that Lauren was with them. I was wrong. There is no sound for a moment, no breathing. And then a muffled scream, like she has pressed something to her mouth. The kind of scream you try to hold back because you feel like you don't know it.

And I know once I say it to her, once I tell her about Lauren, that it is too late. Too late for this all to be a mistake. Too late to have a different ending. I want people to scoff at me, not believe me, think I am overreacting, silly. But someone has screamed. It is almost five in the morning, and for all I know the story is already on the news. It isn't mine anymore, and Pinky's. It is everyone's now.

By early morning the news programs have preempted all regular programming. They are showing viewers the choppy water off of Gay Head. We have the television on in Effie's room. We don't want to watch, to listen, but they might know something before we do. ABC News Special Report: *A small plane carrying John F. Kennedy Jr., the son of the late president, is reported missing at this hour. We have confirmed that the coast guard has launched a search-and-rescue operation. We will have more as details become available.*

By noon they are showing file footage of his father and the famous boyish salute. They are speaking of them in the past tense. I hear myself tell people, until late Sunday, that we are *hoping for the best.*

5

There are many theories. There is the motel theory: that they checked into a motel without telling anyone, to get away by themselves for a weekend. There is the gas theory: that the plane ran out of gas and they were forced to land on one of the small islands and their phones aren't working and they are cursing their luck waiting to be spotted. This is the one I cling to, but by the time the sun comes up I have, for the most part, let it go.

There is that time after something happens when you can tease yourself with other possibilities—flirt with the chance you're mistaken, tell yourself it can still be fixed, that someone can fix it. When it was just Pinky and me on the phone, making guesses about whom to call, we could still pretend nothing was wrong. But now they are saying it out loud, all over the news.

I sleep on the couch most of the day, all of the night. On Sunday I take a long walk down to the beach and then to John's cabin on the far side of the property—a small one-room shack with a wood-burning stove. I fall asleep on the bed in the cabin to the sound of helicopters. There is nothing left to do.

Monday, the coast guard changes its effort from search and rescue to search and recovery and we begin to plan the funerals.

There is a meeting in New York on Monday night and Carolyn's mother asks me to go with her. The heads of the families—each of the Kennedy families, and the Bessettes—are assembling to decide *where* and *how* they will be buried, assuming they are found, and she does not want to go alone.

"I'll go with you," I tell her. But there is a hierarchy. There are rules, after all, and not everyone involved in the situation understands them. It is carefully, delicately, explained to me that I cannot go. *I'm sure you understand, Carole. We just can't have* everyone *there.* I decide I will go anyway, for Carolyn's mother, but then my plane is fogged in at the Vineyard and I don't get to New York in time. Someone suggests that John be buried in Brookline, Massachusetts, in the family plot, alone. We are all confused, stunned. Private thoughts are spoken out loud.

Lisa, Carolyn's other sister, meets me at my apartment and we go to John and Carolyn's on North Moore. We go over the list of who should be invited to the funeral. A group of their friends are here; no one wants to leave. Lisa and I spend the night. There is a crowd of mourners outside the apartment. Some of them spend the night there on the street, with their candles and prayers. When I leave in the morning the news crews are interviewing the people on the sidewalk and filming the wall of flowers. Diane charters a plane and flies Anthony to Holly's house in East Hampton, so I rent a car and drive out to meet him.

They are found seven miles from the Vineyard on Tuesday.

Anthony and I learn this from the television, from CNN. It is a sickening sort of relief, this news. We don't say anything to each other.
We focus on process, on times and locations, and on who is reading
what at the memorial services.

There is one task force in Hyannis and another at Caroline's house
in Bridgehampton. People come and go. Everyone, it seems, is on the
phone. There is no end of decisions to be made; we bury ourselves in
the grim practicality of it all. I am thankful to be assigned a task, to
type the interstitials—small prayers to be read at intervals during the
mass. I type a master list, along with the names of the people who will
read.

Father Charles is called in to help us navigate. He is steady and
calm, suggests different readings and prayers. He handles the logistics
of the church. There are questions about cremation, about whether
he can perform the service outside his jurisdiction. There are questions about a burial at sea. He quietly takes care of all of it.

There will be a mass for John and Carolyn at St. Thomas More,
the small church in the city where masses are said for John's mother
and father each year on their birthdays. There will be a mass for Lauren in Connecticut. We will scatter their ashes into the ocean.

There is the question of who will eulogize them at St. Thomas
More. Who will speak about *him*, who will speak about *her*. There are
rules, it seems, about everything. They do not, in the end, have a
eulogy together. Carolyn's mother suggests that I speak about Carolyn. I don't have the strength. I decide to read a prayer and I can
barely do that.

I believed—a belief not entirely lost—that this is how it goes: girls and
boys grow up, they get married, they grow old, and they die. And
though I came to know *growing old* wasn't likely for Anthony, I still
harbored this dream. I could not have imagined the small blue boxes.

Thursday, a group of family members take a coast guard boat out
to the Navy destroyer *USS Briscoe*.

There is a card table on the deck of the ship, in front of rows of metal folding chairs where we sit, and Father Charles brings out three pale-blue cardboard boxes and sets them down. Tiffany blue.

He says a brief mass and I don't hear any of it. I am too stunned by the size of the boxes there in front of me, so small they take my breath away. We recite a prayer as their ashes are scattered into the sea.

At the funeral mass the next morning Senator Kennedy speaks about John, and Hamilton speaks about Carolyn. Anthony reads the Twenty-third Psalm, and I stand at the altar and read a prayer from the Book of Ruth—the same prayer that the Senator read at their wedding. The church is silent. I'm sure people are crying but I only hear her voice. *I miss you, too, Lamb,* she says, and I look up, startled, and then down again at my index card. I see her long easy stride on the sidewalks of Bethesda, unbroken by anxiety or by Anthony's gym bag bumping her leg. I see her curled up in a metal hospital chair.

The tragedy whores come out in full force. It seems there is no end to the stories of *where I was when they died.* No end to the stories of when they were last seen.

One of the news anchors makes a comment about Anthony's health, because in the footage of the coast guard boat, he is the only one sitting down. "In a wheelchair," one network reports. But it is not, it is just a chair. A reporter from the *Daily News* calls to confirm he is dying. People ask me who was on the boat, instead of saying, simply, "I'm sorry." Everyone wanted an invitation to the funerals. It seemed to be the hottest ticket in town.

These are all small transgressions, really. Carolyn and I would laugh if she were here, but she is not. It will take me years to forgive anyone that they have died.

6

Anthony knows I have given up. He hates me, I think. It's a temporary state, of frustration and despair, but it needs more time than we have. We have been staying at Joan and Pete's house in Bridgehampton since we left the Vineyard, and I spend the afternoons drifting on my back in the pool, staring up at the sky, tears running into the chlorine water.

Joan arranges to have a car pick Anthony up and drive him to dialysis three times a week; he spends his afternoons in Bridgehampton at Caroline's. I go there to pick him up one day, and her daughter is looking at pictures, some of Carolyn and John. I lose my composure for a moment and fall into tears.

"We've got to go on. You have to snap out of this," Anthony says that night, standing over me, angry. I am curled into a ball. "We still have each other, and we have to go on," Anthony says.

He is angry with me for deserting our routine, for not wanting to pretend any longer that things will be fine, for letting on that I know he too will die.

He cried the night the plane went down. He sat at the kitchen table and folded his arms to support his head, and then dropped it down and cried. It was the first time I'd seen him like that, and I knew we were beyond doing anything for each other. We were beyond going on. He was in a place only John had access to, all those years of *I got you.* A place of vacations and holidays and summer camps. Of letters, of dinners, of endless competition. Of rolling their eyes, of weddings, of hope, of toasts, of brilliantly wicked and funny tricks that only the two of them understand, of all the things they whispered to each other with their heads down. *I got you, you got me. I got you.*

As for me, I could not yet believe that she would let something like this happen to her when she knew how much I needed her. Suddenly there was nowhere to go.

Anthony's birthday dinner is not what Carolyn and I had planned. It is a scaled-down, untimely celebration in the wake of untimely deaths. There are cake and candles and a toast from the birthday man. I give him a gold locket with a picture of us on one side and of John and Carolyn on the other. "I'm so proud of you. I love you," I write on the card. We have suspended reality for the evening.

He looks forty years older, hollowed out, sitting in his chair. There is a small group of us at Pete and Joan's. Anthony stands up and addresses the room. He struggles through his words.

"Thank you for sharing my birthday with Carole and me. For being so supportive after everything that has happened. It's been important to both of us. I know we'll be able to get through what has happened, to go on, with all the support in this room, with all your friendship."

I barely recognize his voice. Whose creaky, shaky voice is this? Whose thin arms, one holding on to a cane, the other gesturing half-heartedly behind his words? The room echoes with the absence of John. Anthony's frail state and his staggered breath notwithstanding, John would have heckled him, would have waved away every awk-ward trace in this thick air. John would not have left Anthony stand-ing and alone, to search for words. He would have made a joke in his own toast about Anthony's tireless work on behalf of old people and children. *I got you, Tonypro,* he'd say. *You got me. I got you.*

John was lecturing me on the five stages of death the week before he died. Insisting we tell Anthony that he was going to die. For all that, I like to think he would have humored Anthony. With Carolyn and John both gone, I am unable to. I stare at my plate. I know how much it has taken for Anthony to do this, to get up and speak, to thank everyone, his frailty in full view.

Anthony goes swimming in the ocean the next day at his mother's, and I watch from the beach. Herbert holds him by the arm on one side, his friend Mark on the other. He swims a while and then they help him back out.

On Monday morning we drive back to the city, then to Staten Island for Anthony's appointment. He's been undergoing radiation here, at Staten Island University Hospital, and we are scheduled to have a CT scan. This hospital has always reeked of despair, even more so today in the gloomy rain. They take the scan and it is good news. The tumor hasn't grown since our last appointment. We drive back to our apartment and I make an excuse to leave.

"I'm going for a walk," I say. "I'll be back in an hour, okay?" And then I call Holly from a pay phone on the corner. "I can't do this," I tell her, my voice raised. "I can't do this anymore. I have to find a way to get out because I just can't do it." The tumor hasn't grown, and the future, this stuttered death, stretches out in front of me. Anthony and I, dying like this forever.

We have an appointment at New York Hospital in the afternoon to talk about an experimental therapy Anthony wants to start, and when we arrive Dr. Ruggierio looks concerned.

"Maybe you should check into the hospital tonight," he says to Anthony, then looks at me. "No," Anthony says. "I'm not checking in. I have dialysis tonight. I'll do my dialysis, and then maybe. I'll think about it." I stare back at the doctor. *What?* I think. *The tumor hasn't grown. He was swimming this weekend.*

"It would be best, just to be safe. I'd just feel better if you were in the hospital tonight." He is looking at me, trying to get me to go along and I just stare back at him. *Are you okay?* he seems to be asking. *Do you hear me?* "We're going home," I tell him. "We'll check in with you tomorrow."

Since the accident I'm afraid of everything, and nothing. I float between hysteria and delusion. Nothing can get my attention, not even my husband's death. I have already seen it.

I order takeout from Sant Ambroeus when we get home, and

leave Anthony alone while I walk to Madison to pick it up; a short walk but it feels good. I return and put the food on TV trays. We don't say a lot, we don't eat much, and after a while I help him to bed. I stay up late and watch TV.

The next morning Anthony wakes up at six, as he does every morning. His breathing is difficult. He is taking tiny, shallow breaths, but I have seen this before, this breathing. It is his language that startles me. The words aren't making sense. He is stringing them together haphazardly. He is speaking sometimes in French.

"I have to take a shower," he manages to say. So I help him into the bathroom.

I wash his hair then, help him lean against the sink to brush his teeth. He does the whole routine—the shower, brushing his teeth—because he has done it every single day of his life. He is mumbling things, but they are disconnected, like someone talking in his sleep. I struggle to understand him. I think it is just another thing. *There are so many things*. I have completely lost my perspective.

I call Hamilton. "Something's not right," I say. "I think you should come over."

When he arrives he goes straight to the bedroom, where Anthony is sitting on the edge of the bed and I am in a chair watching him. Anthony's eyes are empty. He is still trying to talk. I wait for Hamilton to say something.

We walk into the other room.

"Carole," he says, "you need to call the hospital. This isn't something we can manage right here."

"What?" I don't understand.

"I think you need to call his doctor, right now."

Dr. Ruggierio answers the phone as if he's been waiting right next to it for me to call. "There are two things we can do," he tells me. "I can arrange for a hospice group to go to your apartment, but it might take a while to put into place. Or we can send an ambulance and I can have it there in five minutes." And before I can respond: "I recommend the ambulance."

I pack Anthony's gym bag—a pair of shorts, an extra T-shirt, his sneakers—and the ambulance arrives minutes later. Our doorman does his best to keep people back, but even late morning on a quiet weekday, we gather a crowd. We are a small parade, flanked by people who don't know Anthony, making up their own minds about this man getting buckled onto a stretcher chair, a man they have never seen marching across the beach or running in the park or biking thirty miles to Montauk.

"Make sure someone calls Carolyn," I say to Hamilton before we leave. "Call Carolyn and John so I won't be at the hospital alone."

He stares at me, expressionless.

Dr. Ruggierio is waiting in the ER. "We need his living will," he says. I have forgotten it. *How could I forget it?* I call his lawyer to have one faxed over. There is nothing the doctors can do until they get it. I have forgotten the sound machine, with the ocean waves and waterfall. It is so careless, I think. I am irritated with myself. I've had so much time to prepare for this. I start making phone calls at the nurses' station down the hall, managing the details, and Dr. Ruggierio comes over.

"Carole, you should stop that and come into the room." I don't want to go into the room. I am afraid of what is happening there.

Anthony is sitting up on the bed, swatting away an oxygen mask. He is confused and looks at me. I don't know what to say to him. I can't move; I just stand there frozen with fear. A nurse gives him a shot of something, a tranquilizer to calm him down, and then we sit there, him on the bed, me in a chair, and I cannot believe that this is how it ends. That this is what it boils down to—a small room in the ER, nurses bringing in chairs as people show up. I excuse myself and walk down the hall to the bathroom to throw up.

They move us upstairs to a private room and the nurses lift him into bed, pull a blanket up to his chest, and give him a shot of morphine. "It will ease his anxiety about not being able to breathe," they say to me. "You understand what that's going to do, right?"

I remember his aunt and the IV morphine drip, and I understand what they are saying to me. The morphine will slow his breathing; it will make him sleep. I also know he may not wake up.

I climb into bed with him and we are spooning, me in back with my arm around his chest. He falls asleep and then I fall asleep. When his system shuts down, so does mine.

I drift in and out, humming a tune in my head. It is peaceful, sleeping here like this, Anthony warm and so calm. I hum the tune, not thinking about anything. Hours tick by unexpectedly. It feels as if everything has stopped.

Then he wakes up briefly, remembers he has an appointment. "Call Marty Adelman," he says. "I'm supposed to meet him at three. Can you reschedule it?" Anthony is the executor of John's estate and he is meeting with the lawyers this afternoon to go over the will. I leave the room to call and reschedule.

When I return, the nurse is standing over his bed. "Stop, that's enough," I say while she is giving him another dose of morphine. She looks at me, surprised. "Okay. I'll come back later."

I have a feeling he will wake up again. I am willing him to wake up, because this can't be it. This can't be an ending. And he does, just after three o'clock. He sits straight up and leans on the bed tray, supporting his head with his arms. There is a small group in the room: his mother, Mike and Diane, Hamilton and Caroline. Anthony stares at Diane with a confused look on his face.

"What's happening to me?" For the first time I see that he is scared.

"You're fine." She has a soft smile on her face. "You're just going to get very much-needed sleep." He looks slowly around the room, and he winks. Then he lies back down and closes his eyes.

I crawl back into bed with him. My head is resting on his chest, and I am listening to his heart. His breathing is shallow, but I can hear it. His heartbeat is strong. Then, as the hours pass, it beats fainter. Slower, like a song fading out. It beats and then I count and then it beats again. Friends and nurses come and go. An entire day passes. The clock on the wall says 7 p.m. when Dr. Ruggierio taps my shoulder. I have forgotten there are people in the room. "Carole," he says softly. "I'm sorry."

But I can still hear his heartbeat, so I wave him off. "Don't touch me." He apologizes and sits down. I listen to Anthony's heartbeat until it is so faint I can barely hear it and then it's gone. I don't know who is in the room. I can't look. I can't look at Anthony. I don't move. It is quiet, and I'm lying next to him, tears streaming down my face, and that's how they know his heart has stopped.

Father Charles arrives and starts the prayers and I become aware, as though it is something I have overheard, that Anthony is dead. I kneel by the bed with Father Charles. I listen to the prayers, then leave without looking back.

I have left the hospital so many times before, and come back, that it feels natural to leave. *He's sleeping now,* I think, *and I'll leave but I'll see him later.* This is how I am able to walk out.

I make phone calls from my apartment. I sound practiced. "We went to the hospital today," I say. "Only this time Anthony didn't come back."

7

We are in a room at The Mark Hotel on Madison. Lee and Tina, Caroline and Ed, and I. We have been wearing black, it seems, for three solid weeks. We are getting good at this, the funerals. As Father Charles leads us through the same process, there is a sense of déjà vu. *Which readings do we want? What gospel should we choose? Who will say which prayers?* I don't register the words, only the soothing timbre of his voice.

Anthony is at Frank E. Campbell funeral chapel on Madison. They are waiting for me to send over a suit, to pick out a coffin. They send a salesman to the hotel with paperwork: the death certificate, cremation permit, a catalog of urns and coffins. I remember the late president's white dress shirt in Anthony's closet. He kept it in a box folded neatly, the collar stamped "1600 Pennsylvania" from the dry cleaner. I ask Holly to take it and his perfectly tailored navy suit to the funeral home. The ceremony is a closed casket; the shirt is symbolic, a gesture. *He would have liked that.* We say this after each decision. I pick out an urn and the salesman shows me "The Presidential" coffin. "This is the model Jackie Onassis was laid to rest in," he says. It is a beautiful dark mahogany with shiny pewter handles. I can almost hear Anthony gasp: *Twelve thousand dollars for a coffin? Are they out of their minds?!?*

We plan a ceremony in East Hampton. Most of the people who come will remember the white clapboard church from our wedding. Lee will have a reception at her house, and before the sun goes down we'll scatter his ashes. John is not here to eulogize Anthony, so Diane will, and Caroline. I pick out the floral arrangements, assign pallbearers, and choose the hymns.

Holly calls me at Lee's house the night before the funeral. "You need to come over," she says. "There's something here for you." When I arrive she hands me a small box from Tiffany. My birthday is the next week and Anthony had my present delivered to Holly's because he didn't know where we'd be. "To my Peanut," it says on the gift card. "Happy Birthday." Inside is a diamond pendant cross on a thin platinum chain.

And then the next morning as Lee, Herbert, and I walk into the church, Carolyn's mother pulls me aside and hands me something, too. "She would want you to have this," she says. It is Carolyn's amethyst ring, inscribed with her initials in front of mine—*secret friends forever*. I put it on and I think of her hands, always fluttering, always moving. I see her getting in and out of cars, walking down the street, leaning her head against John. I see us driving down the Beltway, singing along with the radio. I see a room at the Hyatt, with Poptart crumbs in the bed. I see those big bold eyes and smell the faint scent of musk oil she leaves behind. I see her smiling, holding a glass paperweight with the Dogwood bloom, at the small crafts store in Georgetown.

I follow the pallbearers down the aisle and sit silently in the pew at the front of the church.

We scatter Anthony's ashes in the ocean from the beach in front of his mother's house. I stay for two days and then go home. The doorman gives me a package of Anthony's things from the hospital: his sneakers, his Swiss Army watch, his gold wedding band.

He was handsome and serious, bent over scripts in a hotel room, and then he stood and reached for my hand.

Fortune

And another regrettable thing about death
is the ceasing of your own brand of magic,
which took a whole life to develop and market—
the quips, the witticisms, the slant
adjusted to a few, those loved ones nearest the lip of the stage . . .

—JOHN UPDIKE, "Perfection Wasted"

Christmas 1998

We're late but not very, and it doesn't matter, because it's Christmas and we've all been to church and the city smells of pine and I'm happy because we'll all be together tonight. They are driving from Carolyn's mother's house in Connecticut, and we're on our way from Suffern. It's one of those moments when I open the door and they are there, like racing to the top of the hill and you've earned the chance to stop and catch your breath.

Our tradition. We are starting it this year. "We need our own tradition, don't you think?" she said. I like the idea that we will all come back to something. It is Christmas, you are supposed to let the rest go for a bit. Suspend reality.

"Merry Christmas!" John shouts, and the quiet apartment is scattered with noise. He unbuttons his coat and drops it on a chair. Beneath it, corduroy pants and sweater; Carolyn, a black turtleneck, like mine, and skirt. Traces of Egyptian musk follow her in. I will smell it on my clothes after she leaves, on Anthony's sweater.

"Merry Christmas, Lamb," she says, and kisses me, putting her coat on a hanger. I pick John's up off the chair, and he puts his arm around me and motions to the shopping bag in his hand. "I need to borrow wrapping paper," he says, and I laugh, because of course he does. Anthony helps Marta unload bags of groceries. She sets to work right away, chopping and measuring. Rack of lamb—from Lobel's with tiny parachutes—is already marinating in the refrigerator.

I take John into the bedroom and hand him paper and scissors and tape, and then take them back and wrap the gifts myself. I add his to the small pile under the tree.

I have Christmas carols on—Bing Crosby—and John makes a

face. He changes to a jazz station and Chet Baker floats in over our heads like a cloud. I have stockings hung by the fireplace, one for each of us, with our names in sparkles.

Anthony pours vodka tonic for himself, a beer for John. I open a bottle of champagne for me and Carolyn. It is five o'clock and the city is already dark, but it feels like a lazy afternoon.

Marta comes out to set the table, and Carolyn and I shoo her away. We love this part. We are intent. We get out the good china, the Baccarat crystal, the special Cartier salt and pepper shakers that were a wedding gift and only come out on days like this. Carolyn sets the silver candelabra down carefully.

I hear John's voice in the other room, Anthony's laugh.

In the living room I hand out gifts. For Anthony there is a thick pullover fleece from John and an engraved silver bell. "So you can summon the servants, Principe," he says in his best British accent. This running joke between them: Anthony, the prince, the proper English boy, John the mischievous scamp. Anthony and I give them breakfast trays, because Carolyn loves to eat in bed. They give me a gold band engraved AMOR.

Over dinner we talk about trips. "Let's go to Cuba next year," John says. "I'll fly us."

"I'll risk commercial," Anthony says, not missing a beat.

John moves past it. "We'll go in November; it's the best time of year."

Out loud we imagine sunbathing on the white sand, strolling along the Malecon, by the sea, smoking Cuban cigars with Castro—this gets a laugh. "And let's go to Greece in the summer," John says. "Wouldn't it be fun, Anthony, to go back to Skorpios? I'd love to see it again. We'll show the girls what they missed working at Caldor." Anthony smiles. Carolyn and I roll our eyes.

"You have to charter it now," I say, referring to *Christina,* the Onassis yacht. "You better call early."

John is serious. "Maybe I could arrange to stay in the pink house, on the island."

We use the word *tradition* over and over. Our new tradition, Carolyn says. We'll do this every year. And we talk breezily, brazenly, about the years ahead, our futures and where they'll take us. Anthony wants to build a log cabin in Alaska. John offers to cut down the trees. These are the sorts of things you talk about when one year is ending, another waiting to begin.

After dinner we sit in the living room for a little while before they leave. John on the tiger-print couch, Carolyn snuggled drowsily on his lap. I squeeze next to Anthony on his chair and he kisses my cheek. I could stay here like this forever, but we're all leaving in the morning to get on planes and so we stand and stretch and start the motions of ending the night.

"It was nice, wasn't it?" she whispers in my ear as I help her with her coat. "We should do it again next year, shouldn't we?"

"Yes, we will," I say.

ACKNOWLEDGMENTS

Where to start is the problem.

This book would not exist without the encouragement and love of the incomparable Teresa DiFalco, my closest friend and sister-in-law, who had the temerity to marry into my family and who taught me that families are all pretty much the same; who was trapped with me on a small island off the Canadian coast and persuaded me to write my story; and whose guidance nurtured words on paper into a coherent narrative. And I thank her for keeping this author's faith alive when it so often flickered.

Also I want to thank my brothers and sisters for sharing their memories, and in some cases, allowing me to steal them, especially my brother Anthony, who let me live with him in Oregon while I wrote this book; he rescued me during the blizzard of '04 and never complained when Teresa and I stayed up nights laughing and "being geniuses together."

My love and gratitude to my father for his wry sense of humor; to my mother, who nudged me past the town-limits sign and taught me to be an independent woman. Endless thanks to all my assorted aunts and uncles for the late, late show, and whose laughter I can still hear.

A heartfelt thanks to my Oregon reading group, especially Janis Bozarth, who not only read the early drafts but transcribed the twenty hours of audiotape that formed the framework for this memoir, and to Melanie Kaufman and Sridhar Venkatapuram, whose thoughtful early reads of the manuscript and notes were invaluable. A very special thanks to Dave at Coffee a la Carte, my Oregon "office," for the unlimited cups of coffee, BLTs, and free internet access.

Thank you to Steven at Prince Street Copy, who printed out countless versions of my manuscript and gave me breaks on copying and never

263

complained when it was always a rush job; the entire staff at 12 Chairs Café, who kept me fed and allowed me to use their space as my New York "office."

Many thanks to Bill Whitworth, the "Nijinsky" of editors, whose endless wise counsel kept me focused and sane; who introduced me to the jazz trumpet, the perfect hard-boiled egg, and the power of a well-placed comma. And who made me feel like one of the "big boys," if only for a moment.

Special thanks to my agent, Lynn Nesbit, for her extraordinary belief in my story. And her uberefficient and lovely assistant, Tina Simms.

And to Nan Graham for shepherding me through the publishing process; though I could never quite summon the proper appreciation for "pagination," I did appreciate her patience and guidance and great judgment. To Alexis Gargagliano, for her meticulous eye and for keeping everything moving forward, and the rest of the dedicated team at Scribner: Erin Cox, Suzanne Balaban, Erica Gelbard, Mia Crowley-Hald, Anna deVries, Kyoko Watanabe, and John Fulbrook.

I am enormously grateful to my friends who were brave enough to agree to read a very early draft: Alison Hockenberry, who started at ABC News with me and who lived through it all, twice. Bryan Lourd, whose insight never failed to inspire. I gave Mike Nichols the first thirty pages and then he gave me the confidence to "just keep writing." Diane Sawyer, whose guidance in life, love, and writing I treasure. Meredith White, whose unflinching and honest eye made me a believer.

I am indebted to my friends Christiane Amanpour, Lisa Heiden, Charles O'Byrne, Holly Peterson, Narciso Rodriguez, Michael Rourke, Jamie Rubin, who gave the manuscript thoughtful reads and whose friendship never wavered.

I will always admire Lee Radziwill for her courage and her steadfast faith during difficult times. And Hamilton South, whose humor kept us all laughing against the bleak backdrop and whose unfailing generosity of spirit and friendship I will always cherish.

To Tina Radziwill, Marta Sgubin, Marc Burstein, Joan Ganz Cooney, Sheila Nevins, Pete Peterson, Richard Plepler, and Mark Robertson, whose love, affection, and friendship helped us survive every day.

I will be forever grateful to Dr. Steven Rosenberg and his entire staff at the NIH for giving Anthony and me more time than we ever thought possible.

ABOUT THE AUTHOR

Carole Radziwill worked as an award-winning journalist with ABC News for fifteen years. She is writing a novel and lives in New York City.